MOROCCO
THAT WAS

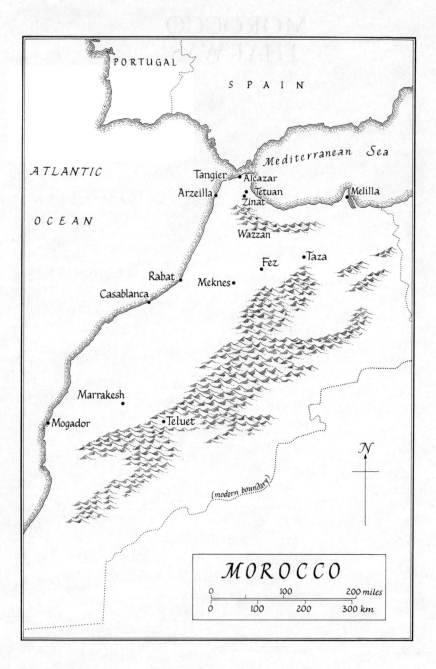

PORTUGAL

SPAIN

Mediterranean Sea

ATLANTIC

Tangier • • Alcazar
Arzeilla • • Tetuan
• Zinat
• Melilla

OCEAN

Wazzan

• Fez • Taza

Rabat •
Casablanca • Meknes •

Marrakesh •
• Mogador • Teluet

N

(modern boundary)

MOROCCO

0   100   200 *miles*
0   100   200   300 *km*

WALTER HARRIS
(Photographed soon after his release from captivity)

MOROCCO
THAT WAS

WALTER HARRIS

WITH A NEW PREFACE BY
PATRICK THURSFIELD

ELAND BOOKS, LONDON
&
HIPPOCRENE BOOKS, INC., NEW YORK

Published by
ELAND BOOKS
53 Eland Road London SW11 5JX

First published by
William Blackwood in 1921

ISBN 0 907871 40 2
First issued in this paperback edition 1983
Reprinted 1984

Printed and bound in Great Britain
by Redwood Burn Ltd, Trowbridge, Wiltshire

Cover design © Philip Wills

*Cover photograph. Haj Absalam Ould Haj Maati Mayanzi,
Kaid of Shaomia, taken by the Hon. E. Loch in 1896.
Reproduced by kind permission of
the Royal Geographical Society*

Frontispiece photograph © P.V. Harris

Index © Sarah Matthews

Map © Reginald Piggott

CONTENTS.

THE MOORISH COURT—   PAGE

    I. THE ACCESSION OF MULAI ABDUL AZIZ .   .   1

   II. LIFE AT THE MOORISH COURT   .   .   . 32

  III. THE ROAD TO RUIN 65

  IV. THE BEGINNING OF THE END   .   .   . 91

   V. THE LIQUIDATION OF THE SULTANATE .   . 119

  VI. THE SULTAN AT HOME 140

 VII. THE SULTAN IN FRANCE   .   .   . 160

RAISULI 179

SAINTS, SHEREEFS, AND SINNERS .   .   . 265

CHANGES AND CHANCES   291

INTRODUCTION

THE tomb of Walter Harris is to be found not far from the entrance porch of St Andrew's Church, Tangier. Behind a simple tesselated pavement of cut Fes tiles there is a head-stone of ivory-coloured marble representing two Moroccan arches crowned by a roof of green pantiles. Carved in the headstone are the words "WALTER BURTON HARRIS. Born 1866, He came to Tangier in 1886 and was associated with The Times as correspondent in Morocco and elsewhere from 1887 till his death April 4th 1933. He loved the Moorish People and was their friend". Nearby are the tombs of his friends SirReginald Lister, the British Minister to Morocco who died en poste in 1912 and of Kaid Sir Harry Maclean, the British officer who was for many years Instructor to the Sherifian armies. The graves are surrounded by wild iris, acanthus, yucca, hibiscus and plumbago and shaded by false pepper trees, cypress and datura festooned with wysteria, passion flowers, night flowering cereus and the delicate sweet-smelling rose known here as the Shah of Persia's Pet. The churchyard is like a tropical garden, a controlled jungle of parched scents and rare plants, in itself an echo of the garden Walter Harris planned and planted at the villa he built four miles west of Tangier, then a lonely and dangerous region apt to be infested by wild tribesmen from the Anjera hills nearby. The Villa Harris is now a Club Mediterranée, surrounded by modern hotels, while Harris's other house in the Medina, made from two small old mer-chant's houses, stands forlorn and empty just beneath the wall of the Kasbah. After being considerably enlarged by Mr. Maxwell Blake, the United States Minister, into an exotic

Arabian Nights palace, it was acquired by the late Barbara Hutton. Harris would probably have approved.

As with so many eccentrics – and among these Walter Harris must certainly be classed – it is to-day hard to disentangle the truth from the legend. Harris loved to tell stories, especially about himself, and there can be no doubt that many of these stories were improved out of all recognition by repetition and by the enthusiasm and invention of their author.

The basic facts of his life are simple, and can be checked. Born to a well-to-do shipping family, he had no material worries and was free to lead whatever life he pleased and travel wherever his whim dictated. By the age of 18 he had been round the world and was only 20 when he first arrived in Morocco and 21 when he accompanied the British Minister, Sir William Kirby Green on an official mission to the Sultan Hassan I who was then residing at Marrakesh. At the age of 23 he published his first book "Land of an African Sultan" which includes accounts of this journey, a visit to the fanatical Muslim towns of Wazan and Sheshouan (since much visited and now called Ouezzane and Chaouen). In the same volume he describes a journey to Meknes and Fes and there exists, by chance, another account of the same trip, written by the French artist Georges Montbard. It is clear that the two men, though travelling companions, neither liked nor appreciated each other and while Harris is content with a few faintly scornful remarks about the Frenchman's preference for remaining in camp if it should happen to rain and nervousness at the approach of unknown tribesmen when on the road, in "Among the Moors" Montbard allows an almost paranoid dislike of Harris to pervade every chapter of an otherwise by no means un-attractive and detailed account of the trip and description of Moorish people and way of life as it then existed. While Montbard sneeringly recounts Harris's love of good living and lists the contents of his travelling hampers sent from Fortnums (of which he was only too pleased to have the benefit) and is forever jeering at Harris's forages after hares and partridge, both accounts show that, while Montbard occasionaly took a pot shot at a lark while the sun was shining, Harris, with another English companion, would be out in all weathers seeing that their table was furnished with fresh meat. When the party arrives at a new town, it is Harris who vists the Kaid and the Pasha and who organised, not without frequent difficulty and ill-will on the part of such local functionaries, their accommodation and proper reception. Montbard, one feels would not have got far with-out Harris's combination of enthusiasm, panache, sheer effrontery and local knowledge.

The other side of the coin would seem to have been Harris's love of making his own part in any yarn he was telling into a hymn to his own cleverness, cunning, bravery, popularity and importance. All his geese had to be swans and his over-vivid imagination made sure that his listeners were never allowed to forget this. The more prosaic Frenchman could not stomach the "Tartarin" aspects of Harris's character and made clear he thought him, as did others, a braggart and a liar.

We should remember however that, when these two books were written and published in 1889, Harris was still very young and that his written account of their experience is verified in almost every detail by that of the man who questions his truthfulness. We should also remember that Harris throughout his life was a trusted and valued corres-pondent of *The Times,* and that august journal, especially in those days, would not tolerate any divergence from strict accuracy. In his obituary *The Times* stated that his long association with that newspaper was "fortunate both for the journal and the Nation which received early and trust-worthy information all through the years when Morocco was a storm centre of European politics". If his campfire stories and afterdinner yarns got slightly out of hand and began to resemble the Thousand and One Nights, his despatches and serious books can still be relied upon.

In "Tafilet", (1895) in which Harris describes his visit to the camp of the Sultan Hassan I at the oasis of that name, the return of the Sherifian army over the high Atlas, the death of the Sultan and the event leading to the choice of his successor, and in "France, Spain and the Rif", (1927) the maturity and seriousness of Harris's approach, though it does not obscure his gaiety, shows why the Times held him in such high esteem. "Tafilet" especially would merit a reissue, though "Land of an African Sultan" is marred by the racial prejudices of Harris's youth and upbringing. "Morocco That Was" falls between the two categories. Like "Land of an African Sultan" it is primarily autobiographical. Harris's friendship with the two ex-Sultans, Moulay Aziz and Moulay Hafid, is an established fact, but his stories, especially those referring to Moulay Aziz, who was exceptionally intelligent but overcome by circumstances he could not control, go far beyond the limits that loyalty and truthfulness should have dictated. Here Harris, regrettably, allows his passion for a funny story to overcome his judgement, and though *The Times* wrote that "he was want to describe the ludicrous incidents that were constantly occuring in such a way that the serious side of them as illustrating an impractical regime was never obscured by their absurdity," gratitude and fairness should not have permitted that the reputation of Moulay Aziz should have been so smirched. The chapter of Raisuli (first published in two parts in Blackwoods Magazine) is typical. No one will ever know if there really was a headless body in the hut into which he was thrust after being captured by the bandit. But there might well have been; and it was totally in character that, headless corpse or no headless corpse, Harris should a few weeks after his release have visited Raisuli as a friend who had been invited for a few days shooting in the hills near Tangier.

Walter Harris's personal life was always the subject of rumour and speculation. His marriage to Lady Mary Savile was anulled after a very few years. The late Miss Jessie Green, niece of Sir William Kirby Green, who knew Harris well and who was present when the Anjera tribesmen returned him after his capture and imprisonment by Rasuli, used to tell a story of how Harris was once attacked in the street by a man with a knife. When she asked Harold Nicolson, whose father was then British Minister, what this affray was about, he refused to give details as being unsuitable for a young umarried lady. Many years later he told her that it was an act of revenge by the father of a young boy sent to Harris as a house slave.

Despite such stories Harris seldom seems to have made real enemies. He was sensitive, witty and gifted, but completely unconcerned with consistency. As *The Times* pointed out he could make a famous jest about the armies of Moulay Aziz and Moulay Hafid being largely composed of deserters from each other, but would not have been disconcerted if anyone has twitted him for changing sides himself.

If Walter Harris's descriptions of Morocco at the close of the nineteenth century – and even in the first two decades of the 20th century seen far-fetched and improbable to those who know Morocco today, it should be remembered that until well after the Treaty of Fes in 1912 and the establishment of the French and Spanish protectorates – the country was as closed and unknown to foreigners as was Tibet. Morocco had been an independent kingdom since the arrival of Moulay Idrees, a grandson of the Prophet Mohammed, in the 8th Century A.D. This independence had been fiercely guarded through the centuries and it was only due to the inevitable decadence of a closed society that refused to admit new ideas that it fell at last, in the closing years of the rush to colonise, to outside influence. The life and customs that Harris describes had not changed for hundreds of years. Today Morocco is a rapidly developing modern country. The decadence that attracted the cupidity of foreign powers has been overcome and it should not be forgotten that foreign control lasted only 44 years, long enough for new ideas to permetate and be assimilated but not long enough to eliminate or even erode a pride of race and a sense of historic destiny unknown in the other Arab counties of North Africa. Egypt was never really independent from the death of Cleopatra until the rise of General Nasser, Libya until Ghaddafi, Tunis only briefly in the late middle ages and Algeria never until General De Gaulle decided to cut the metropolitan link with France; but Morocco's isolation and independence was only interrupted for less than half a century – and that within living memory. It was Walter Harris's privilege to witness and record the greater part of Morocco's remarkable transition from a medieval to a modern state. Though it was not until 23 years after his death that Morocco regained its full independence, it should not be forgotton that the then reigning monarch, King Mohammed V, came from the same dynasty, never displaced and was the nephew of the two Sultans whom Harris had known, and that the Grand Vizir el Mokri, in office in 1912 was still officially, though over a hundred, still in power, History in Morocco, though coloured by ancient tradition, was still very recent and luckily Walter Harris was there to watch it happen.

The funeral of Walter Harris in Tangier rivalled that of his older contemporary Kaid Sir Harry Maclean as a demonstration not only of international official mourning but also of universal local affection. After his death in Malta his body was brought back for burial to the town where he had spent most of the previous 50 years. After a brief service at the port conducted by the head of the Franciscan mission, the coffin was taken to the Anglican Church for internment. Though it was market day in Tangier, businesses and shops closed and the cortege passed through the crowded *souks* amid total silence and general signs of mourning. Never before had Tangier seen so unanimous a tribute of respect from Moroccans and foreigners alike.

© Patrick Thursfield, Tangier, May 1983.

MOROCCO THAT WAS.

THE MOORISH COURT.

I.

THE ACCESSION OF MULAI ABDUL AZIZ.

MY first introduction to the Moorish Court was in 1887, only a very few months after my arrival in Morocco, when I was invited by the British Minister, the late Sir William Kirby-Green, to accompany his special Mission to the Sultan.

Mulai Hassen was then at the zenith of his power. He was a "strong" Sultan, probably cruel, and certainly capable. His energy was never-failing, and he maintained order amongst his lawless tribes and stamped out the constantly occurring revolts by an almost unceasing "progress" through the country, accompanied by his rabble of an army. He seldom spent six months together in any of his several capitals, and the Moors had a saying, "The Imperial tents are never stored."

The great labour, the enormous transport that these journeyings necessitated, is difficult to appre-

A

ciate. Not only was the Sultan accompanied by
his numerous ladies and all his viziers and their
families and suites, but he had with him as well
some ten thousand soldiers and a rabble of camp-
followers. A large number of native merchants
also joined the throng, for trade flowed to the
region in which the Court was residing.

Some idea of the results upon the country
passed through can be imagined from the fact
that the very name of these expeditions in Arabic
is " Harka," " the burning." No matter whether
the tribes were in incipient rebellion, in open
revolt, or in peace, they had to provide the food
and fodder of this great horde, whose ravages
more nearly resembled those of a flight of locusts
than the passing by of human beings. Not only
such " legal " taxation as could be extorted was
collected, but the viziers and the Sultan's entourage had to be bribed and paid as well, while
every soldier and every camp-follower pillaged on
his own account. On receiving the news of the
coming of one of these Imperial expeditions, as
many of the population as could, or as dared,
fled to other regions ; and the Sultan often passed
through a deserted country, except that the
Governor and tribal representatives had to be
there to pour the little wealth of the countryside
into the royal coffers.

Morocco was still an almost unknown country
in those days. Europe paid little attention to
what was passing within its boundaries, and so
long as the Sultan's actions didn't threaten to

complicate international questions, he was allowed to go his own way. The rivalry of Great Britain and France was its outstanding feature, together with the constantly recurring quarrels and petty local wars of Spain with the tribes that surround her " Presidios " on the northern coast. Morocco lived its life apart. True, it was at the very gates of the Mediterranean, but it might have been in the Pacific for all the attention that it attracted. From time to time the European Governments despatched special Missions to the Sultan—gigantic picnics to one or other of the capitals, during which the pending claims would, or would not, be settled ; a commercial treaty was possibly discussed ; eternal friendship was sworn where only hatred on one side and indifference on the other really existed, for in those days the general feelings of the Moors toward the Europeans and Christians amounted to hate.

Sir William Kirby-Green's special Mission proceeded by sea to Mazagan, conveyed by a British warship, and thence overland to Marrakesh, the Sultan having, as the custom was, sent an escort, transport, and tents to the coast for this purpose.

However rotten the state of Morocco may have been at that time, Mulai Hassen's strong hand held its fabric together, and presented to the outside world a front of great dignity. The British Mission travelled amongst the tribes in perfect security, and was received with all honour and with pretended rejoicings. Compliments flowed as fast as mountain streams—happy in their wording, sonorous in their utterance, and absolutely insincere.

And then, in mingled dust and sunshine, the entry into the southern capital; the threading of its narrow streets; the throng of onlookers; the almost hopeless crush of horses and mules and men; and our arrival in the great garden of olives and oranges which surrounded the kiosks of the Maimounieh Palace, in which the Mission was housed during its stay at Marrakesh.

The reception of foreign envoys by the Sultan formed a pageant of much magnificence. Only a very few years later the whole formality was changed, and the representatives of the Governments of Europe were no longer received as vassals bringing tribute. But as long as the old etiquette lasted, there could be no question about the splendour of the ceremony. It may have been derogatory, and no doubt was, for the representatives of the Great Powers of Europe to stand bareheaded in the sun while the Sultan, under a crimson parasol, remained on horseback; but no one could dispute the picturesqueness of the scene or its oriental dignity.

The great square of the palace, covering many acres, in which the reception took place, was surrounded by yellow walls, here and there pierced by gateways. At one end, above these walls, appeared the flat terraces and green-tiled roofs of the palace, at the other extremity the cypress- and olive-trees of the great park of the Agdal;

while away to the south, towering high into the morning sunlight, rose the snow-covered peaks of the Atlas Mountains. A fitter *mise en scène* for a great pageant could scarcely be imagined.

The great square was lined with troops, ragged and parti-coloured, some in uniform and some out of it, and some in uniform so ragged that they were as much out of it as in it. Others, again, in brilliant costumes of every colour, evidently made and served out for the occasion. In detail much was wanting, perhaps; in general effect it was a rainbow. Into the centre of this square the British Minister and his suite were ushered by high white-robed functionaries of the Court, while close behind the little group of uniformed Europeans were piled the cases of presents sent by the British Government to His Shereefian Majesty. In fact, the whole traditional ceremony was based upon the reception of vassals and the offering of tribute.

A blast of trumpets, and the great green gates of the palace are hurled open, and a hurried throng of Court attendants, in white robes and crimson-peaked fezes, emerges. A band of shrill music—pipes and drums—bursts into noise. Banners and wand-bearers and spear-bearers follow, and black grooms leading horses, saddled and caparisoned in gay silks and gold embroideries, which prance and neigh at the dust and noise. Then the Sultan, a stately figure in white, on a white horse trapped in green and gold. Over his head is borne the great flat parasol of State, of crimson velvet and gold, while at his side attendants wave long white scarves to keep the flies off his sacred person. After him follow his viziers, portly gentlemen swathed in soft white hanging garments, and then more Court attendants and slaves.

As the sacred presence of the Sultan passes into the public square a great shout rends the air, and the bowing crowd cries, " May God protect the life of our Lord."

As the procession approaches the group of the British Mission it divides to right and left, and the Sultan advances, accompanied only by his Chamberlain and one or two attendants, and followed by his viziers. The members of the Mission bow and salute, and the Chamberlain presents the Minister to His Majesty, who bids him welcome. Sir William Kirby-Green then read his speech, and handed his credentials to His Majesty, wrapped up in silk. The Sultan took them, holding the folds of his cloak between his sacred fingers and the infidel documents! The suite is presented, and after another word or two of welcome on the part of the Sultan, His Majesty turns his horse and retires again to the precincts of his palace, amid the cries of his people, the booming of cannon, and the shrill blast of native music.

It may not be out of place to give here a brief account of how this ceremony came to be abolished. I was attached, in 1902, to Sir Arthur Nicolson's special Mission to the Sultan Mulai Abdul Aziz at

Rabat. There had for some time been a strong feeling on the part of the European Governments that some new ceremonial should replace the traditional form of the reception of the representatives of the Powers, and I was sent to Rabat, a week in advance of the Mission, to urge upon the Sultan the expediency of this change. I was at that time upon very intimate and friendly terms with His Majesty, and had ample opportunity to put these views before him. Mulai Abdul Aziz always had, and has, the true instincts of a great gentleman, and he agreed readily that the form of reception in vogue at his Court was derogatory to the position and dignity of a special envoy from the Sovereign and Government of Great Britain. At the same time, he maintained that it was extremely difficult to introduce radical changes in Court etiquette without creating a hostile feeling amongst the people, or at least running the risk of much criticism. For a few days he hesitated ; but the evening before the arrival of the Mission he authorised me to inform Sir Arthur Nicolson that the old ceremonial would no longer be carried out, and that his reception would take place in a room in the palace. In order to explain the change of procedure, it was allowed to be whispered in the town that His Majesty was a little unwell, and unable to stand the fatigue of the great function in the open air.

The reception accordingly took place in an upper room of the palace. The young Sultan was seated

cross-legged on a pale blue Louis XV. sofa, the
greater part of which was covered by his out-
spread robes. At his side stood his Minister of
Foreign Affairs and his viziers. The Chamberlain
introduced the British Minister, who read his
speech in English, the interpretation being made
by an official of the Legation. The Sultan whispered his reply to the Foreign Minister, who spoke
it out aloud.

The scene was attractive, and of course much
more " intimate " than the great ceremonial of
the past, but was never lacking in dignity. The
" audience," confined strictly to the reception,
lasted only a very few minutes, when the Minister
and his suite retired. As we were proceeding
down the staircase, I was hurriedly called back
into the Sultan's presence. He had thrown off
the great white cloak in which he had been almost
enveloped, and discarded his heavy turban of
State for one of much less weighty dimensions.
His viziers and courtiers had departed. Calling
to me to come quickly, he cried, " Climb up here
with me, on to the back of the sofa ; we shall
be able to see the Mission ride out of the palace
square " ; and he clambered up and stood on the
gilt carving of his throne, whence, by pulling himself up by his hands, he could just see out of a
little window high up in the richly-decorated wall
of the room. Following his example, I mounted
beside him, and together we watched the Minister
and the Mission mount their horses and depart
from the palace, to the booming of guns.

At the time of my first visit to the Court, Si
Ahmed ben Moussa, better known as Bou Ahmed,
was the predominant figure amongst the native
officials. He held at this time the post of Chamberlain, one of great importance and influence,
as its holder was in constant contact with the
Sultan, and could gain his private ear. He was
undoubtedly devoted to the Sultan's interests, and
served him faithfully and well. His father had
been a palace slave, and he himself was very
dark in colour, and of most unattractive appearance. He was a man of no particular intelligence,
but of indomitable will, and cruel. He made no
pretensions to understand the foreign relations of
Morocco; and except in so far as he was anti-
European, more from political than religious
motives, he seems to have had no fixed policy.
Even later, when he became, under Mulai Abdul
Aziz, Grand Vizier, he was content to leave the
discussion of all affairs of foreign policy to the
other viziers, though no doubt he took part in
the decisions arrived at. Mulai Hassen's Foreign
Minister was Sid Fadhoul Gharnit, a wily and
intelligent gentleman, who is still living. When
the Government of which he was a member fell
—and the falls of Government in those days often
meant the falling of heads too—Sid Fadhoul
Gharnit was seized by a stroke, and disappeared
into the recesses of his house. For years he was
supposed to be paralysed, and was no doubt in
bad health; but another change of Ministry came
about years afterwards, and he emerged again,

miraculously cured and looking younger and more spry than ever, to become Grand Vizier for a time. He has now retired from public life, and resides in Fez. No doubt his paralysis, real or feigned, saved his family from ruin, his fortune from confiscation, and probably himself from prison or even death. Difficult as was the work, great as were the responsibilities of Cabinet Ministers in Morocco, they were not pestered by an Opposition, for if—rarely—any members of the outgoing Government survived, they were always in prison.

In 1893 Mulai Hassen determined to visit the desert regions of Morocco, including far-off Tafilet, the great oasis from which his dynasty had originally sprung, and where, before becoming the ruling branch of the royal family, they had resided ever since their founder, the great-grandson of the Prophet, had settled there, an exile from the East.

Leaving Fez in the summer, the Sultan proceeded south, crossing the Atlas above Kasba-el-Maghzen, and descended to the upper waters of the Wad Ziz. An expedition such as this would have required a system of organisation far in excess of the capabilities of the Moors, great though their resources were. Food was lacking; the desert regions could provide little. The water was bad, the heat very great. Every kind of delay, including rebellion and the consequent punishment of the tribes, hampered the Sultan's movements; and it was only toward winter that he arrived in Tafilet with a fever-stricken army and greatly diminished transport.

Mulai Hassen returned from Tafilet a dying man. The internal complaint from which he was suffering had become acute from the hardships he had undergone, and he was unable to obtain the rest that his state of health required, nor would he place himself under a régime. For a few months he remained in the southern capital, and in the late spring 1894 set out to suppress a rebellion that had broken out in the Tadla region.

While camping in the enemy country he died. Now, the death of the Sultan under such circumstances was fraught with danger to the State. He was an absolute monarch, and with his disappearance all authority and government lapsed until his successor should have taken up the reins. Again, the expedition was in hostile country, and any inkling of the Sultan's death would have brought the tribes down to pillage and loot the Imperial camp. As long as the Sultan lived, and was present with his expedition, his prestige was sufficient to prevent an attack of the tribes— though even this was not unknown on one or two occasions—and to hold his forces together as a sort of concrete body. But his death, if known, would have meant speedy disorganisation, nor could the troops themselves be trusted not to seize this opportunity to murder and loot.

It was therefore necessary that the Sultan's demise should be kept an absolute secret. He had died in the recesses of his tents, themselves enclosed in a great canvas wall, inside which, except on very special occasions, no one was permitted to penetrate. The knowledge of his death was therefore limited to the personal slaves and to his Chamberlain, Bou Ahmed.

Orders were given that the Sultan would start on his journey at dawn, and before daylight the State palanquin was carried into the Imperial enclosure, the corpse laid within it, and its doors closed and the curtains drawn. At the first pale break of dawn the palanquin was brought out, supported by sturdy mules. Bugles were blown, the band played, and the bowing courtiers and officials poured forth their stentorian cry, "May God protect the life of our Lord." The procession formed up, and, led by flying banners, the dead Sultan set out on his march.

A great distance was covered that day. Only once did the procession stop, when the palanquin was carried into a tent by the roadside, that the Sultan might breakfast. Food was borne in and out ; tea, with all the paraphernalia of its brewing, was served : but none but the slaves who knew the secret were permitted to enter. The Chamberlain remained with the corpse, and when a certain time had passed, he emerged to state that His Majesty was rested and had breakfasted, and would proceed on his journey—and once more the procession moved on. Another long march was made to where the great camp was pitched for the night.

The Sultan was tired, the Chamberlain said. He would not come out of his enclosure to transact business as usual in the "Diwan" tent, where

he granted audiences. Documents were taken in
to the royal quarters by the Chamberlain himself,
and, when necessary, they emerged bearing the
seal of State, and verbal replies were given to a
host of questions.

Then another day of forced marches, for the
expedition was still in dangerous country; but
Mulai Hassen's death could no longer be concealed. It was summer, and the state of the
Sultan's body told its own secret.

Bou Ahmed announced that His Majesty had
died two days before, and that by this time his
young son, Mulai Abdul Aziz, chosen and nominated by his father, had been proclaimed at Rabat,
whither the fleetest of runners had been sent with
the news immediately after the death had occurred.

It was a *fait accompli*. The army was now free
of the danger of being attacked by the tribes;
and the knowledge that the new Sultan was already
reigning, and that tranquillity existed elsewhere,
deterred the troops from any excesses. Many
took the occasion of a certain disorganisation to
desert, but so customary was this practice that it
attracted little or no attention.

Two days later the body of the dead Sultan,
now in a terrible state of decomposition, arrived
at Rabat. It must have been a gruesome procession from the description his son Mulai Abdul
Aziz gave me: the hurried arrival of the swaying
palanquin bearing its terrible burden, five days
dead in the great heat of summer; the escort,
who had bound scarves over their faces—but even

this precaution could not keep them from constant sickness—and even the mules that bore the palanquin seemed affected by the horrible atmosphere, and tried from time to time to break loose.

No corpse is, by tradition, allowed to enter through the gates into a Moorish city, and even in the case of the Sovereign no exception was made. A hole was excavated in the town wall, through which the procession passed direct into the precincts of the palace, where the burial took place. Immediately after, the wall was restored.

Beyond having been presented to Mulai Hassen while accompanying a diplomatic Mission, I never had personally any conversation with him. In those days the isolation of the Court was extreme, and the most rigid traditional etiquette was in force. He was no fanatic, and had he been able to break down some of the great reserve which encircled him, he probably would have been content to do so. In appearance he was extremely handsome, dark, but showing no trace of black blood, with straight regular features, and a most dignified bearing. His most remarkable feature was, however, the sadness of his expression. I saw him on many occasions during the last few years of his reign, for he appeared fairly often in public, and was always struck by this look of weariness and sadness. He died in middle age. Yet apparently he possessed a considerable sense of humour, and was not averse at times to playing practical jokes upon his Court and entourage. It was his son, the Sultan Mulai Abdul Aziz, who told me of the following incident.

It was the custom of the Sultan in early spring, when the first fresh butter of the season came in, to give a feast to his courtiers and to certain distinguished people of the town. Butter with the Moors is like the primrose with us. It heralds the spring, the time of great productiveness in Morocco, when the flocks and herds bear their young and fatten upon the rich grass. A few months later summer comes, and the herbage dries up. The cows cease calving and their milk runs dry, with the result that the people are dependent upon preserved butter—" smin "—for their food; and they are great butter eaters, both in its raw state and in their cooking. So when the first cows calve and butter comes into season, no feast is complete without its " lordly dish " of this much-appreciated article. The poets sing of it, as ours do of the nightingale—not materially, but rather as being the outward and visible sign of the new spring-life of all things, those few months in the year when all is productive, all is increasing, and which give promise of the great crops that are to follow.

Amongst the guests of the Sultan upon one of these occasions was a certain celebrated scholar, a master of religion, who was charged with the education of the Sultan's sons. He had, as well as great knowledge, another characteristic—great meanness.

When the repast was over and the steaming

dishes of cooked meats, or what was left of them, had been removed, there remained great plates of fresh butter, the very first of the season, hard and rolled into large balls. The learned tutor of the Sultan's sons stated that it was much to be regretted that such splendid butter should be wasted by being eaten by the palace slaves and attendants, and forthwith he tore off a length of his fine white turban, rolled up one of the large balls of butter, and replaced the package in the crown of his high-peaked fez, which formed the foundation of his headgear.

One of the slaves told Mulai Hassen what had occurred, and he determined to amuse himself at the expense of his sons' tutor. He entered the great chamber where the guests were assembled and bade them welcome, paying a few compliments to each. When it came to the turn of the learned man, the Sultan congratulated him on his great attainments, adding, "He shall be specially honoured. Bring rose-water and incense."

Now, it is the custom at Moorish feasts to sprinkle the guests with rose and orange-blossom water, and to perfume their robes with incense. So the long-necked silver bottles and the brass incense-burner were produced. From the latter, laid upon red-hot charcoal, the burning sandalwood diffused its smoke in delicious clouds. Having received the regulation sprinkling, the incense-burner was placed before him. Lifting his wide sleeves, the slaves held the censer below them, allowing the smoke to permeate his volum-

inous garments. Then drawing the hood of his
" bernous " over his head and face, the customary
perfuming of the turban was begun. But the
slaves held tight, and instead of the performance
lasting half a minute, it was unduly prolonged.
At first it was only the richly-perfumed smoke of
the sandalwood that entered his nose and eyes ;
but presently the delicious odour changed, for the
butter concealed in his fez, melting under the
applied heat of the red-hot charcoal, was beginning to drop into the incense-burner, giving forth
a penetrating and unpleasant odour of cooking.
From drops to a trickling stream took a very
little while, and soon the whole room was full of
the smoke of burning butter, while the aged scholar
presented the most pitiful sight—half-blinded,
choking, and dripping all over. When he had
been washed and cleaned up the Sultan had
gone.

Mulai Abdul Aziz was, at the time of his succession (1894), about twelve or thirteen years of
age. He was a younger son of the late Sultan,
for Islamic thrones do not necessarily descend by
primogeniture. It is not unseldom a brother who
succeeds, and at times even more distant relations.
The throne is almost elective inside the royal
family, though, as a matter of fact, a Sultan
generally nominates his successor. The descent
from the common ancestor—who in this case of
Shereefian families is the Prophet Mohammed—
is of far greater importance than the relationship
of the deceased and succeeding Sultan. After the

abdication of Mulai Hafid in 1912, his half-brother,
Mulai Youssef, was "chosen" to fill the throne,
and accepted without hesitation. His choice has
been amply justified by the dignified manner and
the constant tact that he has always shown in
his very difficult position.

The mother of Mulai Abdul Aziz was a Turkish
lady, brought from Constantinople to Morocco.
Report states that she was a woman of great
intelligence and considerable force of character.
She was certainly a most devoted mother. It is
even said that she played a part in the politics
of the country, and that she was consulted on
affairs of State by her husband. That she must
have possessed a remarkable personality is clear
from the fact that she maintained her influence
over the Sultan till the day of his death—no easy
task amidst a host of rivals—and so assured the
succession of her son. Her great friend and companion in the harem was another Turkish lady,
the mother of the reigning Sultan Mulai Youssef.
It is curious that these two " strangers in a foreign
land " should both have been destined to become
the mothers of Sultans.

It was only natural that the succession of a
minor gave rise to every form of intrigue at Court.
There were two great factions in the palace—the
party of Bou Ahmed, the powerful Chamberlain,
on the one hand, and that of the Grand Vizier
and Minister of War on the other. These two high
officials belonged to the aristocratic and powerful
family of the Ulad Jamai, and were respectively

Haj Amaati and Si Mohammed Soreir. Now Bou
Ahmed was the son of a negro slave, and therefore could count on no tribal or family influence.
His rivals, on the contrary, were Fez aristocrats,
highly born, and supported by the influential
population of the towns. They came of what is
known as a " Maghzen " family—that is to say,
a family who in the past had held Government
posts, and had a sort of traditional claim to high
employment. It was evident that jealousy must
exist between these two factions.

Bou Ahmed's position of Chamberlain gave him
constant access to his sovereign, whose extreme
youth brought him little into contact with his
viziers. No doubt, too, Bou Ahmed could count
upon the influence of the Sultan's mother. He
had been the constant and trustworthy confidant
of her husband, and instrumental in putting her
son on the throne. His own fate, too, depended
upon his keeping him there, and there can be
little doubt that Mulai Abdul Aziz's mother and
Bou Ahmed worked in connivance.

As soon as the new Government was organised
sufficiently for Mulai Abdul Aziz to travel, the
Court left Rabat for Fez—the real capital of the
country. No Sultan can count upon his throne
as being safe until he has been accepted by the
religious and aristocratic Fezzis, and taken up his
residence in the city; for Fez is the centre of
religion and learning—and also of intrigue—and
the influence of its population upon the tribes is
very great. It was therefore very important that

the young Sultan should reach Fez at as early
a date as possible. His journey through the tribes
to Meknés was very successful. He was well
received on every side, and on his arrival at the
old capital which Mulai Ismail, a contemporary
of Louis Quatorze, had built, the population of
the city accorded him a popular welcome.

Meknés is some thirty-three miles from Fez,
and there remained only this last stage of the
journey to be accomplished.

Bou Ahmed fully appreciated his position. He
knew that once in Fez his influence must decrease.
His rivals could count upon the support not only
of the townspeople, but also of the Sultan's relations in the capital. To the Fezzis he was an
upstart, and there would be no peace from their
intrigues to bring about his fall, and no pity when
he fell. It was a case of now or never for Bou
Ahmed.

There were no signs of the coming storm. The
Ulad Jamai brothers were no doubt waiting till
their arrival amongst their own people in Fez to
begin a more active intrigue, and Bou Ahmed
himself was courteous and a little obsequious to
the influential viziers. A few mornings after the
Sultan's arrival at Meknés, the usual morning
Court was being held. Haj Amaati, the Grand
Vizier, surrounded by his white-robed followers,
rode into the palace square, amidst the bowing
officials and the salutes of troops. He was immediately summoned into the Sultan's presence.

Mulai Abdul Aziz was alone with Bou Ahmed

when Haj Amaati entered. He prostrated himself, and waited for the Sultan to speak. In a rather frightened voice Mulai Abdul Aziz asked him a question. Haj Amaati's answer was not found satisfactory, and Bou Ahmed burst forth in a string of reproaches against the Vizier, and accused him of disloyalty, avarice, extortion, and political crimes. Suddenly appealing to the Sultan, he asked for permission to arrest him. Mulai Abdul Aziz inclined his head.

A few minutes later a dishevelled, cringing, crying creature, amid jeers and laughter, was dragged through the palace square amongst the crowd that only so short a time before had been bowing to the ground. His clothes were torn, for the soldiers were rough, and his turban was all askew. As he passed through the gate, dragged by the soldiery, the sentry at the door seized the Vizier's clean white turban and set it on his own head, replacing it by his own dirty fez cap. A shout of laughter greeted this act.

The Vizier's brother, Si Mohammed Soreir, the Minister of War, had not yet left his house for the palace. He was arrested at his own doorway, and did not attempt to resist, but allowed himself to be led to prison.

The subsequent history of these two men forms perhaps the blackest page of Mulai Abdul Aziz's reign. They were sent in fetters to Tetuan, and confined, chained and fettered, in a dungeon. In the course of time—and how long those ten years must have been—Haj Amaati died. The Governor

of Tetuan was afraid to bury the body, lest he
should be accused of having allowed his prisoner
to escape. He wrote to Court for instructions.
It was summer, and even the dungeon was hot.
The answer did not come for eleven days, and all
that time Si Mohammed Soreir remained chained
to his brother's corpse! The brother survived.
In 1908 he was released after fourteen years'
incarceration, a hopeless, broken, ruined man.
Everything he had possessed had been confiscated ; his wives and children had died, the result
of want and persecution. He emerged from his
dark dungeon nearly blind, and lame from the
cruel fetters he had worn. In his days of power
he had been cruel, it is said—but what a price he
paid !

He settled in Tangier, where I saw him almost
daily. He was in absolute poverty ; but all his
friends assisted him—and he wanted so little. An
old slave woman of the family, who had survived
in some out-of-the-way corner, came to look after
him, and used to massage his tortured wrists and
ankles. At length he died.

Two days before his death I saw him for the
last time. It was clear that a very little span
of life remained for him. I sat with him a long
time, and as I rose to leave him, he said : " Listen.
When they have washed my body for burial, I
want you to see that my chains and fetters are
put back upon my limbs. I desire to appear
before my God as I spent those fourteen years
of my life, that I may appeal to Him for the

justice my Sultan refused me, that He in His great mercy and forgiveness may open to me the gates of Paradise."

It was impossible to replace the chains and fetters, but I believe a link was sewn up in his winding-sheet. With the cruellest cynicism he was given an official military funeral, attended by all the native authorities and functionaries—for after all he had been Minister of War !

Sir Ernest Satow represented Great Britain in Morocco at the time of Mulai Abdul Aziz's succession. On learning of Mulai Hassen's death, the news of which Kaid Maclean—who was with the Moorish army—had managed to send to Tangier with almost incredible rapidity, Sir Ernest sent for me and told me that he proposed to send some confidential agent to Fez upon a mission, which would certainly be difficult and very likely dangerous, for, as the news of the Sultan's death spread, there would no doubt be disturbances on every side. I naturally volunteered to go, and my offer was accepted. The same night at twelve o'clock I left, accompanied by one of my men, both of us well mounted and armed. I am averse to carrying arms in such countries as Morocco, and have very seldom done so ; but the occasion was unusual, and bands of marauders might be looked for. I was dressed as a native mountaineer, my head shaved except for one long lock of hair, which I, native fashion, wore at this period of my life ; my legs bare, and my feet thrust into yellow slippers. A rough brown-hooded cloak

covered my scanty clothing. I, no doubt, looked
a brigand—my companion was one. Luckily I
had good horses in my stable, and we chose the
two most likely to stand the fatigue. It was most
important to start at once and travel fast, in
order, if possible, to keep ahead of the news of
the Sultan's death, which was now publicly known
in Tangier. I could not take the direct route for
Fez, for part of my mission was to visit certain
influential Shereefs *en route* to whom I was personally known, and to exhort them to use all
their influence in the interests of peace, law, and
order.

It was midsummer, and dawn was early; but
before the sun had risen we reached Arzeila,
twenty-six miles from Tangier. Here I breakfasted with the Shereef of Abrish, a brother-in-
law of the famous Raisuli, and himself a man of
considerable renown. He promised to exert all
his influence to keep the tribes quiet. After a
short halt I left the town, and at night arrived
at Alcazar, having covered, by the route we had
travelled, well over sixty miles. From Alcazar to
Wazzan was a matter of some eight hours' ride,
and I reached the holy city of that name early
the next afternoon. I was most cordially received
by the very influential Shereefs who inhabit that
little mountain city, so rarely visited by Europeans, as it is holy ground. It was a feast-day;
but in spite of that the Shereefs at once got to
work, sending numerous letters to the tribes to
remain quiet. This work kept me at Wazzan till

the middle of the following day, when I started once more, reaching the Maizerieh, a village on the hills above the Sebou Valley, that night. Here we slept, to start again before daylight.

It was clear that the tribes here had learned the news of the Sultan's death, for all night long there was desultory firing, and in the early dawn we could distinguish groups of horsemen in the valley below. A general wiping out of old scores had begun, combined with organised pillage.

Avoiding as far as possible the districts where firing was taking place, my man and I rode on. The situation was uncomfortable, and I forgot for a moment what brigands we ourselves must have looked; but on suddenly coming upon a long line of laden camels, the half-dozen caravan men in charge took to their heels and ran for their lives. We soon, however, reassured them, and rode on. The fourth day's travelling after leaving Tangier I arrived in Fez, having by our detours covered from 190 to 200 miles. My horses were tired, but not done up. At midday I presented the British Minister's despatch, and my verbal message, to a council of the native authorities sitting in the house of Amin Haj Abdesalam El-Mokri, the father of the well-known Grand Vizier, Haj Mohammed El-Mokri, perhaps the most intelligent and capable of all the Moorish authorities of to-day.

I remained in Fez for several weeks. Meanwhile, Mulai Abdul Aziz had reached Meknés, where, at the moment of the arrest of the Grand

Vizier and the Minister of War, I arrived, returning to Fez with the young Sultan.

I have always looked back upon that period
with great pleasure. I was engaged upon a mission
of some delicacy, and I was thrust into the very
midst of native affairs. With that hospitality for
which the Mokri family is so well known, I was
a guest in their great house, one of the sights of
Fez, with its terraced gardens and its many fountains. It required no little courage in those days
to harbour a "Christian," and I think this was
the first time on which a European had ever
been made welcome to stay in one of the great
Fez houses. I wore the native dress—I had, of
course, arrived without even a change of shirt—
and lived in the company of the sons of the family,
and was treated as one of them. My wants were
amply supplied from the voluminous wardrobes of
my hosts.

My mission was a success. On 14th July Sir
Ernest Satow wrote me agreeing to my request
to be allowed to return to Tangier. His letter is
before me now :—

" The Foreign Office has much approved of my
having sent you to Fez, and will not be unmindful
of the services you have rendered on the present
occasion. I sent copies of the greater part of
your long report (which I copied out myself) to
Sanderson, and Lord Kimberley read it with great
interest. I will only add now that I feel myself
under a great obligation to you for having undertaken an important and, to all appearances, peril-

ous mission. But I felt you were the man to accomplish it. . . . Many thanks for all you have done. It has been most successful."

My mission had lasted many weeks, and necessitated riding several hundreds of miles in the great heat of midsummer in discomfort, and often in danger. The British Government remunerated my services by presenting me with a cheque of £100. I did not complain, nor do I now, for it has been so unusual to be paid at all when employed upon these unofficial missions, that it seemed almost extravagant. Only on one other occasion during my whole Morocco career have I ever been paid even my out-of-pocket expenses for tasks undertaken at the request of the British authorities. I never realised myself the extent of the work I have done in this connection until I began to write this book, when I unearthed the voluminous correspondence that a succession of British Ministers had addressed to me, and which seem to treat of every mortal question pertaining to Morocco.

I have quoted Sir Ernest Satow's letter, not from any desire to boast of the utility of my work, but because it represented one of the very few marks of appreciation and encouragement that I ever received from official sources, or, rather, I should perhaps say, in which the credit of my work was allowed to me. It was only years later that I learned that from the day of Sir Ernest Satow's departure from Morocco, over a period of many years, all my work went home anonymously—that is to say, contained in official despatch as " I understand," or " I am informed." In my own particular case it didn't matter much ; but I confess that it hurt a little to be told long afterwards that the mass of information that I obtained—often by undertaking journeys at the direct instigation of the British authorities, often by my own personal relations with the tribes, and always at my own expense—went home without its origin being disclosed, and without identity. I have quoted Sir Ernest Satow's letter ; I will give one or two quotations from those of his successors.

" I want you particularly to find out and let me know the following things . . ."   " It would be interesting, as you are in that part of the country, if you would go a little farther and visit . . ."   " I want you to impress upon the Sultan the importance of . . ."   " I would like you to return here as soon as possible, to consult you about the . . . question."   " You are the only authority on the . . . tribes and what is passing there. Could you therefore return . . ."   " I hope you will arrange not to be long away, as I want to consult you about . . ."   " Please give the Sultan clearly to understand that we will not . . ."   " You are the one and only authority on these questions."   " When you have time would you make me a full report on . . ."   " As a private individual it will be easier for you to get the Maghzen [Government] to agree to . . ."   " I bow to your superior knowledge on all these

questions, and now agree with you that . . ."
" Do come back. I am lost without having you
to consult." These are a few extracts of what
was written ; the verbal instructions and requests
were naturally far greater.

I am glad of having been able to be of use,
and would not hesitate to act again as I acted
in the past ; but the policy of depriving the
unofficial and unpaid workman of the little crumbs
of credit is wrong. It ought rather to be the rule
to tempt young men of adventurous disposition
to live the life I led, and, if necessary, to assist
them—not to use them perpetually and keep them
outside the pale. It is contrary to human nature
to be absolutely disinterested in the personal success of one's work, and the suppression of its
origin—more particularly when its origin is a life-
time of travel and of study, as well as a proficiency
for making friends amongst such people as the
Moors—can only tend toward discouragement. In
any branch of life but that of diplomacy such
action would be considered incorrect.

Since 1912, when the French Protectorate was
declared, and even before that date, from the
time when England had abandoned all political
aims in Morocco except to assist French policy,
my information became of more value to the
authorities of our friend and ally than to ourselves. I was invited to accompany more than
one French special Mission, and have on many
occasions been consulted on questions of great
confidence, not only by French Ministers in Tan-

gier, but also by the highest authorities of the
French Protectorate. My little dossier of French
official correspondence compares very favourably
with that of our own people. Sir Ernest Satow's
letter, which was quoted, is the one and only
expression of appreciation I ever received from
the British Government, while I have a dozen
letters of thanks, simple and full of appreciation
and encouragement, from Paris. My duties as
' Times ' correspondent often brought me into more
or less acute discussions with the Spanish Government, but this has not deterred their high authorities from expressing to me on several occasions,
in letters which I much appreciate, their thanks
for information given, and their satisfaction at the
large and fair way I have treated certain diplomatic questions, not only in the ' Times ' but also
elsewhere.

In such a life as I have led there have been
necessarily moments when one has been disheart-
ened and depressed, perhaps owing to fever, perhaps to events. In my case, happily, they have
been few and far between, and I look back over
those past years in Morocco as a period of great
pleasure ; but there have been moments when a
little word of encouragement, a few lines to say
that one's work had been appreciated at home—
another letter, for instance, like Sir Ernest Satow's
—would have been so welcome and have done so
much. I can honestly say the occasions have not
been wanting.

I have enjoyed throughout the confidence of

our representatives, and a very intimate and much appreciated friendship with them all. I have had every opportunity of seeing the inner workings of their diplomacy, and I can state that Great Britain has been fortunate in her Ministers in this country. Some left Tangier to fill more important posts elsewhere—Sir Ernest Satow, Sir Arthur Nicolson, and the late Sir Gerard Lowther, the best and kindest of men. One, perhaps the most brilliant of all, rests here for ever, the last British Minister to Morocco, Sir Reginald Lister, whose loss to his country was so great, and to his friends irreparable.

LIFE AT THE MOORISH COURT.

MULAI ABDUL AZIZ'S stay in Fez, the northern capital, in 1894, was not of long duration, for it was important that the Court should move to the south to consolidate his throne in those regions. While Northern Morocco has always been the unrestful and most seditious part of the country, it has never presented such a serious danger as the south is capable of becoming, for the northern tribes are poor, numerically in no great force, and always at war with each other. But in the Marrakesh region it is different. The rich agricultural land, and the great harvest reaped from it, render the tribes affluent ; they are well horsed and well armed, and very prolific. Again, beyond the plains, the great range of the Atlas Mountains is inhabited by spirited and warlike Berber tribes, to all intents and purposes unconquered. Fortunately for the welfare of a long succession of Moorish Sultans, these great tribes, governed by hereditary chiefs, were nearly always on bad terms with one another ; and one of the most important results accomplished by the French Protectorate Govern-

ment in the last few years has been to form a
league of the southern tribesmen. Any one who
knew the old Morocco could scarcely believe that
the great chiefs—the Glaoui, the Mtougi, the Gindafi, and the Rahamna Kaid—would ever join
hands, even in the interests of the country. But
to-day it is so.

Mulai Abdul Aziz was able to leave the north
in a state of peace and security. New Governors
had been appointed, and Bou Ahmed's firm hand
had made itself felt, and it was indispensable that
the Court should move south : there were already
signs of unrest that could not be ignored.

The arrival of the Sultan in the southern capital
had a tranquillising effect, and Bou Ahmed set
to work to restore order amongst the restive
tribes and to build himself a palace—at the public
expense. For six years he continued building,
and every available workman and artist was
employed. The result was grandiose, and the
building now forms the " Residency " of the
French Protectorate Government. The " Bahya "
—that is to say, " The Effulgence," as the palace
is called—consists of a succession of handsome
courtyards, one planted with cypress, orange,
lemon, and other fruit trees and flowers, leading one out of the other. These courts are
surrounded by arcades, on to which the great
rooms open. Everywhere are fountains and tanks
of water. This palace must cover many acres of
land, and though quite modern, is a building of
singular interest. There is one courtyard which

is particularly beautiful, where the Moorish architect based his art on the traditions of the past.
The walls are higher; the woodwork is not painted,
as is usual, in polychrome; while the court itself
is not nearly as large as some of the others. The
rooms themselves are perhaps less interesting than
the courtyards into which they open, though in
many cases the elaborately carved and painted
ceilings are very good.

On a very recent visit to Marrakesh I was able
to wander at leisure over this great palace, accompanied by a native who was in charge, and who
knew its every corner and turret, for he had been
employed on its construction. I had seen it years
before—or, rather, a portion of it—for I had twice
been entertained at dinner by its owner, the famous Bou Ahmed. I recall now one of those evenings: the hot, jasmine-scented air of the courts,
for it was late in spring, and the great dinner
served in one of the saloons, while a native band
discoursed anything but soft music just outside;
and Bou Ahmed himself—short, dark, and of
unprepossessing appearance, but none the less an
excellent host. He has been dead now for twenty
years, and his property, confiscated by the Sultan
on his death, has passed into other hands. His
name is only a memory of the past. In Morocco
it was not, " How are the mighty fallen ! " but
" How are the mighty falling ! " for almost month
by month some great Kaid, some Vizier, or some
Prince fell—and fell far indeed.

Bou Ahmed had other things to think of besides

his house. There was grave dissatisfaction amongst some of the tribes, particularly amongst the Rahamna, whose extensive territory lies immediately to the north of the city of Marrakesh. A leader, Taher ben Suleiman, had arisen, and under his influence the tribes revolted. The local authorities were murdered or driven out, and the rebellion became general. Its suppression took long, and cost much in lives and money. On one occasion the rebels arrived at the walls of Marrakesh and took possession of the northern suburbs of the town, but were driven back. Bou Ahmed showed considerable ability in the suppression of this revolt : not only was his energy unceasing, but he knew also how to utilise the jealousy and mistrust that always exists among the rebels. He worked tribe against tribe, and division against division. The Maghzen, by its superiority of organisation, and by the means at its disposal to obtain men, arms, and ammunition, prevailed. The Rahamna rebellion was repressed, and hundreds of square miles of country were given up to fire, the sword, and pillage. The tribe was almost wiped out ; hundreds died in prison ; the women and children became the prey of the soldiery, and were sold or driven away to starve, and devastation reigned supreme. A few years later I travelled through the Rahamna country. It was still deserted, and the fields were grown over with thick weeds and thorn-bushes. Only a few most miserable black tents, with half-starved inhabitants, remained where once the rich and flourishing Rahamna tribe had dwelt. Taher ben Suleiman was captured. He was imprisoned in a cage made of the barrels of his partisans' rifles—a cage so small that he could scarcely move in it,—and was exhibited to the public of Marrakesh, to be spat upon and reviled. He died in prison.

As long as Bou Ahmed lived the young Sultan remained in the palace. True, he appeared at ceremonies and celebrated the religious feasts in public, but he was a nonentity. Bou Ahmed alone governed Morocco.

In 1900 he died. I was in Marrakesh at the time of his last illness, when he lingered on day by day, kept alive by inhalations of oxygen. No one cared, unless it was a few of his personal followers and attendants, who would naturally suffer by his demise. As for the rest, there was a general indifference. He had never been popular, and the immense fortune he had amassed and great palace he had constructed awoke the jealousy of others who had the same desires but not the same opportunities. He was feared certainly, for his will was indomitable, and he was cruel. A sort of superstitious reverence had encircled his life, but it disappeared when sickness laid him low; and when he breathed his last, the pent-up feelings of the people burst forth, and they rose up and cursed him.

The death of a great personage in Morocco is terrible, and for several days as the Vizier lay expiring, guards were stationed outside his palace

waiting in silence for the end. And then one
morning the wail of the women within the house
told that death had come. Every gateway of the
great building was seized, and no one was allowed
to enter or come out, while within there was
pandemonium. His slaves pillaged wherever they
could lay their hands. His women fought and
stole to get possession of the jewels. Safes were
broken open, documents and title-deeds were extracted, precious stones were torn from their set-
tings the more easily to be concealed, and even
murder took place.

While all this was proceeding within the strictly
guarded walls, Bou Ahmed's body was borne out
and buried. The Sultan, weeping, followed the
bier of the man who had put him on his throne
and kept him there through those difficult years
of his youth. He must, indeed, have felt himself
alone as he stood beside the grave of his Vizier,
who, whatever may have been his faults, however
great may have been his extortions, had been
loyal throughout. When Mulai Abdul Aziz, still
weeping, had returned to his palace, his first act
was to sign the decree for the confiscation of all
Bou Ahmed's property. It was now organised
loot, for officials and slaves were turned loose to
carry out the royal commands. For days laden
baggage animals, half-concealed under great masses
of furniture, heaped with carpets and bedding, or
staggering under safes, bore Bou Ahmed's property into the Sultan's palace. His women and
his slaves were made to give up their loot, and

the house was left empty and its owners penniless. A few days later nothing remained but the
great building—all the rest had disappeared into
space. His family were driven out to starvation
and ruin, his slaves were taken by the Sultan to
be kept or sold, and his vast properties passed
into the possession of the State. It was the
custom of the country. The belongings of all
State functionaries passed at death to their lord
and master the Sultan. I see Bou Ahmed's sons
now and again. They are in complete poverty,
and accept as presents with real gratitude the
little sums which an upper servant in England
would despise.

The accepting of small presents of money is, in
Morocco, not considered by any means derogatory,
much less the accepting of large sums. I remember
well a great-uncle of the reigning Sultan, a man
who had been Viceroy in his time, who regularly
toured the country with a slave or two, collecting
alms. He was a pleasant genial old gentleman,
and had no hesitation in asking any one he met
to help him, or in accepting the smallest of coins.
On one occasion he arrived at the residence of a
native ex-official of the Moorish Court, who lived
in Tangier. There was a tennis-party going on,
and the guests, amongst whom were a certain
number of the representatives of the European
Powers, were at tea. His Highness called me aside
and asked who all these Europeans were. "They
are," I replied, "largely the Ministers of the
foreign Powers." "Aha," said the Prince, "they

ought to be good for a pair of shoes if not for a cloak. Rich people, rich people." I was able to deter him, much to his surprise, by explaining that it was not the custom in Europe for members of the royal families to ask total strangers for coats, or even shoes, and I added that if he would wait a little I would see what could be done. I mentioned the Prince's request to a few of my friends, and we subscribed between us the six francs necessary to purchase a pair of yellow slippers, the only footgear of the country. He was graciously pleased to accept them with the dignity of a Prince of the Blood.

The death of Bou Ahmed naturally brought about changes at Court. Whatever jealousies there may have existed amongst the viziers, and no doubt they were many, they realised that common action was necessary. Each might have, and probably would have, to defend his own particular position from the others, but collectively they had to defend their united positions from all the world. They must either succeed or fall together, and they determined to succeed.

The Sultan was now about twenty years of age, and might at any moment desire to assert himself; and the self-assertion of young monarchs of auto- cratic power and no experience is dangerous. The viziers realised that in all probability the dis- appearance of the strong hand of Bou Ahmed would tempt the young Sultan to become more independent, and it was necessary to come to some arrangement as to how he should be led to think and act. Certainly it must not be in the direction of affairs of State—those the viziers meant to keep to themselves. An occupation must be found for the inexperienced and hitherto secluded monarch.

It was the exact reverse of all the traditions of Morocco; but the situation was an unusual one, for there had never been a Sultan in a similar position. The viziers felt that should influence be brought to bear to keep him in his palace he might rebel against this enforced seclusion, and rid himself, and probably in no gentle manner, of the men who had instituted it. No; it was clear the Sultan must be amused, and his amusements must be so numerous and so varied that his entire attention would be distracted from affairs of State. Morocco itself could not supply the novelties that would be required. Such pleasures and such luxuries as the country could produce were his already—women, horses, jewels, and the whole paraphernalia that goes to make up an oriental potentate's surroundings. For further distractions appeal must be made to Europe. It was not made in vain. It was the beginning of the great debacle, of the reckless extravagance, of the follies and the debts that led to foreign loans, and step by step to the loss of Morocco's independence.

A strong and good adviser might have prolonged the life of an independent Morocco, for although possessed of no great attainments or will-power, Mulai Abdul Aziz was thoughtful, intelligent, and desirous of doing well. It was no easy matter, however, at Marrakesh, the southern capital, where the Court was at this time in residence, to keep the young Sultan amused. Situated 100 miles from the nearest port, which itself was 300 miles down the Atlantic coast, communication with Europe was necessarily very slow, and the Sultan's ever-increasing orders of European goods took long to carry out. Often, too, the heavy Atlantic swell rendered communication impossible between the ships and the shore for weeks together.

The Sultan's caterers were at their last resources. Fireworks were played out ; bicycle tricks had led to bruises and sprains ; and even photography had lost its pristine interest. At this critical moment came word of a belated circus at one of the coast towns. It must naturally have been a very poor circus ever to have found itself at that dreary little port, but its advent was welcomed as enthusiastically as if it had been Barnum's entire show. Imperial letters were directed to the local Kaids and Governors, agents rushed wildly to and fro, and eventually the circus, bag and baggage, consisting of a dozen people and three or four horses, started out across the weary plains of Morocco to obey the royal command. It all took time, and meanwhile in Court circles it was the absorbing topic of conversation. One or two serious rebellions among the tribes, and an acute quarrel with the Government of a European Power, passed into temporary oblivion.

Now, the proprietress of this circus was an

extremely stout Spanish lady of uncertain age,
on whose corpulent body the rough jogging on a
mule for more than a hundred miles had left almost
as painful an impression as the discomfort, heat,
and worry of the journey had upon her temper.
She herself took no active part in the performance, and it was on this account, to her intense
indignation and wrath, that she was refused admit-
tance to the court of the palace in which the
Sultan was to witness the show. His Majesty's
orders were that none but the actual performers
should be allowed to enter.

So the fat lady and one or two of the employees
of the circus remained in an outer courtyard
adjoining the enclosure in which the Sultan, seated
under a gorgeous tent, was witnessing the performance. A wall some twenty feet in height
separated these two courts; and in the outer one,
where the fat lady found herself, the Sultan had
been building some additions to the palace, and
a pile of stone, mortar, and other material reached
almost to the top of the wall. The lady was both
angry and bored, nor were a herd of gazelle and
a few fine specimens of mouflon—Barbary wild
sheep—that roamed about the enclosure sufficient
to keep her amused.

To have received a royal command to come all
that way to the Moorish capital, and then to be
deprived of the glory of seeing her own circus
performing before a real Sultan, was more than
she could bear, and she straightway began to
climb the great heap of building material that lay

piled against the wall. It was hard work, nor was her figure suited for such mountain-climbing ; but she was to receive assistance from a source undreamed of. Affected, no doubt, by her slow progress in a sport of which he himself was so proficient, the old ram mouflon lightly bounded after her. Balancing himself for a moment on his hind-legs, he lunged forward and butted the fat lady so successfully from below that her ascent was materially assisted. In a series of repeated bounds, owing to no voluntary action on her own part, she found herself pantingly grasping the top of the thick wall.

Meanwhile the performance of the circus was progressing to the Sultan's satisfaction. Suddenly, however, an expression of wrathful consternation became visible in his face, and, speechless, he pointed at the wall. There, far above, was the agonised and purple visage of the fat lady, peering down at the Sultan and his Court. In a moment the officers of the suite were shouting and gesticulating to her to retire. But the only reply they received was a sudden vision of a considerable portion of her immense body, as a playful mouflon, himself invisible, gave her another hoist up. At last all her body was on the wall, to which she clung for dear life with arms and legs, as she lay extended on its summit. It was at this moment that the mouflon appeared. With a majestic bound he leaped on to the summit, stood for a moment poised on his hind-legs, then suddenly dropped, and with a terrific prod from his wide

horns, butted the fat lady at least a yard
along the wall. He was evidently intent upon
taking her round the entire circuit of the courtyard.

For a few moments there was turmoil. The
Sultan sat silent and amazed, while the Cabinet
Ministers all shouted to the lady to disappear,
which she was certainly most anxious to do. The
slaves, more wisely, pelted the mouflon with stones,
and drove him from his point of vantage. Then
slowly the lady disappeared—the fat legs first,
then the heaving mass of body, and finally even
the purple face was seen no more.

It was in 1901 that I became personally ac-
quainted with the young Sultan. I had seen
him once or twice, for I had accompanied Sir
Arthur Nicolson's special Mission to Marrakesh in
1896 ; but at that time the Sultan had not emerged
from his shell of reserve. He was still a young
boy, evidently very shy, and entirely under the
thumb of Bou Ahmed, the famous Grand Vizier.
One audience that we had with him on that occasion was not without interest. We had ridden
far into the depths of the great Agdal gardens
to a summer-house, where His Shereefian Majesty
was waiting to receive the British Minister. A
tangled jungle of orange-trees ; vines climbing
over broken trellis, and clinging in festoons to
great cypresses ; here and there a broken marble
fountain or a tiny stream—such were our surroundings. With our escort of white-robed Moorish
cavalry, led by the Master of the Ceremonies, we

rode through the great garden to dismount before
a kiosk of arches and pillars, of green-glazed
tiles and red geometric frescoes on a yellow wall.
Everywhere the tangle of vegetation had overgrown its borders. The cypresses shot up, pillars
of dark green, above the building, while vine,
jasmine, and geranium strove for the supremacy
below. Outside the building, and out of sight of
its occupants, sat a row of Moorish officers, the
Sultan's attendants. At the door of the one room
that the kiosk contained — for it seemed all
arches and pillars without—stood Bou Ahmed, the
Vizier, a dark, stout, short man, showing his black
origin in every feature.

Within, opposite the doorway, on a Louis Seize
settee, was Mulai Abdul Aziz. He was seated
cross-legged, with his hands folded in his lap and
half-hidden in his soft white raiment. I remember
being particularly struck with his pale complexion
and his evident shyness. At the side of the divan
was a chair, where the British Minister was invited to be seated, while we who were in attendance stood around the door. The Sultan himself
said little, and that little was addressed to his
Vizier in almost a whisper, and repeated by him
to the British Minister. In a few minutes Mulai
Abdul Aziz had largely recovered his self-posses-
sion, and was busy taking in every item of the
uniforms worn by the Minister's suite. He could
scarcely keep his eyes off one man—the present
Lord Loch—whose six feet five, capped by an
enormous busby, was of evidently entrancing in-

terest to His Majesty. Four years later, talking
to Mulai Abdul Aziz in the intimacy of personal
friendship, I reminded him of this episode. He
laughingly replied that he had certainly been more
struck with his height and uniform than anything
else on that Mission, and requested me to ask the
British Minister whether it would not be possible
for Lord Loch to accompany a second embassy
that was to start a few months later. This message
duly reached the authorities at home, and in
January 1902 Mulai Abdul Aziz, no longer shy,
had the pleasure—and it was an evident pleasure
—of once more welcoming Lord Loch at his Court.
I little thought at their first meeting, when I
watched the young Sultan's shy interest in the
big Guardsman, that a few years later I should
witness the same Guardsman instructing the same
Sultan in the mysteries of " tip-and-run " in an
enclosure of the Shereefian Palace.

My first private audience with Mulai Abdul Aziz
was in the summer of 1901. After a considerable
delay, largely owing to the discussion of the kind
of obeisance I was prepared to make in entering
His Majesty's presence, I was honoured with a
private audience. I found His Majesty courteous,
pleasant, and intelligent. He was easy to amuse,
and by my departure from the austere etiquette
of the Court in not confining my remarks to
replies to His Majesty's questions, although at first
it seemed a little to surprise him, I succeeded in
gaining his attention and amusement. I had been
told that my audience would be very formal and

last a few minutes. It lasted over an hour. The
Sultan was seated, and I remained standing the
whole time—to which I could not very well object.
In any case, I had overcome the difficulty of my
reception by refusing point-blank to go down on
my knees and to touch the floor with my forehead—a form of salutation which was being practised by the Europeans in His Majesty's service,
for already he had begun to increase his Christian
entourage. I had stated that I was prepared to
enter the Sultan's presence in adopting the same
formalities as I did in the presence of my own
sovereign, and the Sultan had accepted that
formula. Almost the first question he asked me
was if I had ever been received in private audience
by my own King. I replied that I had experienced
that honour. He then asked what obeisance I
had made. I replied that I had bowed on entering the room, and again on approaching His
Majesty's person. The Sultan seemed surprised,
and demanded why it was the Englishmen in his
service carried out the Moorish form of etiquette
by kneeling and touching the floor with their
foreheads? I could only protest that I didn't
know, except to surmise that, as they were in the
service of a Moorish Sultan, they probably thought
they ought to adopt the traditional Moorish form
of obeisance. The Sultan gave orders that it was
to be discontinued, though, as a matter of fact,
the Europeans in his service still continued to use
it on the great feast-days of the year until the
end of his reign. A few years later, on one of

these occasions I saw a long line of Englishmen
drop on to their knees and bow their foreheads
to the ground as the Sultan approached. It is a
matter of personal option, based on prejudice. It
seems to me that any human being has a right
to act in such matters just as he thinks right.
That he demeans himself or his country by so
doing appears to me ridiculous. An Englishman,
and much less England, cannot be demeaned by
any fantastic gymnastics. I preferred not to do
it solely for the reason that it seemed to me to
be absurd, just as half the ceremonies at a British
coronation would appear absurd and meaningless
to a Moor. Nearly all etiquette is ridiculous, only
we are more or less accustomed to it, and have
largely modified its eccentricities. I have experienced things nearly as absurd as this Moorish
custom in other Courts. Some years ago, on one
of the very hottest days of a hot summer in a
country of Southern Europe, I had the honour to
be received by the sovereign. I arrived at the
palace at half-past ten in the morning and left it
at one o'clock. The king in question was dressed
in the heavy blue uniform of an admiral; I was in
a frock-coat. The thermometer, even in the room,
must have been in or very near the nineties.
Yet we stood the whole time—for two hours and
a half. At half-past two I was summoned back
to the palace to complete this long but interesting
audience. With a sigh of relief His Majesty said,
" I think this time we can sit down." And we
did. Why on earth we hadn't sat down in the

morning during all those perspiring hours Heaven
only knows. I could have understood a king
sitting and his visitor being made to stand, but
mutual discomfort and fatigue in such a case and
for such a length of time appears to me to be
almost childish folly.

The Moorish protocol would have compared
favourably with this European etiquette. The
Moorish visitor would have made his lowly obeisance to the sovereign, but this done he would
have squatted down, more or less comfortably,
in his Sultan's presence, and remained seated till
the end of the audience. It seemed to me to be
preferable. But etiquette is all a question of
custom and habit. Take kissing, for example.
How well every man must remember how, when a
small boy, he feared that his mother might kiss
him in the presence of his schoolfellows. In after
years, when it is too late, how he would have
treasured those lost kisses were they now obtainable ! What amusement, too, the kissing of foreign
men on the railway platforms of the continent
has caused us ! But witness the meeting of two
great Morocco chiefs—the stately approach, the
last few more hurried steps, and the graceful embrace as each bends forward and kisses the other's
shoulder. I have seen the meeting of great men
in Morocco in the hour of sorrow, when they
have fallen upon each other's necks and wept.
How few soldiers know that the origin of the
salute they give to-day comes from the East, and
is really no more than the movement of the sub-

D

ject to shield from his eyes the effulgent glory of his sovereign, only to-day it applies equally to the effulgent glory of his second lieutenant as well. Habit is everything, and prejudice scarcely less.

These were the first days of the toys and fireworks at the Moorish Court. For a time the latter were paramount, and almost nightly the southern capital was illumined by the reflection of Catherine-wheels and startled by the flashing of the many colours of marvellous rockets. A man was brought especially from England to show and prepare the fireworks, and he became a permanent member of His Majesty's suite. The natives were partly amused, partly shocked. Thrifty as the Moor is by nature, he could not overlook the wild extravagance of this manner of spending money, and the fireworks by the time they had arrived in Marrakesh had cost a pretty price. Freight, insurance, and the long caravan transport from the cost had to be added to the original cost, and there was an item known as commission. They were certainly very beautiful fireworks and very expensive. I was present at a display given to amuse a British Minister, who highly disapproved of this extravagance, but could not refuse the invitation. There was a set piece of an enormous elephant, and the show concluded with a waterfall of fire in a new shade of pink, just discovered, and accordingly of elevated price. It was certainly very beautiful, but it was very useless and very dear.

One afternoon the Sultan informed me that

there would be a display that night in the palace grounds, but that it was for the " palace "—that was to say, the ladies—and no men would be invited ; but if I went up on to the roof of the house in which I was living, I should no doubt be able to witness something of it. I watched the beautiful rockets of every colour rise in their streaks of fire into the wonderful sapphire blue of the sky of the southern night, to burst with their thousand stars, filling the whole scene of the flat house-tops of the old city with the pale glow of greens and pinks and yellows. In the " Jumma el-Fenaa "—the open place that lies in the centre of the city—the crowds stood and watched the rockets as they rose over the high walls of the palace half a mile away.

The next day the Sultan asked me what I had thought of the display. I spoke of its beauty, and hinted at its waste. I mentioned the crowd in the square. " What did the people say ? " asked the Sultan. " I didn't hear much," I replied ; " but on several occasions some one would cry out, ' There goes another thousand dollars of our money.' "

Mulai Abdul Aziz had expected to hear his own praises sung for having presented the brilliant spectacle to the people of his city, and my answer surprised him. It was, however, not without effect, or perhaps he was growing tired of coloured fires, for there was a great diminution in these displays, although the professional exhibitor remained for some time later at the palace.

Throughout the many months that I spent at
the Moorish Court, I always felt that a catastrophe
must eventually happen. The Sultan was evidently
being led upon the road to ruin, and near him as
I was, all my efforts to persuade him of the fact
were in vain. On more than one occasion, particularly towards the end of 1902, I implored him,
in language which he smilingly told me no one
had ever ventured to address to him before, to
pull himself up in time. He was kind, thanked
me for being so outspoken, and continued his
pro-European proclivities and his extravagances.
Had he at that time dismissed the greater number
of his European employees, leaving only his doctor,
an engineer or two, and any one who had been
in his father's employ, and ceased spending his
money, the whole future of Morocco might have
been changed.

His afternoons in Marrakesh were given up to
play. More than once, always accompanied by
Menebhi, the Minister of War, and some of his
European employees, we rode in the immense
wilderness of gardens of the Agdal Palace. At the
edge of a great square tank we would dismount,
and sometimes went for a row in one of the various
boats that he kept there. On one occasion His
Majesty and his Minister rowed—very badly indeed—while I, the only other occupant of the
boat, steered. The Sultan, who rowed bow, caught
several crabs, and splashed poor Menebhi all over.
The Minister of War rowed about one hundred
short strokes to the minute, whilst the Sultan,

struggling with his oars, rowed about ten extremely long ones. But both were hugely delighted with the performance, and our spirits were of the highest.

"We are both boatmen, and you are the passenger. We are crossing a Moorish ferry," cried the Sultan.

Entering into the Sultan's little joke, I replied "that they were the worst ferrymen I had ever seen, and that on landing I should complain to the authorities of their incapacity."

"Oh, you will, will you?" replied Mulai Abdul Aziz. "Then all I can say is, we won't put you ashore until you pay us."

"Then I'll stop here."

"All right," replied the Sultan; and he promptly began to splash me with all his might and main, though poor Menebhi was getting as wet as I was.

"Will you pay?" asked His Majesty.

"Willingly," I laughed. "How much?"

"Half a peseta each" (about 4d.), answered the Sultan, and they duly pocketed their fee. It was the first time in my life I had tipped a Sultan and a Minister of War.

In the autumn of 1902 I was invited to accompany the royal progress to the northern capital, Fez.

The Sultan's departure from Marrakesh, where he had now been in residence for some six years, had been expected earlier in the autumn; but constant delays occurred, and although the imperial tents had been for some time pitched out-

side the city gates, it was not until late in November
that a start was made. Early one morning, surrounded by all the characteristic pomp pertaining
to the Sultanate of Morocco, Mulai Abdul Aziz
left his palace in the southern capital for the first
camp of his northward march.

There is no necessity to describe day by day
the Sultan's progress. The etiquette and formalities of each were almost identical, though the scene
was an ever-varying one, changing with the nature
of the country traversed. An account of one day,
picked out at hazard, will be sufficient to give
an idea of the whole. Long before daylight the
great camp was astir, and when, soon after 3 A.M.,
the morning gun was fired, a number of tents
had already been struck, horses saddled, and mules
and camels packed for the march. In the moonlight and early dawn the scene was one of great
beauty—an indistinct medley of white tents, here
silvery in the moonlight, there ruddy with the
glow of camp-fires, whose tall red columns of
smoke rose pillar-like into the still air. In and
about the tents passed the shadowy forms of men
and animals. As if by magic the scene was ever
changing, as tent after tent silently fell to the
ground, until with the first glow of dawn there
remained of the great encampment only the canvas-
walled enclosure containing the Sultan's tents, and
a plain covered with horsemen and thousands
upon thousands of baggage mules and camels.
Already the cavalry were massed near the Sultan's
enclosure, the horsemen forming an open square,

in the centre of which, surrounded by the Ministers of State, lay a crimson-curtained palanquin with its couch of turquoise blue. From the entrance of the Sultan's tents to the square of cavalry a double line was formed by white-robed, red-capped officials, awaiting His Majesty.

A bugle sounds clear in the still atmosphere, and a moment later a great cry rends the air. There is a beating of drums and a sound of trumpets, as a solitary white figure, erect and dignified, walks slowly through the bowing lines of officials, enters the square of horsemen, and seats himself upon the blue divan. Again arises the cry of welcome, as, bending forward, the tribes greet their Sultan with the salutation, "May God prolong the life of our Lord."

The sun has risen now, his first rays falling upon the gold-orbed banners, heavy with brocades and silks that wave high above the heads of the cavalry; then upon the wild horsemen themselves, their saddles of brilliant reds and greens, half-hidden in the heavy folds of their long white garments, and the scene becomes one of indescribable beauty. One by one the Sultan's tents are struck, and the great canvas-walled enclosure vanishes under the hands of hundreds of skilled tent-pitchers. Sometimes His Majesty gives an audience to an official, a local governor of a tribe, who, barefoot, approaches the Sultan, falls upon his knees, and three times touches the ground with his forehead, remaining crouched before his lord and master during the few seconds that

such audiences last. Again a bugle; and through
the line of horsemen run dusky soldiers leading
saddled horses, trotting them past the Sultan
that he may choose upon the back of which
he will perform the day's march. With a slight
motion of his hand the choice is made, and the
honoured steed is led up to the palanquin. Sometimes it is a white, saddled and trapped in turquoise blue; sometimes a grey, decked in rose-
coloured silks; sometimes a black, his head half
hidden in primrose-yellow tassels.

As the Sultan mounts, the scene becomes for a
few minutes one of wild confusion. The banner-
bearers, the spear-bearers, the cavalry, the scarlet-
and-blue mounted infantry, the high officials on
their saddle-mules, the artillery, even the Sultan
himself, seems hopelessly mixed in a struggling
crowd. It is only for a very little while, and then
from the medley emerges the royal procession,
forming into order as it proceeds. The vanguard
is formed of an escort of cavalry, headed by the
standard-bearers, carrying flags of every hue and
colour, the poles topped with glittering balls.
Next come the artillery, the guns carried upon
the backs of mules, and after them a troop of
mounted infantry. Two mounted men, carrying
long slender spears, precede the led horses, five
or six of which, trapped in rich silks, always form
a feature of the procession. Riding alone is the
Grand Master of the Ceremonies, a dark man of
fine presence, wand of office in hand. Then, after
a space of some forty yards, the Sultan, a solitary

white figure on horseback. At his side run negroes, waving long white scarves to keep the dust and the flies off his holy person. Immediately behind His Majesty rides a soldier, bearing aloft, so as to shade the Sultan from the rays of the sun, the Imperial parasol of crimson and gold. The red palanquin, borne by sturdy mules, follows, and behind it a long wide line of standard-bearers, the banners rich in gold thread and brocaded silks, and the poles of one and all crowned with gilded orbs. Immediately behind the flags ride the viziers and great officers of State, followed by a rabble of smaller officials and soldiery, of black slaves and tribesmen from all over Morocco.

There are no roads, and the procession of men and animals spreads widely out over the plains and undulating hills. Often as far as the eye can reach one can trace the great migration stretching from horizon to horizon, a rainbow of colour upon the green plains. Sometimes to cross a valley the procession narrows in, to spread out again in the open country beyond, till the whole land is dotted with horsemen and mules, and slow-gaited lumbering camels.

Now and again a tribal governor, with his escort of horsemen, comes to salute his sovereign. Drawn up in a long line they await the Sultan's approach. At his approach the governor dismounts from his horse and prostrates himself before his lord, to rise again at a signal from His Majesty. Bending low, he approaches and kisses the Sultan's stirrup, then mounts again, and with a hoarse cry of

welcome the tribesmen dig their spurs into the
flanks of their barbs and gallop pell-mell hither
and thither, now singly, now in line, firing their
guns the while, until the horses are brought to
a sudden standstill in a cloud of smoke and dust.
These tribesmen are not the only people who
come from afar to greet the Sultan on his march.
There are beggars and representatives of all the
dervish sects, from cymbal-beating negroes from
the Sudan to the Hamacha of Meknés, who cut
open their heads with hatchets. There are snake-
charmers and acrobats, and men with performing
apes; little deputations of country Jews and
Jewesses; groups of white-robed scholars from
local mosques, bearing white flags; veiled Arab
women, uttering shrill trembling cries of welcome,
and offering bowls of milk; lepers with their
faces swathed and wearing great straw hats, bearing bowls of wood to collect alms in, for none may
touch them—a thousand scenes of human life,
with all its pleasures and all its tragedies.

On the sixth day's march one of the largest
rivers in Morocco, the Oum er-Rebia, had to be
forded. Fortunately the autumn rains had not
yet fallen, and the river presented no great obstacle
to the passage of so large a caravan. Almost the
first to ride across was the Sultan, his horse surrounded by negroes on foot, while a line of expert
swimmers were held in readiness, linked hand in
hand, stretched from bank to bank. For over
three hours the procession steadily waded through,
and though many a mule fell and many a man

and pack were soaked, no serious accidents occurred. It was a scene of wild confusion as the
horsemen and laden animals climbed down the
steep bank to the water's edge and entered the
swiftly-flowing river ; but in the end all got across
in safety, and great were the rejoicings and many
the congratulations that night in camp, for it is
seldom that a Sultan and his vast following have
crossed the Oum er-Rebia without paying a toll in
human lives.

Usually a ride about four hours brings the
Sultan to his next camping-ground. A quarter
of an hour before reaching the selected spot the
bands commence to play, and the tribesmen, the
cavalry, and mounted infantry gallop ahead, forming into two lines, between which His Majesty
rides into a square of horsemen drawn up in the
same formation as that of the early morning.
The crimson palanquin is quickly unharnessed, the
blue divan arranged, and Mulai Abdul Aziz seats
himself in solitary state to await the pitching of
his encampment.

No tent might be raised in the camp until the
gilded globe which surmounts the Sultan's principal tent is in position ; but it required only a
very short time for the skilled tent-pitchers to
pitch the great mass of canvas crowned with its
glittering orb. It is a signal to the rest of the
camp, and almost as if growing from the ground
arose the white canvas town. There was no confusion, no noise. Every one knew the right position to pitch in, and the whole system worked

without a hitch. Probably the Moors are alone in the pitching of these great camps; it seems a hereditary trait in their characters. Sultan after Sultan, ever since the Empire of Morocco first came under the dominion of the Arabs, had travelled in exactly the same manner as that in which Mulai Abdul Aziz was making the journey from Marrakesh to Rabat. In no detail had it changed. The very shape and decoration of the tents had never varied, and to such an extent had conservatism been maintained, the Sultan told the writer, that, so far from travelling with all the luxury that one could imagine, he was forbidden by the unwritten laws of tradition to cover the floor of his State tent, except for three small carpets. The rest of the floor-space must consist of the soil of the country, and this, on the day which His Majesty narrated the fact, was perhaps four inches deep in almost liquid black mud. Outside his tent he may lay down straw or matting, or any covering he may please, but within there must be nothing.

The Sultan's principal tent once up, the tent-pitchers turned their attention to the remainder of his camp, consisting of some half-dozen large marquees, the whole—an acre perhaps of ground —being enclosed with a nine-feet wall of white canvas, decorated in patterns of dark blue. This private encampment of His Majesty formed the centre of the camp, which stretched away on all sides, often for nearly half a mile in every direction. At the outer extremity were pitched the tents of the infantry, so close to one another that entrance and exit to the camp was only possible at certain intervals, where spaces were left for the purpose.

The greatest interest naturally attached to the immediate surroundings of the Sultan's tents. No one but his ladies and their female slaves might enter the walled enclosure, with the exception of one small portion of it divided off from the rest, retained for unofficial audiences. His Majesty transacted all his affairs of State outside the enclosure, in a tent of scarlet and green cloth, pitched at the end of a large open square, and visible from a considerable distance. Here before the eyes of the public His Majesty received his Ministers, attended to his correspondence, and sealed official documents. Near this tent, known as the " Siwan," were two large marquees, one used as a mosque, the other the office of the viziers. In this quarter, too, were the offices of the other Ministers of State and high officials. Behind these were the private encampments of the more important personages, often consisting of several very large tents leading to one another by covered passages of canvas. Directly opposite, on the farther side of the Sultan's enclosure, were the royal stables, where a quantity of fine barbs were tethered, their number constantly being added to by the presents brought to His Majesty by the tribal governors.

As soon as his tents were ready, the Sultan remounted his horse, and amidst the playing of bands and the shouts of the tribesmen, rode into the seclusion of his private camp. It was generally not long after His Majesty's disappearance from view that a long line of white-robed and veiled women, mounted upon mules, passed silently amongst the tents and entered the royal precincts. As they filed through the camp every man turned his head away from the mysterious white procession. Usually the whole camp was pitched by midday, and not long after that hour the neighbourhood of the Government quarters became astir with life. The white-robed viziers sought their offices, while soldiers kept order amongst the throng of people that were always crowding near the tent doors awaiting audiences with the Ministers of State. Only the "Siwan" was deserted, but not for long. A bugle sounds. There is a hurrying to and fro of officials and soldiers, and again the cry, "God prolong the life of our Lord," is heard, and the solitary white figure, round whom all this great camp revolves, is seen slowly entering under the shadow of the tent of scarlet and green.

His Majesty usually gave some two or three hours a day to the consideration of affairs of State, though, on the occasions on which the great caravan did not travel and no journey was made, a considerably longer period was put aside for public business. Meanwhile, in another quarter of the camp, provisions and fodder were being distributed to the vast concourse of people who follow His Majesty upon these royal progresses. Yet, in spite of the fact that some thirty thousand persons and probably twenty thousand horses and mules had to be fed, the commissariat worked without a hitch, and food and fodder were supplied in an incredibly short period of time to all those who had a right to receive it. The local tribes alone were dependent upon their own resources, and, with this exception, the Sultan feeds the whole camp. Up till the time of this journey of Mulai Abdul Aziz the march of a Sultan through a district was sufficient to bring ruin upon the people, so extortionate were the demands made upon them. But he would have none of this, and most of the provisioning was paid for, not by local taxation, but from the Imperial Treasury, and His Majesty showed throughout solicitude for the welfare of his subjects. He allowed them to approach him, and listened attentively to their complaints against the local officials.

At sunset gunfire, His Majesty prayed, and retired to his tents for the night, though almost every evening he gave unofficial audiences to his friends in the divided-off portion of his private encampment reserved for this purpose. As night fell the camp became dotted with the little lights of lanterns, often gaily decorated with coloured glass, while here and there a camp-fire showed up ruddily amongst the tents. Now and again could be heard the tinkling of stringed instruments and the soft murmur of a singer, who seemed afraid to raise his voice in the stillness that pervades everything,—a stillness only broken now and again by an order to the guards and sentries—of whom

400, shoulder to shoulder, encircled the Sultan's enclosure—or by the long-drawn accents of the mueddin as he called the Faithful to prayer.

The " last post "—and as the note of the bugle dies away, a wonderful silence fell upon the moonlit camp.

III.

THE ROAD TO RUIN.

By the end of 1902 Mulai Abdul Aziz had returned
to Fez, desirous of introducing reforms, and reck-
lessly extravagant. His intentions were the best;
but if there was one thing his viziers did not
desire to see introduced it was reform, for their
livelihoods and their fortunes depended upon a
continuance of the state of corruption which they
had every interest to see prolonged. So they
closed their eyes to the young Sultan's extravagances, watched him waste his own and his country's money on every sort of folly, and shared in
the profits.

All sorts of rumours and stories were current
amongst the tribes as to what went on in the
palace. For instance, the Sultan, finding the white
walls of one of the interior courtyards too dazzling
for his eyes, had them painted blue—an innova-
tion unheard of at a Court where tradition ruled.
Now the walls of this courtyard were visible from
the hills above Fez, and the patch of bright blue
soon attracted the attention of the tribesmen
attending the local markets. To them, as it was

E

contrary to Moslem tradition, it must be of Christian origin, and a story was soon being circulated that Mulai Abdul Aziz had lost his fortune playing cards with his Christian friends, and was now staking the various parts of his palace in lieu of money. He had lost this particular court, which the Christians had taken possession of and painted blue. As a matter of fact, at this period playing-cards were unknown inside the palace, and with all his extravagances Mulai Abdul Aziz never showed the least propensity to gambling. All play for money is forbidden by the Moslem religion, and the young Sultan was strict in the observances of his faith.

The rumours of Christian influence spread fast, and were soon taken advantage of. The Moors are essentially opportunists, and one, Omar ez-Zarhouni, was more opportunist than the rest. He was an educated man who had been a scribe at Court, but a forgery had put an end to his career in the precincts of the palace. For a time he was a sort of secretary to Hammou el-Hassen, the Berber Kaid of the Beni Mtir tribe, when I knew him. In 1901 he left the Kaid and disappeared into the country. Amongst other useful attainments he was a skilful forger, and knew a certain number of rather ordinary conjuring tricks. He possessed as well a most fluent tongue. By the aid of these accomplishments he was able to make a living, travelling from tribe to tribe on a she-donkey, from which fact he became known along the countryside as " Bou Hamara "—literally, the "Father of the she-donkey." It was amongst the simple tribesmen of the Rif that he met with his principal success. Starting with the idea of merely earning a livelihood, he soon saw the possibilities of a career on a larger scale. His conjuring tricks, his wily tongue, and his forgeries —to say nothing of the she-donkey—encircled him with a sort of religious prestige; and one day he suddenly declared himself to be Mulai Mohamed, the first-born son of the late Sultan Mulai Hassen, and therefore the elder brother of the then reigning sovereign, Mulai Abdul Aziz. For a time he did not discard his donkey, and the humility of this means of transit added attractions to his prestige in the eyes of the devout.

In the late autumn of 1902 Mulai Abdul Aziz left Fez for Rabat. His departure had been de-layed on account of this incipient rebellion of Bou Hamara's; but affairs seemed to have quieted down, and the departure of the Court took place in November. An army had been meanwhile sent in the direction of Taza to put down the rebellion. The choice of a Commander-in-Chief for this army was typical of Morocco of those days. The situa-tion was critical, and the future depended largely upon the success of His Majesty's troops. The Sultan was leaving North Morocco, and by this fact alone his position would be weakened; but the tradition of corruption—accepted and per-mitted—was too great. I asked the Sultan, for I was at Fez with him at that time, whom he had chosen as Commander-in-Chief. To my aston-

ishment he replied, "My brother, Mulai el-Kebir."
"But he is still a boy," I replied, "and has never
been a soldier." "True," replied the Sultan, "but
my other brothers have all commanded expeditions. It is Mulai el-Kebir's turn. He has never
had a chance of making a little money." The
making of a little money was, of course, the
abstraction of the soldiers' pay and extortion
everywhere. I accompanied the Sultan when he
left Fez in November. The Court proceeded, with
all its pomp and majesty, to Meknés, where we
stayed a few days, and then on into the Zimmour
country, where rebellion was rife. It is impossible
to say of how many people the rabble which
accompanied the Sultan consisted, but we were
probably 18,000 or 20,000 in camp, with at least
half perfectly useless for warfare. A number of
Fez merchants, who followed the Court from
capital to capital, accompanied the Sultan, and
each had his family and retainers with him.
Amongst other strange groups were hundreds of
beggars, for the most part blind, who also migrated
with the Court.

There was some fighting in the Zimmour country,
but still more in the Sultan's camp. The incidents
which occurred were typical of the time and
country. The Zimmour tribesmen decided to resist the Sultan's progress at a deep ravine which
crossed the plains at right angles to our line of
march. This ravine was perhaps 400 feet in depth,
a few yards wide only at the bottom, where a
little river flowed, and half a mile across at its

summit. Aware that the army was likely to meet with resistance at this spot, a halt was called on the edge of the valley. Half-way up the steep slope on the opposite side was an open ledge of green grass, on which was a group of black tents and thatch huts of the Zimmour villagers. From the thick brushwood opposite a few rebel shots were fired at the army. The Sultan's artillery and machine-guns were brought up to the edge of the ravine, and began firing promiscuously into the brushwood. It was soon clear that the valley was not strongly held. The Zimmour tribesmen are horsemen, and their attack was more likely to be made on the plain across the ravine, at the moment when the army was extricating itself from the precipices and brushwood.

A regiment—the Doukkalas—was ordered to clear the valley in preparation for an advance, and started down the steep hillside with much noise and singing. A few shots were fired at them as they descended. The river crossed, they began the ascent, and soon reached the little deserted village. Here temptation was too strong, and instead of mounting higher they began to loot. The villagers had carried off all their movable property, but their stores of grain remained, and grain is valuable in the Sultan's camp. The question was how to transport it. The Moorish soldier is not easily foiled, and the brave Doukkala regiment was quite up to the occasion. In the presence of the Sultan and of the whole army they laid down their rifles, took off their baggy uniform

breeches of bright blue cotton, tied up the holes
through which the legs ordinarily protruded with
string, and filled the rest with wheat. This done,
they loaded up their booty on their backs, picked
up their rifles, and started to return to the army.

Nothing would make them go on : bugles were
blown, signals made, orders shouted ; but the
Doukkalas felt that their day's work was done,
and steadily climbed homewards. In exasperation
the Abda regiment, equally famous and equally
brave, was sent to support them, and to see if
they couldn't be persuaded to turn once more in
the direction of the enemy and abandon their
loot.

With music and singing the Abda regiment set
out. They met the Doukkalas struggling up under
their heavy loads near the river-bed. A collision
was inevitable, and the Abda charged. The Doukkalas threw down their loads and commenced
firing, and in a few minutes a little battle was
raging far down below us in the ravine between
the two loyal regiments. A ceasing of the firing
bespoke a compromise. The two bodies of troops
fraternised, the Doukkalas temporarily abandoned
their breeches' loads of grain on the river-bank,
and returned barelegged to the Zimmour village
with their comrades the Abdas. Once there it
was the latter's turn to step out of their nether
garments, and the Doukkalas assisted them to
load up the remaining grain. This done, the two
regiments, except for a few killed and wounded,
returned together, every man bearing on his back

his voluminous baggy blue breeches stuffed to bursting-point with wheat and barley. I shall never forget the sight of these troops struggling up the steep slope, puffing and perspiring, dressed in the scarlet " zouave " coats, with just a fringe of shirt encircling their waists—and nothing else,— and on the summit the enraged Sultan and his Court and the rest of the army, impotent to change the course of events. The afternoon was well over, and all thought of crossing the ravine that night was out of the question, so the camp was pitched on the side we were on.

I have passed many strange disturbed nights in Morocco, but this one was perhaps unique, for the Doukkalas and Abda regiments quarrelled over the division of the spoil, and fought on and off all the night through. Bullets were flying in every direction, and one had to lie as low to ground as possible. Eventually things quieted down, and one of my servants came and announced to me that " it is all right. The army is now being flogged,"—which was a fact, for the energetic Minister of War had managed to arrest the survivors of the two regiments concerned, and was having them individually severely flogged one after the other by soldiers of other regiments and slaves and volunteers.

We never crossed that ravine. The next day the news reached the Sultan that the army under his brother had been defeated by Bou Hamara near Taza. In all haste we turned back, and proceeded once more to Fez. That return journey

over the track of our advance brought to light
many things of which nothing apparently had been
known, or at least cared about, in camp. The
road was strewn with dead—stragglers from the
Sultan's army who had been cut off by the rebel
Zimmours; for woe betide any one who lagged
behind. We found in the precincts of a country
mosque a dozen corpses, decapitated and mutilated; and even the blind beggars on foot, whose
afflictions made it almost impossible to keep up
with the army, fell a prey to the tribesmen, and
not a few were found stripped of their poor belongings and with their throats cut. Woe betide the
wounded, too—left to die where they fell—for the
Sultan's army possessed no hospital installation of
any kind, and no ambulances. Every effort of
the few doctors who from time to time were
employed at the Moorish Court was almost in
vain. Only if a fallen soldier's comrade chose to
carry him to the camp did he escape death on the
field of battle; but the question of his transport
and of his subsequent care rested entirely with his
comrades, and the Moorish soldier's comrades were
not always prepared to make sacrifices for a
wounded " pal." Often they waited his death in
order to steal his clothes; often they stole his clothes
and left him to perish without awaiting his death.
In camp, if there was a doctor, medical attendance was given, but it was given almost without
any encouragement or any help from the Maghzen,
but none the less given whole-heartedly. Even
when the whole army was attacked with malaria,

it was often the doctor who supplied the entire quantity of quinine required out of his own pocket. The idea of the value of their men's lives never seems to have entered into the heads of the authorities.

Often the soldiers, if they took the trouble, buried the wounded alive, to prevent their heads being carried off as trophies by the enemy. I remember being told, while spending an evening with some of the riff-raff of the army—who, in spite of their characters, were often the most jovial and cheery of companions—the story of a recalcitrant wounded comrade who didn't want to be buried alive. The incident had happened the same day. The man was badly wounded, the camp was a long way off, and his " pals " didn't mean to have the trouble of carrying him there. So they dug his grave, and began to push him in. He naturally protested. " I am not dead," he cried ; " don't you see I am living ? " " Be quiet," said a companion ; " you were killed at least an hour ago. Don't you realise that you are dead ? " The poor man still cried out till the earth covered him and put an end to his protestation and his life. The soldier who narrated the incident added, " The Moorish soldier is an ungrateful and unbelieving individual. This man, for instance, had no confidence in us, his comrades, when we assured him he was dead. I hate ingratitude,"—and he filled up his little " kif " pipe and handed it to us for a whiff.

Life was of no value, but the Moorish soldier is.

I have seen him often under all circumstances;
and in spite of all his faults, I have an admiration
and a liking for him. He considered his "pal's"
life as nothing, and his own almost as valueless;
and yet on my many journeys I have often
experienced kindness, and never rudeness, from
these outcasts of the old régime. Murderers often,
generally thieves, and always blackguards, yet
there existed amongst them the undercurrent of
the pride of race, and a sense of honour in their
dealings with a sympathetic European, which they
would have considered quite unnecessary with a
compatriot. In all life and on all my journeys
in Morocco I have made a point of trusting every
one, and seldom, if ever, have I been disappointed.
I have put natives taken from the wild mountain
districts into positions of confidence; I have given
them every facility to rob, but I have trusted to
their honour, and they have not failed me. I am
often told I have been and am foolish, and that
some day!—but that some day has not come yet,
and my life has been rendered far easier and far
happier by the mutual confidence that has always
existed, and still, I am glad to say, exists, between
the people of this country and myself. I start
out on my journeys with this certain knowledge,
that wherever I choose to go I am known at
least by name and sure of a welcome.

A few days after taking the hurried decision to
return, the Sultan reached Fez, where he remained
for several years, unable to leave these disturbed
regions where revolution was rife. In the summer

of 1903, having returned to Tangier meanwhile, I was captured by Raisuli's tribesmen, and spent three weeks in captivity at Zinat and in the Anjera mountains. My experiences are narrated in the chapter which deals with the famous brigand and his doings.

In 1904 an arrangement was come to between France and England regarding Morocco. This book does not in any way pretend to be a history, and important as this event was, it need only be referred to here in a few words. France was permitted by this agreement to intervene in Morocco, on the condition of not changing the political status of the country, and was given a free hand to preserve order and to grant such assistance for the introduction of certain reforms as might be required. France at the same time agreed to come to terms with Spain. All British commercial rights and privileges were to remain intact.

Raisuli was all this time in communication, if not in league, with Bou Hamara, who remained in the Taza and Oujda districts. While I was a prisoner of Raisuli's in 1903, I managed to abstract from a secret cupboard in the room in which I was confined a number of documents of considerable interest. One of these was the " dahir " of the Pretender appointing Raisuli Governor of the mountain tribes of North-West Morocco. This dahir is stamped with the great seal of the Pretender under the name of Mohamed ben Hassen. No doubt Raisuli, who was at this moment Mulai

Abdul Aziz's Governor in the same districts, was keeping this alternative appointment up his sleeve in a case of the necessity arising of having to proclaim the Pretender as Sultan.

It was only natural that this Anglo-French agreement should bring about a general spirit of unrest in the country, and in May 1904 Raisuli captured Mr Perdicaris and his stepson, Mr Varley. They were released seven weeks later against a ransom of £14,000 and political advantages for Raisuli, who obtained from the Sultan, Mulai Abdul Aziz, his own appointment of Governor of the north-west tribes as one of his terms.

Meanwhile the situation in the interior became so serious that all Europeans were withdrawn to the coast, and even at Tangier security was threatened. In December my country villa was attacked during the night, and I narrowly escaped a second capture. The soldiers guarding my house were seized and disarmed in the verandah; but the brigands, under a young chief called Ould Bakkasha, failed to force an entrance into the house. The telephone wire was cut, but I had just time to get a message through, and a few hours later troops arrived. Our total losses were one soldier killed and one wounded. I had to abandon my villa and come and live nearer the town.

Ould Bakkasha, the chief of this new band, was killed a few weeks later. He was a young man, of attractive manner and appearance, who evidently wanted to become a second Raisuli; but fate was against him. During a raid which he and his men made upon a village, he was shot. He was forcing his way into a house, the owner of which was holding the door on the inside. Unable to leave the door, the owner of the house called to his son, a mere boy, to bring him his rifle, which was hanging on the wall. The boy in hurrying to his father fell, and the rifle went off. The bullet pierced the closed door, and killed Ould Bakkasha, who was attempting to force an entrance from without. The band fled, leaving their chief's dead body on the threshold.

The year 1905 saw the famous visit of the Kaiser to Tangier, the result of the Franco-British agreement of the previous year, and of the subsequent action of France in sending a special Mission to Fez to insist upon the introduction of reforms. It was on 31st March that the Kaiser landed. At the last moment he had hesitated to come ashore, partly on account of the roughness of the sea, and partly perhaps because he may have appreciated the far-reaching effects of this hostile demonstration to France and indirectly to England, and partly because he feared assassination at the hands of anarchists.

The Emperor looked nervous as he rode through the decorated streets to the German Legation. Immense crowds of natives, who had been told that this visit meant the saving of the independence of their country, had gathered on the open market-place in front of the Legation, and volley after volley was fired by them as the Emperor arrived and left. Many of the guns and rifles contained bullets, one of which, in its downward course, struck and indented the leather helmet of one of the suite, but fortunately no accident occurred. I was in the room while the diplomatic corps and the native officials were presented to the Kaiser, and heard both his words to the French Chargé d'Affaires, Comte de Cherisy, and to the Moorish authorities. To both he announced his intention of considering Morocco as an independent country, and of treating its Sultan as an independent sovereign.

Fez became a few months later the scene of action, for three special Missions—a British under Mr (afterwards Sir Gerard) Lowther, a French Mission under Monsieur Saint René Taillandier, and a German under Count Tattenbach—visited the capital. The French Government was insisting on the acceptance of its reform proposals by the Sultan, and every assistance was being rendered by the British Government to obtain this desirable result; but German influence was too strong, and the Sultan Mulai Abdul Aziz definitely refused the French proposals on 28th May, only a day or two before the arrival of the British Mission in Fez. The moment was cleverly chosen. Mr Lowther's Mission was *en route* to the Court, and only learned of the Sultan's decision on his arrival at Fez. He was too late to influence the Sultan, and too late to abandon his Mission. This check to France led indirectly to the fall of Delcassé and the agreement to hold an International Conference on the subject of Morocco.

Meanwhile there was no improvement in the interior situation of Morocco. Bou Hamara maintained his rebellion in Eastern Morocco, and Raisuli governed in north-eastern tribes. Everywhere there was insecurity, and two British officers, Captain Crowther and Lieutenant Hatton, were captured in October on the shore of the Anjera coast, where they were employed in the salving of H.M.S. *Assistance,* which had gone ashore there. The brigand who made this coup was the Shereef Ould Boulaish, an important Anjera tribesman. Their release was fortunately obtained without much difficulty.

The Court had lost its prestige. The Sultan was openly scoffed at and despised, and anarchy reigned on every side.

This final stage of the history of independent Morocco had begun and ended in the early years of this century, when the young Sultan, Mulai Abdul Aziz, entered upon that period of his reign which may be deservedly known as the years of the *commis voyageurs.* It was a pitiful period and one best forgotten, except that every now and again some incident would occur worth recording on account of its perfectly unintentional humour, which only rendered more pitiful still the depressing interludes. It was the last decadence of the decadent Moorish Court. The Treasury was fast being emptied, the revenues were being wasted, foreign loans were being raised, and the palaces of the Sultan were littered with packing-cases, the contents of which the British Press once seri-

ously described as "evidences of Christian civilisation at Fez." Everywhere it was packing-cases,
and even to-day on some of the tracks from the
coast to the interior lie the wrecked fragments of
machinery and other rusty forsaken goods, which
the weary camels could transport no longer.

Of what did these "evidences of Christian civilisation" consist? Grand pianos and kitchen-
ranges; automobiles and immense cases of corsets;
wild animals in cages, and boxes of strange theatri-
cal uniforms; barrel-organs and hansom-cabs; a
passenger lift capable of rising to dizzy altitudes,
destined for a one-storied palace; false hair;
cameras of gold and of silver with jewelled buttons;
carved marble lions and living macaw parrots;
jewels, real and false; steam-launches and fireworks; ladies' underclothing from Paris, and
saddlery from Mexico; trees for gardens that
were never planted, or, if planted, were never
watered; printing-presses and fire-balloons—an
infinity of all that was grotesque, useless, and in
bad taste. As each packing-case gave forth its
contents they were looked at, perhaps played with,
and the majority speedily consigned to rust and
rot in damp stores and damper cellars. It was,
indeed, a glorious period for the *commis voyageurs*,
but it was the "agony" of Morocco. Every
incident in Europe was seized to push their wares.
The coronation of King Edward VII. brought
crowns to the fore. The Sultan was told he must
have a crown. He objected. It was contrary to
his religion to put gold or jewels on his head.

But escape was impossible. A coloured oleograph was spread out before him representing King Edward in his coronation robes, standing by a small table, with his index finger lightly resting on the summit of the Imperial Crown. This at least was a purpose to which the Sultan, without infringing the tenets of Islam, could put a crown. So the crown came.

The crown, it was rumoured, came from Paris; but the State coach was British, and London's best, built by a famous coach-builder, and of fine workmanship. The afternoon that it arrived, transported in packing-cases carried on platforms, which in turn were slung between camels, the Sultan was playing bicycle-polo with some of his European suite, which included at this period an architect, a conjurer, a watchmaker, an American portrait-painter, two photographers, a German lion-tamer, a French soda-water manufacturer, a chauffeur, a firework expert, and a Scottish piper. All these enjoyed the personal friendship of His Majesty, and the *entrée* into the presence of the ruler who, with the exception perhaps of the Grand Lama of Thibet, should have been the most exclusive and the most secluded of sovereigns. It is no wonder that the tribesmen looked askance on the high palace walls.

It was a gorgeous coach, of crimson lacquer, with gilded ornamentation. The inside was lined with rich green-brocaded silk, and the hammer-cloth was of scarlet and gold, and bore what were supposed to be the Royal Arms of Morocco—as a

F

fact, non-existent. Like the coach itself, the purple harness, with its gilt fittings, was of the very best; and together they formed an ensemble as expensive as it was utterly useless, for there were no roads in Morocco.

The bicycle-polo ceased, and the Sultan invited the Consul of a great foreign Power, who happened to be at the Court, and the writer, to come and inspect his newest purchase. In the centre of an immense field of swampy grass, surrounded by high crenellated walls, stood the scarlet carriage. In this field of many acres were opened all the packing-cases which were too large to pass through the gateways that led into the interior courts of the palace; it served also as a grazing-ground for His Majesty's menagerie. In a wide circle at some little distance from the State coach stood a ring of zebras, emus, wapiti, Hindu cattle, apes, antelope, and llamas, with a background of more timid flamingos and strange storks and cranes—one and all intent on examining, from a position of safety, the extraordinary scarlet addition to their numbers which had suddenly appeared among them.

The Sultan was evidently pleased. As usual, he said little; but he called to one of his officers, and ordered four horses to be harnessed to the coach. It had to be explained to him that no horse in the Imperial stables had ever been in harness, for the Sultan's previous purchases of carriages and hansom-cabs lay rotting idle and neglected in stores and cellars. But His Majesty was not going to be deprived of the pleasure of seeing his coach in movement. Men—soldiers and slaves—were harnessed and told to pull. Slowly the lumbering, useless, expensive but glorious State coach began to move.

" We will ride in it," said the Sultan ; and, beckoning to the Consul of a Great Power to get up behind, he himself mounted to the scarlet-and-gold seat of honour on the box. The writer rode inside. When all were seated, the vehicle started on its first and last progress of State. The soldiers and slaves sweated and puffed as the wheels sank deeper and deeper into the swampy ground, and the " progress " was slow indeed. Slow, too, were the paces of the procession that followed us, for, doubting but fascinated, the whole menagerie was in our wake, led by an emu whose courage had already been proved by an unprovoked attack upon the Scottish piper, and by having danced a *pas-seul* on the prostrate form of the expert in fireworks a few days previously. Close behind the emu followed a wapiti—with the mange—and then in turn the zebras, the Hindu cattle, the apes, gazelles, and lastly, the timid llamas, with their great luminous eyes and outstretched necks. Away in the background half a dozen cranes were dancing and performing the most absurd antics.

It rained that night, and the next day the little lake of water in which the State coach stood was purple from the dye of the harness, and the beautiful hammer-cloth of scarlet and gold flapped limp and ruined in the wind. Inside there was a pool of water on the green-brocaded seat.

The great fault, or misfortune, of Mulai Abdul Aziz was his extravagance. He was never able to realise the value of money. He spent, in the few years since he emerged from the seclusion of his palace to take up the reins of government, not only the whole revenue of his country, but also the savings of his predecessors. And what had he got for it all ? A lot of rubbish, bought at fabulous prices, which was lying rotting and rusting in the gloomy cavernous stores of his various palaces ! He was to blame for this extravagance, no doubt, but others were to blame still more. Those to whom he looked for advice left no stone unturned to exploit him. They made their fortunes, and left a broken unhappy Sultan, whose whole country was in rebellion, whose Treasury was exhausted, to bear the brunt of their sins. Mulai Abdul Aziz, full of the vigour of youth, anxious to learn, anxious to reform his country, anxious to do what was right, had a future before him of much useful work. His advisers took his education in hand—and his education cost him dear, for his fortune, his influence with his subjects, and his reputation had all gone. He was weak and young and sometimes stubborn ; but no man ever lived whose intentions were better ; but these intentions were warped and frustrated by his advisers. The Sultan had no disinterested person about him ; no disinterested advice was given him. He was told, when he spent his money in ordering useless goods from the various European countries, that it gave satisfaction to the Governments of those respective countries that he made his purchases in their markets.

Few of the things that he bought gave him any pleasure. Photography amused him for a time; but even this was made a means of exploiting him. A camera of gold at £2000 came from London; 10,000 francs' worth of photographic paper arrived in one day from Paris. His Majesty once informed me that his photographic materials, not including cameras and lenses, for one year cost him between £6000 and £7000! He naturally did not know what was required, and left it to his commission agents to purchase the " necessary " materials. They did, with a vengeance.

But it must not be thought that the Sultan lived no other life except this. His frivolity was of short duration—an hour or two perhaps every day; but at other times affairs of State took up his attention, though scarcely as much as ought to have been the case. He could, too, on occasion be remarkably serious in his conversations; and as he possessed a quick intelligent mind, much prone to speculation, his talk was often exceedingly interesting, and there were many occasions when, alone with him for an hour or two at a time, he let his words flow on from subject to subject. On the question of religion he was by no means a fanatic, though in every way a strict and orthodox Moslem, in spite of many stories to the contrary. His faults have been against the traditions of his predecessors, and never against his religion, though the two are so indissolubly mixed in the minds of the people that they are incapable of distinguishing one from the other, and so the untrue rumours which were spread broadcast all over Morocco appeared as based on fact. He would never have attracted attention and suspicion had he been a little better advised. The men who bought him European boots and European saddles, to their own profit and to his unmaking, were almost guilty of high treason. The men who ordered fancy European uniforms for him in the European capitals, as well as the men who photographed him in them, and allowed his photograph to appear in the illustrated papers of Europe, could almost have been tried for attempted regicide. From the newspaper to the picture post-card, the " Commander of the Faithful," the religious head of Islam in North-West Africa, was exhibited in a variety of costumes in the Tangier shop windows and sold for a halfpenny: and this in a country where pictures are considered as contrary to religion. That Mulai Abdul Aziz was weak there is no doubt ; but how easy it is to be weak in such circumstances, for every one was pushing him on, helping him day by day to become more and more unpopular, seeing his authority and his country slipping away from him—" educating " him, in fact, for so they called it, until in the end they left him with an empty Treasury to bear the brunt of the coming crisis. Every commission agent had his vizier-partner, who recommended that particular agent and his goods, and shared the profits. There was no one, actually no one, who could make his voice heard in the surroundings of intrigue and—" education."

Had the men who really influenced him pressed him to stop buying instead of to buy, he would have done so, but such was not their object. They kept back from him the state of the country, and made little of the rebellion which was smouldering all around him. The one man who realised more than the rest how badly things were going was the only man of energy at the Moorish Court, Sid Mehdi el-Menebhi, who had been a special ambassador at London and Berlin. He ventured once or twice to speak seriously, but the mass of intrigue against him was too great. I remember one incident so well. It was in December 1902. I was leaving Fez in the course of a few days for Tangier, when I received from an unknown country Moor news that the Pretender's forces, which, my informant said, were very numerous, were on the point of attacking the camp of the huge disorderly army which Mulai Abdul Aziz had sent out of Fez a day's march to the eastward. I had reason to believe this news then, and I have reason to believe to-day that it was sent me in order that I might leave Fez, for the Pretender at that time intended to follow his attack on the camp with a march on the capital. My informant, an uneducated countryman, mentioned, as a guarantee of good faith, an incident which had happened some years before at Meknés, in which I had apparently been able to render some small service to a Moor whose name at that time I did not know. It was Jilali Zarhouni, the Pretender himself, who four years afterwards, mindful of my little act, sent me this word of warning.

I reported the whole matter to the Sultan, whom I saw alone that night, but I could make no impression upon His Majesty. He laughed at the rebellion and at my fears for his troops, at the Pretender and his reputed forces. " Go," he said, " to Menebhi, and tell him from me to give you a good dinner, with musicians and ' kooskoosoo,' and don't worry yourself. Your fears are groundless." Menebhi gave me the good dinner, but he knew my fears were not groundless. We sat late into the night talking—he was Minister of War at the time—and I think he was persuaded that some steps must be taken. Before we parted we had further evidence of how serious things were becoming, for a Shereef, who had relations at Taza, had received news which confirmed my estimate of the Pretender's forces, though not of his proposed attempt to attack the Government troops.

The next day I bade farewell to Mulai Abdul Aziz. He was standing under a great archway in the palace. He tried to persuade me to stay, but for many reasons I had to be back in Tangier in eight or ten days' time. We stood there a while talking, and nothing could have been more kind than he was.

" I shall miss you much," he said ; " good-bye," and with a shake of the hand he left me. I turned and watched his tall figure, draped in white, until he disappeared into the palace through a gate in the garden wall. It was Monday, 22nd December 1902. That very evening, some forty miles away, his whole army fled in a panic before the Pretender's forces, leaving their entire camp, artillery, stores, ammunition, money, and transport in the hands of Bou Hamara.

The commander of the Sultan's forces that suffered this severe defeat was Mulai Abdesalam el - Amarani, His Majesty's uncle. He was an elderly and much-respected member of the royal family, who, with a brother, Sid Mohamed el-Amarani, had played a considerable and worthy part in Moorish politics. That he possessed any military capacity is doubtful ; but his name and his already proved political influence rendered him a suitable person to command such expeditions, on which diplomacy was always, if possible, preferred to fighting.

On my next visit to Fez, Mulai Abdesalam el-Amarani described to me the attack of Bou Hamara's forces upon the camp of the Sultan's army. His description of his own terror was pathetic. " I had no time," he said, " to collect my valuables, but there were two things I did not want to leave behind—a sack of money and the pills Dr Verdon had given me for my indiges-

tion.   The money was beside my bed, the pills
under the mattress, and I couldn't find them at
once, and between this loss and my terror and the
sound of firing in the camp I had to flee.   It was
not until I was on my mule that I discovered that
in my excitement I had forgotten both the money
and the pills."

IV.

THE BEGINNING OF THE END.

In spite of his extravagances, the life which the Sultan led was a very simple one. He rose early, and after prayers at dawn left the privacy of his palace for the buildings in which he held his Court. Here he took his seat, generally upon a settee or divan, in a private room, a little way removed from the great courtyard in which his viziers carried on their business. This courtyard was surrounded by a colonnade on to which opened a number of small rooms. In these were seated the various viziers and their secretaries, while without in the shade of the colonnade sat those who sought interviews with the various Secretaries of State. A gateway, guarded always by gatekeepers, led from this courtyard to the Sultan's private offices, and messages and letters passed to and fro. From time to time he would summon one or other of the viziers to his presence on affairs of State, and discuss with them what course it might be best to pursue. It can be understood from this slight intercourse that His Majesty held with the outside world, for he seldom had more than this, how easy it was for the people of his entourage to withhold from him all reliable information, and to paint the existing state of affairs in the colours that might suit their own views, or, more often, their own pockets.

"Court," which commenced in the early morning, was finished by noon, and the Sultan retired into the palace, where he dined. He ate always alone, and, as is the custom all over Morocco, with his fingers. This habit, which seems almost revolting to Europeans, is by no means an unclean one, for the hands are washed in warm water both before and after the meal, and the food is always cooked in such a way that it can easily be broken. A habit of our own, which we consider far more cleanly than eating with our fingers, is looked upon by the Moors as filthy—that is, washing our hands or face in a basin, and, still more, taking a bath where the water is not running. The cleaner we become, they say, the dirtier the water we are washing with must necessarily be, and eventually we step forth as cleansed from water which is no longer clean. A Moor to wash his hands has the water poured from a vessel over them, and never by any chance dips them into the dirty water. The same way in their baths: the water is thrown over their bodies out of bright brass bowls, and flows away through holes in the marble or tile floor.

His midday meal over, the Sultan would rest for a while, generally issuing from the palace about three o'clock. There was no afternoon

" Court," and on this account Mulai Abdul Aziz
was free to spend the rest of the day as he pleased,
and generally did so in the company of his European employees and friends. Bicycle-polo, cricket,
and tennis were the order of the day.

One evening, after a longer game of tennis than
usual, we commenced to take in the net, as rain
seemed probable. His Majesty had just retired
into the palace, but had left his pocket-handker-
chief tied to the top of the net, where he had
fixed it, as the light was waning, and it was difficult to distinguish the net's height. I unfastened
the handkerchief, but feeling something large tied
up in a corner of it, I examined it more carefully.
It was a cut diamond, about the size of a small
walnut, which His Majesty had lately purchased.
Carefully secreting the handkerchief and its valuable contents in my pocket—for there is no means
of getting at the Sultan once he has entered the
recesses of the palace, where women only are
allowed—I proceeded to leave the precincts by the
usual exit. I had crossed one courtyard and was
near the outer gate when I became aware that
some one was pursuing me. I took in the situation and ran ; but I was no match for the Sultan,
who, stirred to more than usual activity by the
loss of his valuable jewel, came down upon me
like a whirlwind. Almost before I realised that I
was caught, I was lifted off my feet and thrown
to the ground, while Mulai Abdul Aziz, his knees
pinning down my elbows, was rifling my pockets.
He soon discovered his diamond, still tied in the

handkerchief; but, not content with that, he deprived me of a pocket-book, a ring I was wearing on my watch-chain, a necktie-pin, and a cigarette-case. He let me go at last, laughing at the adventure, but I never saw my property again.

On another occasion I was present when one of the Court officials came to offer his respects to the Sultan on receiving a high appointment. This man was the now famous Haj Omar Tazzi, the present vizier of Government domains.

I was standing talking to His Majesty alone in a courtyard along one side of which were situated the cages of the Sultan's wild beasts, when Haj Omar entered. Prostrating himself barefoot on the marble floor, he touched the ground with his forehead. The Sultan, scarcely heeding him, made a few formal remarks, and then turning to me, asked abruptly, " Do you know this man ? "

I scarcely did, but aware of His Majesty's love of humour, I thought I saw the opportunity for a practical joke upon Haj Omar, whom, being a Fez town Moor, I rightly guessed to be a coward.

" I know him well," I replied. " Only to-day he was at my house begging me to ask a favour of your Majesty on his account."

Haj Omar, who was still prostrate on the ground, looked uneasily in my direction, not understanding what was passing.

" His favour is granted," replied the Sultan, to whom I had made a slight signal to allow me to continue.

"He asked," I went on, "that this afternoon, when summoned to your Majesty's presence for the first time in his new position, he might be allowed to give some proof of his fidelity."

"Certainly," replied Mulai Abdul Aziz.

"He proposed," I continued, "with your Majesty's permission, in order that his fidelity and courage might be put to the test, to spend half an hour in the lions' cage."

Haj Omar, still prostrate before the Sultan, squirmed uneasily, and lifted a fat pasty face toward the Sultan and myself.

"Certainly," replied the Sultan.

"If your Majesty bids me die, I am ready to do so," came a feeble voice trembling with emotion from the ground.

"Call the slave who has the keys of the lions' cage," replied the Sultan, and at the same time he moved in the direction of the wild beasts, Haj Omar following him on all-fours.

The slave arrived; but Haj Omar's terror was now so evident that the joke could no longer be kept up. Seizing me by the hand, the Sultan led me away, and Haj Omar fled.

We played another joke on Haj Omar before I left Fez, and on this occasion Menebhi was my accomplice, if not my instigator.

Haj Omar was pointing out to the Sultan the arrangement of a new flower-garden then in course of construction. His Majesty stood somewhat in advance, and the rather stout, pompous little courtier a little behind him on his right. Menebhi and I, who had wandered a short distance in another direction, soon made a discovery—a pump and a long hose! Standing the pump in the water-tank, I proceeded with the hose till I reached Haj Omar, and just as I put the nozzle down the back of his neck, Menebhi began to pump. The rich Moors never wash with cold water, and the voluminous stream which began to flow down Haj Omar's back nearly caused him to have a fit. The water poured out of his baggy trousers into his yellow slippers, but he daren't say a word, for His Majesty was addressing him. "It shall be done as your Majesty commands," he replied, when the Sultan had ceased speaking; but his voice was so trembling, so truly pitiful, that Mulai Abdul Aziz turned hurriedly to see what had happened. It was a sad object that met his view —Haj Omar Tazzi standing shivering and dripping in a pool of water. Etiquette forbids the Sultan to laugh in public, but etiquette couldn't help him covering his face with the long sleeve of his jelab to hide his merriment, and walking hurriedly in another direction.

The mention of etiquette recalls to my mind one or two of the "traditions" of the Moorish Court. In comparison with the barbaric splendour of the Sultan's State appearances in public, when, in the shade of the crimson-and-green velvet umbrella, he receives his tribesmen, his private life is simple. There is perhaps no more picturesque sight in the world than one of these Morocco processions. The ragged troops in blue

and red, who, with a background of crumbling
yellow walls, line the palace squares; the blue
sky above; the led horses in their gorgeous trap-
pings of coloured silks; the white-robed Court
officials on foot; the splendour of gold-embroidered
banners; and in the centre of it all the Sultan himself, swathed in flowing white robes, the only
figure on horseback—all help to form a picture
that, once seen, can never be forgotten. Then
suddenly a great cry rends the air, " May God
bless the life of our Lord the Sultan ! " and the
motley company bow low as His Majesty, still
shaded by the great umbrella of State, rides into
their midst. Compared in picturesqueness to this
gorgeous pageant, European State ceremonies are
poor indeed. But in his private life the Sultan is
simple enough. No man, of course, crosses the
precincts of the inner palace, where women only
are allowed to enter; but Mulai Abdul Aziz on
several occasions spoke to me of the boredom of
his domestic life. He recounted one or two facts
which show that, autocratic monarch as he is, his
actions are much restricted by precedent. One
of these referred to his bedroom, which must be
furnished in the greatest simplicity, and one colour
alone must be used, a deep, beautiful, indigo blue.
The silk hangings are made and dyed in Morocco,
and no European material must be employed.
Curtains, bedcovers, carpets, and wall-hangings
must all be of this one colour and manufacture.
Again, when out in camp his sleeping-tent must
contain but three carpets, and he must sleep on

G

a mattress on the ground, and not on a bedstead. His viziers and courtiers cover the floor of their tents with straw, over which they lay matting and piles of rich carpets; but the Sultan may have nothing but the bare earth and the traditional three small carpets. In wet weather he is obliged to wade ankle-deep in mud, while slaves wait to wash his feet as he steps on to the rug on which the mattress is spread. No doubt this simple sleeping-tent owes its origin to days when constant dangers threatened the Sultans on their camping expeditions, and when they were liable to be called up at night to lead their troops into battle; but however it may have originated, the custom—a particularly uncomfortable one—remains unchanged to-day. During the daytime the Sultan may spend his time in other tents, where no restrictions are placed upon his luxuries and comforts.

There is a certain room in the palace at Fez to which a recognised tradition pertains. The construction dates from a remote time, and there is supposed to exist, somewhere built into its walls, a certain charm. The purport of this charm is that as long as this particular chamber in the palace remains intact, no Sultan will die in Fez, and, curiously enough, no Sultan has died in Fez since the room was built. His Majesty described the chamber to me, for it is situated in the interior of the palace, where no men may enter. It is a large hall, richly furnished with its original rugs and divans, and every night special slaves, whose duty it is, light the many candles that are supported in the chandeliers. Two huge candles, brought from Mecca once a year, are the only ones that are lit more than once; all the others are replaced nightly. Nor may European candles be used—they must be of Fez manufacture.

The ceiling, rich in carving, still exists, but the roof above has been replaced again and again, one layer above another, without ever removing the underneath ones, lest the "charm" should be destroyed. In the same way the walls have been strengthened from the outside, until their thickness is immense. So exactly has this room been left in its original state that in one corner of it stands a ladder which has never been removed, while skins for holding water are still hanging upon the walls, little left of them but their gold spouts and pendent cups.

Mulai Abdul Aziz was an expert bicyclist, and there were often great games of bicycle-polo of an afternoon in one of the courtyards of the palace. The only other Moor who played was Menebhi, then at the height of his power and influence. The Sultan was a plucky but careful rider, seldom coming to grief, and handling his machine with the most perfect judgment. Menebhi was equally plucky, but much more excitable, and I have seen him, in pursuit of the ball, charge at full speed into the palace wall, to be rescued from what looked like a lot of broken umbrellas a minute later, as he shouted wildly for a new bicycle. As the Sultan was always supplied with the most

expensive articles that could be purchased, most
of his bicycles were of aluminium, and therefore
not suited to bicycle-polo ; but the more that
were broken the more were required, and his
commission agents reaped their harvest. The
record, I think, was taken by a young secretary
of the British Legation, who successfully smashed
six in one afternoon ! But it was not at polo
alone that Mulai Abdul Aziz was a skilful bicyclist,
for he could perform a number of tricks that would
almost have done honour to a professional. I
have seen him myself ride up a steep plank laid
against a packing-case, then along another plank
forming a bridge to another packing-case, and
down an incline at the end again. On one of these
occasions he fell, and lodged on his head ; but
after being stunned for a minute or two, remounted
his bicycle and successfully accomplished his object.

I only once saw him annoyed, and it was with
myself. We were standing on the summit of an
old outer wall of the palace. Immediately beneath
us, in the shadow of the wall, were a dozen or so
ill-clothed, half-starved members of what was in-
appropriately called the Moorish Army. Many of
the little group were evidently suffering from
fever, very prevalent in Fez in summer, and altogether they formed a pitiful sight.

I spoke, perhaps, too warmly of the neglect
with which the soldiers were treated, of their
stolen pay, of their abject misery, and I failed
to notice that the Sultan was not in a mood at
that moment to listen to my complaint.

" It isn't my fault," he said pettishly.

" It is," I replied. " Your Majesty doesn't take the trouble to see that your orders are carried out."

The blood rushed to the Sultan's face, and he drew himself up. " Remember," he said, " you are speaking to ' the Commander of the Faithful,' " referring to his most coveted title.

" I do," I replied, " remember it. It is your Majesty who forgets that these men are ' the Faithful.' "

Alas ! as far as he is concerned, but few of them were any longer faithful.

He bore me no grudge for what I said, and his look of anger passed into one of great sadness. For a little while he stood looking over the great plain that lay before us, then turned and said very gently, " You don't know how weary I am of being Sultan," and tears stood in his eyes.

On one occasion while visiting Meknés with the Sultan, I took the opportunity to go to the Jews' quarter of the town, to call on an Israelite family who had often hospitably entertained me at a feast on previous visits. The lady of the house was an extremely portly dame, one might almost say of gigantic proportions, but as kind-hearted as she was large. I was received with open arms by my host and hostess, their children and grandchildren, and after the usual salutations they began to pour out their woes. The Jews' quarter had been raided by Berber tribesmen, and my friends' house and stables had been broken into

and robbed. Could I obtain justice for them ?
Now, in spite of the Sultan's good intentions,
justice was about the only thing in the world
unobtainable in Morocco. The Sultan, I knew,
would order the damages to be repaid by the
responsible authorities, but my friends would
certainly receive only a very small portion of
what they had lost; the rest would disappear
en route. I therefore determined to obtain justice
from the Sultan by a little ruse. I told the portly
lady that His Majesty would make his State
entry into the town the following day, and bade
her climb on to the pedestal of one of the great
marble pillars of the famous gateway of Mansour-
el-Alj, and there to await his passage. Immediately
she saw the Sultan appear from under the gateway
she was to cry, " Will my Lord the Sultan allow
me to die in misery ? Will my Lord the Sultan
not protect me ? " I told her to look as fascinating as possible—she was well on for sixty years
of age—and to put on all the finery of gold lace
and velvet to which the Israelite ladies of the
Moroccan towns are so partial, and which forms
their national gala dress.

She promised to carry out my instructions, and
I laid my plans accordingly. An hour or two later
I was received by the Sultan, and ventured to
remark that I had experienced a curious dream
the night before. The Sultan asked me to relate
it, and I replied that I had dreamed that I was
accompanying His Majesty on his State entry
into the town, and that just as we passed under

the famous gateway an enormously fat Jewess, in gala attire, clinging to one of the marble columns, cried out, " Will my Lord the Sultan allow me to die in misery ? Will my Lord the Sultan not protect me ? " The Sultan was by nature super-stitious, and wondered what my dream could mean. Needless to say, I didn't inform him.

Everything occurred as I had planned it, with one ludicrous addition. The Sultan emerged from the gate, and there, on the high pedestal of the column, embracing the marble pillar, was my stout friend, shouting out her petition. The Sultan, struck by the coincidence, turned to see if he could catch my eye, and I naturally looked as astonished as he did. But the lady's anxiety to be heard led her to lean too far forward, her hold on the marble pillar was relaxed, and the last I saw of her was taking a header into the midst of scarlet-and-blue soldiers who lined the gateway. An hour later messengers hurried me into the Sultan's presence. I found His Majesty all excitement at the incident, and I explained that no doubt my extraordinary dream was a revelation in order that the woman might receive justice. The Sultan asked me if I knew who she was.

" I have seen her more than once," I replied.

" Go immediately," said His Majesty, " and find out what she wants."

The delight of my friends can be imagined when I entered their house and, on behalf of the Sultan, asked for a " statement of claim." I fully reported the matter, and Mulai Abdul Aziz sent for one of his own relations, Amrani Shereef, and ordered him to see that the family were immediately refunded for what they had lost, and that their house should be guarded in future. In this manner I knew they would get their money, which they certainly would not have done had the matter passed, in the usual course, through the hands of the viziers. The next day they were paid, and the day after I confessed my plot to the amused Sultan.

The year of the Algeciras Conference (1906) I was back in Fez again after an absence of three years. Everything was changed, for the days of prosperity and " packing-cases " were over, and the Maghzen had fallen upon evil times. Tribe after tribe had thrown off their allegiance. The robbery and pilfering and corruption were worse than ever. Famine reigned in the city.

The " campaign " which I, as ' Times ' correspondent, had carried on in the ' Times ' during the preceding year or two, rendered me no *persona grata* to the Sultan and his Court, and even accommodation was refused me and the palace gates hermetically sealed. I stayed for some months, and enjoyed, as I have never enjoyed before or since, the goodwill of the people of Fez. They knew what had happened. They knew that the ' Times ' had called the attention of the world to the plight of their co-religionists and fellow-countrymen in Morocco, and in their suffering and misery they showed an appreciation that was at once most marked and most valued. They knew that the Sultan had refused to receive me, and that the doors of the viziers' palaces were closed to me; and they knew, too, the reason—that I represented a great newspaper, the columns of which have always been open to the cries of distress of ill-used and neglected peoples, and that their plaints had already reached the British public— and the world's public—by these means. I shall never forget the sympathy and kindness shown to me by the mass of the inhabitants at Fez at this time. And what was this change that was so evident ?

It was famine—that was all ! Bread at sevenpence a loaf, and the loaf the size of a railway-station bun. Famine, because a few of the viziers and officials had taken advantage of last year's poor crops to " corner " wheat, by buying it before it entered the town, and selling it at any profit they liked; famine, because the same little coterie regulated the price at which even meat might be sold, and alternately robbed the poor and the butchers; famine, because every necessary of life had to pass through their hands before it reached the public; famine, because even charcoal, without which no cooking can be done, was " cornered." And the caravans of camels which should have been bringing grain from the coast to feed the starving people were commandeered to transport marble for the floors of the viziers' palaces, built with the proceeds of foreign loans—and of famine.

Yes, three years had brought about a change

in Fez, and it was not a change for the better. Life and energy seemed to have disappeared. The hang-dog starving soldiery, in rags of course, and paid, when they were paid at all, sufficiently well to buy half a small loaf of bread a day, prowled to and fro in the streets,—such few, that is, as were left of them, for the greater part had long ago deserted to the Pretender, who fed his men, or had sold their rifles to the nearest buyer, and gone back to spread sedition amongst the tribes. Really no one can blame them, and those that remained would have gone too, shaking the dust of Fez off their shoes—only they had no shoes, and most of them no strength to walk the distance. The streets were full of starving and half-starving people, many of whom begged only with their eyes, too pitiful to look upon unmoved. For a short time the proceeds of a public subscription did something to relieve these sufferers, but the funds disappeared—into the brick and mortar of palaces, it is said—and by, perhaps, more than a coincidence, the date of the conclusion of the Algeciras Conference was also the date at which the Maghzen ceased attempting to feed the poor. Could it have been that the eyes of Europe were no longer fixed on Morocco, and therefore the poor might starve again ? The long lines of suffering humanity cringed back against the walls of the narrow streets to make way for the camels, and mules and donkeys, laden with marble and mosaics for the palaces which the Court favourites were building—with the money of the people, with the

proceeds of famine. Before, the people bore their
sufferings—for even then they suffered enough
from the exactions of the Maghzen, but consoled
themselves by saying, " Our Lord the Sultan does
not know." Now it was different. Famine had
rendered them a little—a very little—more courageous, and they said, " Our Lord the Sultan does
not care." After all, there is only the difference
of one word. In the country districts they went
a little—just a little—further, and said, " There
is no Sultan." It was not true, of course, for
within the crumbling battlements of the expanse
of palace, Mulai Abdul Aziz, bored by everything,
but still kind-hearted, still with the best intentions,
wandered from court to court and from garden
to garden, giving orders that he knew would never
be carried out, weary with trying to do better
things, and content to await a change—any
change—of circumstances, with implicit trust in
God and a lurking mistrust in Europe. He, too,
had lost his energy. It was not altogether his
fault perhaps ; for at one time he really tried,
and circumstances had been against him. Too
much good nature and too little determination
had led to his failure, until he had handed over
everything to men far less capable and far less
well-intentioned than himself, and allowed them
to rob him as they pleased. He saw no one, and
went nowhere, probably because, with his nature,
he could not but feel the ignominy of his position
and the degradation of his country. The palace
itself resembled the palace of a dream, haunted

by ghosts. Yet even as such it was more fitted
for the residence of a Moorish Sultan than the
palace of three years ago, when the courtyards
were strewn with useless European goods, unsale-
able for the most part in Europe, and piled with
packing-cases—empty and full—and littered with
straw. Probably most of this refuse remained
there still—a poor return, after all, for what was
expended on it.

The scene in the great courtyard, surrounded
by its columns and arches, in which the Maghzen
held its daily Court, was changed too. Under
their respective arcades the viziers sat, sleepily
transacting what they called business—that is to
say, putting off till to-morrow, or longer, everything that they ought to have done to-day. There
was no life, no movement, in this Court now.
Where were the soldiers, who, slovenly as they
were, added a touch of colour to the scene?
Where were the country governors and kaids and
their escorts? Where were the officers of the
Court in their white robes and red-peaked fezes
—where were they all? And where that active
lithe figure whose quick stride and energetic
movements, whose keen eyes kept the whole
fabric together—El Menebhi, where was he?
Gone, faded away like phantoms, leaving to a
handful of incapable and self-seeking men—whose
voices were mocked almost in their own hearing—
the misgovernment of their country. What wonder
that the people all over Morocco said, "We have
no Sultan." What wonder that they disobeyed

and ridiculed the Shereefian commands! What wonder that the Pretender and Raisuli and a score of others had arisen all over the country! No, the only wonder is that the population had not rebelled in a body. But they had no need to do so. They paid no taxes and acknowledged no government. As to the townspeople, years of extortion and suffering had crushed their spirit —though they knew that all the present régime was giving them was famine.

And Mulai Abdul Aziz, knowing something of all this—knowing, anyhow, enough to make him desirous of knowing no more—still talked of what he intended to do for his people, still poured out plans for their betterment into the ears of men whose one object was to frustrate them, and wandered aimlessly from court to court and from garden to garden inside the palace precincts —a kind intelligent gentleman, too good in many ways, and too weak in many more, for the arduous position he had been called upon to fill. If the Pope was a prisoner in the Vatican, the Sultan of Morocco was doubly so in the palace of Fez.

Yet these changes, such as they were, could be apparent only to those very familiar with Fez in former days. To all others the city must be the same as ever, with its narrow tortuous streets overhung by, and tunnelled through, the high projecting houses; full of gloom and mystery; with glimpses, here of orange-trees peeping over a high wall; there, of tiled minarets and the green roofs of mosques and tombs—a city that

extends not a yard beyond the walls that encircle
it. Within, a tortuous maze ; without, mile upon
mile of open country dotted by the thatch huts
and tent villages of the tribes. Yet close to the
walls, along the banks of the river that flows in
so many channels through and around the town,
have sprung up gardens of oranges and olives, of
mulberries, apricots, and vines, that form a setting
of richer green to the grey white city that meanders
down from the plain to the valley of the Sebou,
following all the way the form of the depression
in which it lies.

There is scarcely a view of Fez that is not
beautiful, scarcely a glimpse that is not sad.
Its very colouring, or perhaps lack of colouring ;
its amazing alleys into which the sun never shines ;
its ruined mosques, rich in fast-falling mosaics
and wood-carving, in rotting arabesques and grass-
grown roofs ; its damaged drinking fountains,
from the broken tiles of which the water still
splashes to where once a basin caught it, but now
only to form a channel of mud in the narrow
thoroughfare ; its stately caravanserais with their
galleries of arches and trellis of wood that has
turned purple and grey with age ; its garden
quarter from which rise the modern palaces of
the viziers, built with the people's money and the
people's food—all add a mysterious charm to a
city that stands alone as an unspoiled example of
former prosperity and existing decay.

So it is with the people. They wore the de-
spondent sad expression that came from years of

oppression—hopeless of the future, forgetful of the past, and yet with one solace left to them, and one only: that God had ordained it so. Nothing would shake their belief that all was predestined, unalterably predestined and inscribed beforehand, in their book of life. " It is written " —and for them that was enough.

While the Powers of Europe had been almost on the verge of war over Morocco, while the eyes of the world's public had been fixed upon the Conference of Algeciras, while there still lay before the country a future that was unknown, while one-fifth of the land was in the hands of the Pretender, while the Sultan's authority scarcely extended outside a few walled cities—Fez had remained unmoved. Fatalists one and all, the Sultan and his viziers, the townspeople and the starving poor had scarcely given a serious thought to the future—to the crisis through which their country had passed, and was still passing. Mulai Abdul Aziz wandered from garden to garden and court to court inside the palace walls. His viziers still frustrated the good intentions of His Majesty —there was but little majesty left except in name —and the people still starved; and one and all, firm in their unshakable belief, said " It is written."

The results of the Conference of Algeciras and of the " Acte " which promulgated its decisions were what might have been expected. All Europe sent its delegates to the pleasant little Spanish town lying a few miles from Gibraltar, and every

Government had an axe to grind. They poured new wine—vinegar most of it—into old skins, and the result was inevitable. While the special Ambassadors, whose titles fill a couple of pages of print in the tiny volume that contains the "Acte," were discussing Public Works, International Police, the State Bank, and the differences between "fusils rayés et non-rayés"—and a host of other things—Morocco was sinking deeper and deeper into a state of anarchy, rendered more hopeless than ever by the rumours which were circulated amongst the tribes as to what was occurring on the other side of the Straits of Gibraltar. From the hills above Algeciras on at least one occasion the smoke of burning villages in the Tangier district—the result of this anarchy—was clearly visible. Raisuli was supreme in the north, while to the east of Fez the Pretender, Bou Hamara, still held his own.

Bou Hamara was a native of the Zarhoun tribe, who had been employed at one time as a scribe by a high native functionary of Meknés. His conduct, however, had rendered him quite unsuitable to be maintained as a secretary, for he not only, so rumour says, forged his master's signature, but also caused a replica of the Imperial Seal to be made, by which he obtained a considerable grant of money. He had also in his spare moments learned a few simple conjuring tricks. Already known as a scholar and a devout Moslem, these other acquirements stood him in good stead. But he was found out, and left Meknés hurriedly.

Living on his wits, he made for the Taza districts, situated between Fez and the Algerian frontier, and there acquired, from his scholarship and his conjuring, a very considerable prestige. Almost unconsciously he was accepted as a " leader," and eventually declared himself to be Mulai Mohamed, the eldest son of the late Sultan, Mulai Hassen, and therefore the elder brother of the reigning monarch, Mulai Abdul Aziz. He caused a great Seal of State to be struck, and was proclaimed as Sultan. Mention has already been made of the defeat the troops of Mulai Abdul Aziz suffered at his hands in December 1902. His prestige had now reached its zenith, and caused the greatest anxiety to the Moorish Court. He ruled Eastern Morocco for several years with scarcely varying success. At times, it is true, he was driven back into the mountains of the Rif when Taza was captured by a Moorish army under El-Menebhi, the active young Minister of War ; but Bou Hamara was always able to reassert his authority and regain his lost possessions. In spite of every effort of El-Menebhi to maintain an adequate force, the corruption and incapacity of the Court was such that even his energy could avail nothing. The soldiers' pay failed, and the Sultan's troops melted away. It was not until Mulai Hafid had come to the throne in 1912, after the abdication of Mulai Abdul Aziz, that Bou Hamara was captured and brought to Fez. Confined in a cage carried on the back of a camel, the famous Pretender was brought into the

H

Sultan's presence. The interview was protracted. For several days Bou Hamara, squatting in the small space of his cage, was exposed to public view in the great court of the palace where the Sultan held his receptions—and the Sovereign who held the throne and the Pretender who had so long threatened it were face to face. Eventually the prisoner of State was put into the lions' cage in the presence of the Sultan, while the ladies of the Court lined the roof of the palace to witness the execution. The lions, however, too well fed, refused to eat him, but mangled one of his arms. After waiting for some time longer to see if the king of beasts would change their minds, the Sultan ordered the Pretender to be shot, and he was despatched by the slaves. His body was afterwards burnt, to deprive him of any possibility —for the Moors believe in a corporeal resurrection —of going to heaven. Terrible as was his end, Bou Hamara himself had been guilty of every kind of atrocity, and had regularly burnt, after sprinkling them with petroleum, any of the Sultan's soldiers that he had been able to capture during his campaigns.

The vicinity of the Pretender's jurisdiction to the Spanish port of Melilla, on the Rif coast, had seriously inconvenienced the Spanish authorities and inhabitants of that town ; and at length, in order to obtain supplies for the population, the Spaniards had been obliged to negotiate and to enter into direct relations with him. A mining-engineer told me that he had once accompanied some Spanish capitalists on a visit to Bou Hamara's headquarters at Selouan. They all went with a certain fear and trembling, but the stake was a big one. They wanted to obtain a concession for the working of some valuable iron-mines in the neighbourhood. The Pretender received them cordially enough, and invited them to sit down with him on a large carpet spread in the shadow of a tree. The discussion of the terms of the concession proceeded, and Bou Hamara's demands became more and more exacting. The capitalists hesitated and protested, but were brought to acceptance by the fact that while the conversation was still in progress a number of the Pretender's soldiers arrived carrying the recently-severed heads of a dozen or so of his enemies, which they arranged round the edge of the carpet. At the end of the interview the three or four very pale capitalists had accepted in their entirety the Pretender's propositions, and were thanking him for his cordial reception, surrounded by the ghastly exhibition that had not a little influenced their decision.

The heads of enemies were, until the end of Mulai Hafid's reign, commonly exposed upon the gates of the towns of the interior of Morocco. In 1909, during the official Mission of the late Sir Reginald Lister to Fez, the Bab Mharouk was hung with the heads of rebels. One of these grisly monuments fell, with a resounding thud, as the British Minister and some of his party were passing underneath. The manner of affixing them was

by passing a wire through the ear, which was
fastened to a nail in the wall. Over and over again
during my long residence in Morocco I have seen
the gates and other buildings at the Moorish capitals
decorated with these horrid trophies.

A more serious rival to the Sultan Abdul Aziz
came upon the scene when Mulai Hafid, his half-
brother, set up the banner of revolt in Southern
Morocco in 1908, and proclaimed himself Sultan.
The moment was opportune. The previous year
(1907) the French had bombarded Casablanca—
after the massacre of a number of European
workmen by the natives. These workmen, Italians
and Frenchmen, were engaged upon the quarrying
and transport of stone for the construction of the
port. The little railway used for this purpose
passed through, or close to, a Moslem cemetery.
Native opinion, excited by religious agitators,
burst all bounds of restraint, and the Moors
attacked the train. The labourers returning from
their work were murdered. A French warship
arrived on the scene, and an armed party landed
for the protection of the European population of
the town. The forts and native official quarters
were at the same time bombarded. Scenes of the
wildest confusion ensued, for not only was the
town under the fire of the cannon of the warship,
but the tribes from the interior had taken advantage of the panic to invade and pillage the place.
Every sort of atrocity and horror was perpetrated,
and Casablanca was a prey to loot and every kind
of crime. The European force was sufficient to

protect the Consulates, and the greater part of
the Christian population escaped murder. When
order was restored the town presented a pitiful
aspect. I saw it a very few days after the bombardment, and the scene was indescribable—a
confusion of dead people and horses, while the
contents of almost every house seemed to have
been hurled into the streets and destroyed. The
looting was incomplete: piles of cotton goods,
cases of foodstuffs—in fact, every class of mer-
chandise still lay strewn about the roads. Many
of the houses had been burned and gutted. Out
of dark cellars, Moors and Jews, hidden since the
first day of the bombardment, many of them
wounded, were creeping, pale and terrified. Some
had to be dug out of the ruins of their abodes.
Over all this mass of destruction horses and men
had galloped and fought. Blood was everywhere.
In what had once been the poorer quarter of the
town, where the houses, mostly thatched in straw,
had been burned, I only met one living soul—a
mad woman, dishevelled, dirty, but smiling—who
kept calling, " Ayesha, my little daughter; my
little son Ahmed, where are you: I am calling you."
Turning to me she asked, " You haven't seen my
little children, have you ?—a little girl and a tiny
boy, almost a baby." She didn't wait for an
answer, but passed on, still calling Ayesha and
Ahmed.

There were many people completely mad with
fear. The Jews and Jewesses were perhaps those
who suffered the most. One Jewess, rescued from

a cellar, was brought, stunned with terror, to Tangier on a relief ship. It was only after landing that she remembered that she had hidden her baby, to save it from death, in a corner of the cellar where she had been concealed—three days before.

The bombardment of Casablanca and those days of horror necessitated a campaign to clear the surrounding country of the evil tribes that hovered about, waiting another occasion to murder, rape, and pillage. It was the beginning of the French occupation of Morocco, and the final end of centuries of cruelty, corruption, and extortion.

V.

THE LIQUIDATION OF THE SULTANATE.

THE year 1912 saw the end of the independence of Morocco, and though there must always be present a regret when something very old and picturesque disappears, yet, on the whole, the end of its independence was a matter for congratulation.

Built up originally on the foundation of the religious prestige of its rulers—for the Sultans of Morocco were descendants of the Prophet—the rotten old edifice had stood for many years in a state of imminent collapse. Only its isolation, and the exclusiveness and fanaticism of its people, had postponed its earlier disintegration, and for a long time, in the throes of mortal disease, Morocco had kept up a semblance of life. A young and spendthrift Sultan, Mulai Abdul Aziz, had wasted the revenues of the country and emptied its Treasuries—for the greater part on the most useless purchases of European origin. His reign had been the epoch of the *commis voyageurs*, when caravans converged upon Fez from all the seaports, bearing cages of wild beasts, and the most astounding assortment of every imaginable and unpractical

object of luxury and bad taste. It was the time
of fireworks and barrel-organs, of fantastic uniforms
and beds made of looking-glass, of cameras and
parrots from the Amazons. This expenditure, his
association with Europeans, and the weakness with
which he administered his Government, gave rise
to a rebellion. His half-brother, Mulai Hafid, proclaimed himself Sultan in the southern capital.

The war between the two Sultans was tedi-
ous and uninteresting. The principal object of
both seemed to be how to avoid an encounter,
and they contented themselves by issuing edicts of
mutual excommunication, and, in order to obtain
money, by pillaging the tribes, regardless of their
political opinions. When either Sultan had funds
he had also soldiers; failing resources, the armies
alternately dwindled away almost to the point of
disappearance. In fact, both were dependent for
troops on deserters from each other's forces.

In 1908 Mulai Abdul Aziz left Fez for the scene
of the rebellion, and marching slowly by a very
devious course, so as to avoid any possible encounter with the enemy, he set out for the south.
Meanwhile Mulai Hafid, equally pluckily, set out
to conquer the north—also, and for the same
reason, by a very devious route. In all probability
each would have successfully reached the other's
capital without a hitch, if Mulai Abdul Aziz's
army, when only a short distance from its goal,
Marrakesh, had not suddenly pillaged the Imperial
camp, driven the Sultan to seek refuge, after a
long and dangerous journey, on the coast, and

declared for his rival. A few months later he
abdicated in favour of Mulai Hafid, who, with only
a few followers, for his army had likewise deserted
him, had meanwhile arrived in Fez with little
more than the proverbial half - crown in his
pocket.

Fez accepted him as Sultan, on the distinct
condition that the city was to be exempted from
all taxation. This His Majesty solemnly promised
—and he kept his promise for a few weeks, until,
in fact, he was strong enough to break it—and
then he collected taxes, legal and illegal, with
gusto never before experienced.

His ability to act thus was owing to his having
meanwhile collected a little army. Naturally the
Treasury was empty, and no tribesmen presented
themselves as desiring to take military service, as
no pay was forthcoming. The situation was pre-
carious. Without troops Mulai Hafid could do
nothing, not even collect the taxes he had promised
to forgo ; and without the taxes he couldn't live.
At all costs he must have an army.

So one morning the public criers announced in
the streets and market-places that the Sultan was
on a certain day giving a great feast at the palace
to the adepts of the sect of the " Gennaoua."
Now the confraternity of the " Gennaoua " is
very popular in Morocco, though—limited almost
entirely to the Southerners, who are largely of
negro extraction, and form a class by themselves
of labourers and water-carriers—it is looked upon
as unorthodox by the more educated Moors. The

Sultan even hinted that he himself had leanings towards their particular doctrine.

On the day in question the " Gennaoua," washed and in their best clothes, flocked to the palace, and entered its great walled courts, surrounded by frowning towers. With every sign of holiday-making and joy, they manifested their pleasure at the honour of being invited to the Sultan's religious-garden-party—and sought refreshments. Alas ! there were none—nothing but high walls and closed gates—and the next day a sad but resigned army was being drilled on the palace parade-ground.

Mulai Hafid was not the man to restore the dying Morocco back to health. Tribes revolted ; he himself adopted barbarous methods, and the condition of Morocco became worse than before. In the early months of 1912 the Sultan was besieged by the tribes in Fez. He appealed to the French, already installed at Casablanca on the Atlantic coast. An expedition was hurriedly despatched to the capital, which was relieved, and a few weeks later the Treaty of the French Protectorate was signed, to be followed immediately by a massacre of French officers and civilians in Fez. Mulai Hafid's position became impossible, both in the eyes of France and of his own people, and he decided to abdicate. The Court moved to Rabat, on the coast, and there the final scenes of Moroccan independence took place. They consisted in the most rapacious bargaining on the part of the Sultan, in order to obtain the best possible terms for himself.

Before leaving Fez he had already begun to secure his future comfort in life. He had informed all the royal ladies of his palace—and they were legion—the widows of former Sultans and a host of female relations—that they must all accompany him to Rabat. He gave them stringent orders as to their luggage. All their jewels and valuables were to be packed in small cases, their clothes and less costly belongings in trunks. They strictly followed these injunctions, but on the day of the Sultan's departure the ladies and the trunks were left behind. They are still in Fez : the jewels, there is reason to believe, are in Europe. Mulai Hafid always prided himself on his business qualities.

The last weeks of his reign were one continual period of wrangling with the French authorities. He was still Sultan and therefore dangerous, and the question of his successor had not been settled, so he yet held some trump cards, which he played successfully. Even when everything was arranged, and the letters for the proclamation of his younger half-brother, Mulai Youssef, the reigning Sultan, had been despatched to the interior, Mulai Hafid changed his mind. On reconsideration, he stated, he thought he wouldn't abdicate or leave the country, as had been decided. He had already obtained the most generous terms from the French Government, but the situation was desperate. Instructions had already been circulated in the interior to proclaim the new Sovereign, and the reigning one refused to abdicate ! Then Mulai

Hafid said that possibly he might be persuaded again to change his mind. He was; but it cost another £40,000, which was given him in a cheque as he left the quay at Rabat for the French cruiser that was to take him on a visit to France. In exchange, he handed to the French Resident-General the final document of his abdication. The mutual confidence between these two personages was such that for a spell they stood each holding an end of the two documents, and each afraid to let go of his lest the other paper should not be delivered.

The night before the signing of his official abdication Mulai Hafid destroyed the sacred emblems of the Sultanate of Morocco—for he realised that he was the last independent Sovereign of that country, and was determined that with its independence these historical emblems should disappear too. He burnt the crimson parasol which on occasions of State had been borne over his head. The palanquin he hewed in pieces and consigned also to the flames, together with the two cases in which certain holy books were carried. The books themselves he spared. The family jewels he took with him.

From Rabat, Mulai Hafid proceeded to France, where, as the guest of the French Government, and travelling in semi-state, he made a protracted tour. At the conclusion of this journey he returned to Tangier, where his immediate family and retainers—in all about 160 persons—had meanwhile arrived. The old Kasbah (castle) was placed at

His Majesty's disposal, and there he took up his residence.

Almost immediately after his arrival at Tangier began the discussion of the terms of his abdication, for only its more general lines had been settled at Rabat, and in a very short time the ex-Sultan's relations with the French were seriously embroiled. Mulai Hafid did not apparently regret having abdicated. He knew that his continued presence on the throne in the actual circumstances was out of the question. What he did regret was that he had not made better terms for himself, and he still hoped to be able to extort more money and more properties. Thus the negotiations were being carried on by him in a spirit of grasping meanness, that rendered any solution impossible. At the beginning of his reign, only four years before, he had shown signs of an elevated and patriotic spirit, and really intended to do his best to maintain the independence of the country. But he had quickly realised how impossible his self-set task was. He became unscrupulous, neurasthenic, and cruel. He made enemies on every side— amongst his own people by his barbarities and his extortions, and amongst the Europeans by his cynicism and intransigence.

So it came about that in a very short time after his arrival in Tangier his relations with the French authorities were strained to breaking-point. It was at this moment, when everything seemed almost hopeless, that the writer was asked, independently by both sides, to intervene in the interests of peace.

This invitation to intervene came about as follows. There had been a terrible scene between the ex-Sultan and the French authority charged with the negotiations, and Mulai Hafid had used language so unparliamentary that any further meeting was out of the question.

Early one morning the writer received the visit of a French official, who implored him to become the medium of the conversations and proposals, paying him the compliment of saying that he seemed to be the only person who had any influence over the ex-Sultan, whose conduct was bitterly resented in high quarters.

Scarcely had this person disappeared when the ex-Sultan himself arrived. His nerves appeared to have completely given way, and he was in a state of the deepest depression. Throwing himself upon a sofa, and in tears, he poured out all his woes, real and pretended, attacking the French with a vehemence that was as violent as it was unjust. " You," he said to the writer, " seem to be the only person who has any influence upon these villains. Will you continue the negotiations ? " Under the circumstances there was nothing to do but to accept.

An hour later the conversations had recommenced. The ex-Sultan spent the whole day at the writer's villa, and could scarcely be persuaded to eat or drink. During the writer's absence at the French Legation, Mulai Hafid took his departure—and that was not all he took, for he carried away with him the choicest specimens of the

writer's Arabic manuscripts. Being of a literary
disposition, the temptation of the illuminated
books was too great. The writer never saw them
again, but it is only fair to state that His Majesty
sent a present in exchange the same evening—a
gold and enamelled dagger.

During the following weeks the principal points
of the negotiations were successfully solved—the
question of the pension, funds for the construction
of a palace in Tangier, the retention of certain
large properties in the interior, and the future of
the ex-Sultan's wives and children.

Then came the question of the debts, about
which there ensued a long and acrimonious discussion. It had been accepted on principle that
all debts that had been incurred directly, and in
certain cases indirectly, in the interests of the
State, should be considered as Governmental debts,
and be paid by the French Protectorate Government, while all private debts should be settled out
of the ex-Sultan's private fortune.

Now this distinction of debts was rendered
extremely difficult by the systems under which
Morocco had been governed. The Sultan of
Morocco was always an absolute monarch, and,
as such, the revenues of the country were his.
There had never been any distinction between
public funds and private funds—all belonged to
the Sultan. As a rule, the expenses of the State,
as well as the palace upkeep, were paid by bills
drawn upon the custom-houses of the coast. It
was therefore no easy task to arrive at an agree-

ment as to what were State and what private debts, so inextricably mixed had they been in the past.

There was, for instance, a bill for a fine marble staircase, ordered in Italy for the palace at Fez. The French authorities argued that this very expensive staircase was merely a piece of wild extravagance on the part of Mulai Hafid, and that accordingly he ought to pay for it. The ex-Sultan, on the contrary, insisted that the palace was the property of the State—he had argued just the other way when he had been called upon to explain why he had brought away with him certain valuable fixtures—and that any additions and improvements he had made to it were all to the advantage and interests of the State. It was, he said, his successor and not he himself who would benefit by the marble staircase. The Protectorate Government allowed the justice of this argument and paid the bill.

The sequel to this incident is worth the telling. A few months later, when the ex-Sultan was signing a contract for the construction of his new palace at Tangier, he eliminated one of the several marble staircases marked in the plan. He had, he said, a very superior marble stair which would do admirably in its place. The writer ventured to ask if it was the same one about which there had been so much discussion. " It is," replied Mulai Hafid. " You see, it had not yet left Italy, so I telegraphed and had it delivered here instead of being sent to Fez."

A still more complicated claim was for some hundreds of yards of very expensive and very fine crimson cloth. Naturally the Protectorate authorities scheduled this amongst the private debts. The Sultan protested. The cloth, he said, had been purchased for Governmental purposes—in fact, for the trousers of the Imperial kitchen-maids—for there are several hundred slave-women employed in preparing the palace food. The Protectorate Government refused to be responsible for this debt. The ex-Sultan drew up an historical treatise to prove that Imperial kitchen-maids were part and parcel of the State, and passed, like the palace itself, from Sultan to Sultan. The principle was accepted, but the debt was disallowed, on the ground that these good ladies did not require such expensive stuff for their nether garments. A cotton material, they argued, would have equally well served the purpose. The Sultan's reply was unanswerable and crushing. " In Europe," he said, " it may be the custom for the Imperial kitchen-maids to wear cotton trousers, but in Morocco we have more appreciation of the dignity of their position."

There was nothing more to be said. The debt was paid by the Protectorate Government.

The long discussions which the writer, practically unaided, had to maintain with the Sultan were not always facilitated by the surroundings in which they took place. There were no regular business hours for these conversations or for the examination of the voluminous documents which they often necessitated, and which were always in the wildest disorder, but which none the less required a careful perusal. Whenever and wherever His Majesty felt inclined he would burst out with his grievances, and as at all costs he had to be kept apart from the French authorities, the whole storm used often to fall on the writer's head. At times the ex-Sultan, struck by a brilliant idea how to escape the payment of some small sum, would arrive at my villa at dawn—at others I was hastily summoned to the palace at midnight. The debts were discussed and argued over in every possible situation, and any one present, native or European, high authority or slave, was dragged into the discussion. There were two aged ladies whose opinion was constantly asked. One was an old black slave nurse, the other a Berber woman, quite white, who was the Sultan's soothsayer and fortune - teller. Her advice was always good and to the point, and she never hesitated to tell the ex-Sultan that he was acting foolishly when occasion required, and she rendered distinct services toward the unravelling of these complicated questions.

Sometimes it was when seated on mattresses and rugs in a garden, surrounded by his slaves, that Mulai Hafid would argue that all debts were State debts, and that private property never had legally existed, and that individual responsibility —especially for debts—was contrary to the highest principles of divine nature. He discoursed with

great facility and great literary ability. He had
a classical Arabic quotation at hand—often most
skilfully misquoted—to prove his every argument.
He could persuade others quickly, and himself at
once. Leaning slightly forward, swathed in his
soft white robes, he would speak slowly and with
great distinctness and charm, with an accompanying slow movement of his right hand—and then in
the middle of it all his attention would be attracted
by his elephants or his llamas or a group of cranes
that would come wandering out of the shrubberies,
and turn his thoughts and his conversation into
new channels.

While the two elephants were being brought
from Fez to Tangier at the time of the abdication,
one of them escaped on the road, and being an
unknown beast to the villagers of the countryside,
it met with many adventures. Wherever it appeared arose panic and consternation, and the whole
male population turned out with such weapons as
they could lay their hand on to drive away this
terrible and unknown beast. The country population, however, possessed little but very primitive
firearms, whose range was short, and whose bullets
dropped harmlessly off the sides and back of the
huge pachyderm, thereby increasing the panic.
The elephant, luxuriating in the spring crops,
grazed undisturbed, while from as near as they
dared to approach the outraged proprietors poured
volleys against its unheeding bulk. But one day
it found itself on the road again, and came rolling

along into Tangier none the worse, but remarkably spotted all over with the marks of the spent bullets.

It was during one of these long discussions of claims that news was brought to the Sultan that one of these elephants was lying down in its stable and was unable to rise. This information, of course, put an end to all business, and we set out at once to see what had happened. Sure enough, the female elephant was lying on her side, every now and then struggling but vainly to get up.

After everybody present had given an opinion, and every effort had been made to put the poor creature on her legs—from twisting her tail to lighting a lucifer match under her hind-legs, which failed, of course, even to singe the skin— Mulai Hafid arrived at the conclusion that only by the aid of a crane could the elephant be raised.

A heavy beam was found, and made fast to ropes hung from the roof. Two other ropes were passed under the elephant's recumbent body, one just behind her front-legs, the other just in front of her hind ones, a manœuvre that entailed considerable labour.

When everything was ready the slaves began to haul. With cries and shouts of mutual encouragement they managed to raise the elephant till she was swinging suspended in the air, and then set to work to lower her gently on her feet. In this they would no doubt have been successful had not the forward one of the two ropes slipped back, with the result that the unfortunate pachyderm, suspended now only from aft, stood on her head, and remained hung up in this posture until she was lowered to earth once more, this time with her face to the wall in a more impossible position than ever. But in spite of all the difficulties, after much shouting, swearing, and a good deal of real hard work, she was restored to a standing posture.

There were many occasions when our conversations were in less pleasant places than the gardens. There was a room, for instance, in a hideous villa that Mulai Hafid had bought as it stood, and greatly admired, that seemed haunted by the microbe of irritability. Not only was its decoration appalling, but it was full of a host of objects which the ex-Sultan had brought from Fez, amongst them innumerable musical-boxes, clocks of every shape and form—he evidently particularly fancied a kind made in the shape of a locomotive engine in coloured metals, the wheels of which all turned round at the hours, half-hours, and quarters, and mechanical toys. Everything, or nearly everything, was broken, and an Italian watchmaker was employed in trying to sort out the wheels, bells, and other internal arrangements of this damaged collection of rubbish. It was in this room that he had set up his workshop, and nothing pleased Mulai Hafid more than to sit and watch him.

Now it was not unseldom the writer's duty to break to the ex-Sultan the news that the French authorities refused to pay such and such a debt.

With all oriental autocrats it is best to break bad news gently, for they are usually wanting in self-restraint, and are not accustomed to blunt facts. Often it required considerable time and a neatly-expressed argument, couched in Arabic at once diplomatic and literary, to carry out the task successfully and escape an access of temper. I would begin with a little discourse on the origin of revenues, the ex-Sultan would listen attentively, and then just as the moment arrived to bring generalities into line with actual facts, the Italian watchmaker would meet with an unexpected success. Clocks would begin to strike and chime, or a musical-box, old and wheezy, to play, or an almost featherless stuffed canary in a cage would utter piercing notes in a voice that moth and rust had terribly corrupted—or from near the Italian's chair some groaning mechanical toy would crawl its unnatural course over the carpet, eventually to turn over on its back and apparently expire in a whizz of unoiled wheels. The ex-Sultan's attention would stray. There was an end of business, and it generally led to the ordering of a meal to be served to every one—at any hour and on any excuse—at which the watchmaker, who might have only just finished a repast, was the guest of honour, and was forced to eat incredible quantities of very rich, but very excellent, food. And what was left of the royal repast was handed out of the windows and served to the slaves and gardeners.

Perhaps the most difficult claim to settle was

that of the Sultan's Spanish dentist, for not only
was it extremely complicated, but it also became
almost international. It might naturally be supposed that the dentist's bill was for professional
services; but no—it was for a live lion. In the
early days of his reign the Sultan had engaged the
dentist at a regular stipend, and he had become
a permanent member of His Majesty's household.
For a time he was kept busy patching up the
mouths of the Court, but the task was at length
accomplished, and the ladies' teeth glistened with
gold. The dentist remained unemployed.

Now there is no possible reason in the world
why dentists shouldn't be employed to buy lions.
It is not, of course, usual, and so sounds incon-
gruous. In Morocco, views as to the limitations
of professions are much less restricted than with
us. In Mulai Abdul Aziz's time, a very few years
ago, one of the duties of the Scotch Court-piper
was to feed the kangaroos, the professional photographer made scones, a high military authority
supplied the Sultan's ladies with under-linen, and
the gardener from Kew was entrusted with the
very difficult task of teaching macaw parrots to
swear. And so it was not surprising that the
dentist became a buyer of lions.

In the first flush of his success at the beginning
of his reign, Mulai Hafid was setting himself up
as an orthodox Sovereign by Divine Right, and
this necessitated a menagerie. It is one of the
attributes of royalty which has almost disappeared, except in the East, though at one time

universal. It is perhaps fortunate. The hurried
entrance of an excited rhinoceros amongst the guests
at a garden party at Windsor Castle would prove
embarrassing, and so, to a lesser degree, would be
the presence of a hyena at the evening service
at St George's Chapel; but at Morocco similar
incidents would have attracted little or no attention. The father of Mulai Hafid, Mulai Hassen,
allowed his tame leopards to roam about his
reception-rooms; but his son, more timid by nature,
confined the leopards in cages, and replaced them
in his drawing-room by guinea-pigs. The effect
lost in majesty, but the afternoon callers were less
nervous.

So the dentist was sent to Hamburg to buy wild
beasts from Hagenbeck. But he erred. He should
have returned with the menagerie and shared its
glory. He delayed, and when he arrived in Fez a
few months later the novelty and glamour of the
wild beasts was passed, and the reception that he
and the belated unpaid-for lion—the last of a
series of lions—met with was by no means enthusiastic. Mulai Hafid had discovered that the
upkeep of so many sheep-eating beasts was expensive, as the tribes, on the eve of revolt, refused
to supply the sheep, and insultingly demanded
payment.

So far the claim presented no insurmountable
difficulties, but there were complications; for the
Sultan, immensely attracted by the mechanism of
the dentist's operating - chair, had some time
previously ordered from the dentist, and paid for,

a throne to be constructed on the same mechanical principles. This throne had never been supplied, so there was a counter-claim. The Sultan stated that he had paid for the lion; or if he hadn't, then it was a State debt, for which he was not responsible, and demanded the delivery of his mechanical throne. The question was still under discussion when the term of the dentist's contract expired, and the ex-Sultan notified him that it would not be renewed. But the dentist held a trump card, for the ex-Sultan had lodged him, rent free, in a little villa situated on one of His Majesty's Tangier properties. The dentist refused to quit, and the Spanish authorities upheld him, for by the capitulations each Power protects the interests of its respective subjects. A body of slaves were sent to eject him. They found the villa barricaded, and were met with pistol-shots. The complications were becoming serious, and international in character. The Sultan, the French authorities, the Spanish dentist, the black slaves, the writer, a British subject, and the German lion threatened to cause annoyance to the Governments of Europe if recourse was made to firearms. I made an impassioned appeal for conciliation on every one's part. After much delay and no little difficulty, an interview was arranged between the ex-Sultan and the dentist, at which as mediator I was to be present. Each was studiously coached in the part he was to play: the dentist's plaintive appeals to the generosity of the ex-Sovereign were carefully rehearsed, as were also

the Sovereign's " gracious reply," while the writer's
little speech on the blessing of brotherly love was
a gem of the first quality.

Mulai Hafid was seated on a divan studiously
reading a book when the dentist entered and made
his obeisance, but this obeisance—polite but inten-
tionally curtailed—did not meet with His Majesty's
approval. Instead of, as arranged, smilingly
acknowledging the dentist's salutation, the ex-
Sultan continued reading half aloud in a sing-
song drawl.

A long period ensued, broken by one of the suite,
who said, " My lord the King, the dentist is here."

Without raising his eyes from his book the ex-
Sultan asked in the softest of voices—

" Has he brought my mechanical throne ? "

Now that wasn't on the programme at all!
There was to have been no mention of such dis-
tressing objects as dentist-chair-thrones or lions.
There was to have been purely and simply a
reconciliation : a sum of money promised to the
dentist if he would quit the villa, and a general
abandonment of claim and counter-claim. But
alas ! before any one could intervene the dentist
shouted out—

" Pay me for my lion ! "

And then the fat was in the fire. For some
moments the atmosphere boiled with vituperative
allusions to lions and dentist-thrones, until, while
the writer restrained the infuriated potentate, the
dentist was, struggling and shouting, removed
from the presence-chamber.

By dint of great persuasion the writer eventually brought about a settlement. The Sultan did not get his throne, nor did he pay for the lion, which the Protectorate Government took over, not having been informed that it had meanwhile died. The dentist received a sum of money in payment of all his claims. The writer, whose solution it was, got the thanks of none of them, all three parties concerned expressing themselves as distinctly dissatisfied with the settlement arrived at.

VI.

THE SULTAN AT HOME.

In 1912-1913 the modern palace which the latest
of the abdicated Sultans, Mulai Hafid, has built
himself at Tangier, and which covers several acres
of ground with its immense blocks of buildings
and its courtyards, was still rising from the level
of the soil, and His Majesty was temporarily
housed, with all his retinue, in the old Kasbah
at the top of the town. It is a spacious, uncomfortable, out-of-date, and out-of-repair old castle, and
it formed by no means a satisfactory place of
residence, for it was not easy to install 168 people
within its crumbling walls with any comfort or
pleasure. When, too, it is taken into account
that many of these 168 people were royal ladies
with royal prerogatives as to their apartments—
to say nothing of their pretensions to the "most
favoured ladies'" treatment—it can be realised
that the solution was not easy. Even in the most
luxurious of quarters the ladies of the palace are
said to give considerable trouble, for jealousy is
rife ; and if one of them receives more attentions
—personal or in presents—than the rest, there are

often disturbing scenes—and rumour says that
the " Arifas "—the elderly housekeepers charged
with keeping order—not unseldom make use of
the equivalent of the " birch rod "—a knotted
cord.

The royal ladies completely filled all the available accommodation in the Kasbah, and the Sultan
was able to reserve for his private use only a couple
of very shabby rooms over the entrance. Here
he would, apologetically, receive his guests until
the purchase of the large garden in which he constructed his new palace furnished him with more
convenient apartments ; for there was a villa in
the garden which had been erected by its former
owner, a wealthy and respected Israelite, who had
for years filled the post of Belgian Vice-Consul.
This villa, which still exists, is an astounding
example of extraordinary taste—a pseudo-moresque
copy of a toy-house, over which plaster and paint
of every colour had been poured in amazing pro-
fusion. Plaster lions guard its entrance, more like
great diseased pug-dogs than the king of beasts,
and to add to their attractions they were then
painted all over with red spots. A scalloped archway crowned the front door, and the former owner
had once pointed out to the writer that each of
the thirty-two scallops was painted a different
colour, which was quite evident. Inside, decoration had run riot in the wildest way. The ceilings
dripped with plaster protuberances in reds and
gold. Mouldings pursued their strange courses
all over the parti-coloured walls, enclosing odd-

shaped panels painted with views of lakes and
mountains and impossible fishing-boats—designed
and executed by some local genius. Chandeliers of coloured glass hung suspended from the
ceilings, and the windows were fitted with panes of
green and purple. The Sultan was in ecstasies,
and furnished these astounding apartments with
chairs and sofas covered in red plush trimmed with
blue and yellow fringes, and studded with blue
and yellow buttons. On the walls he hung promiscuously a score of clocks of all sizes and shapes;
he littered tables with mechanical toys; he piled
up musical-boxes in every corner; he hung cages
of canaries in every window, and adorned the
chimneypiece with baskets of paper-flowers—and
then he sat down, happy, to enjoy civilisation.

Amongst many mechanical toys which Mulai
Hafid possessed was one which in its absurdity
surpassed any toy I have ever seen. It was—or
had been—a parrot, life-sized, seated on a high
brass stand which contained music. Moth and
rust had corrupted, and there was little left of the
gorgeous bird except a wash-leather body the shape
of an inflated sausage, with the two black bead
eyes still more or less in place, and a crooked and
paralysed-looking beak. The legs had given way,
and the cushion of a body had sunk depressedly
on to the brass perch. One long red tail-feather
shot out at an angle, and round its neck and
sparsely distributed over its body were the remains
of other plumes, of which little but the quills
remained. On either side were the foundations

of what had once been its wings, consisting of mechanical appliances in wood and wire. Anything more pitiful than this relic of parrotry could not be imagined.

Every now and then, apparently for no reason, this strange toy came to life. The sausage-like body wriggled, the broken beak opened, the tail-feather shot out at a new angle, and the framework of the wings extended itself and closed again with a click; and then after a mighty effort, which gave one the impression that the ghost of a bird was going to be sea-sick, the whistling pipes concealed in the brass stand began to play. The music was at a par with the bird—notes were missing, and the whole scale had sunk or risen into tones and demi-tones of unimaginable composition. To recognise the tune was an impossibility, but the thrill of the performance was undeniable. It seemed as though there was a race between the bird and the pipes to reach the climax first. Both grew more and more excited, until suddenly there was a long wheeze and longer chromatic scale from high to low, and, with an appealing shake of its palsied head, the parrot collapsed once more into its state of petrified despair.

Mulai Hafid was completely content. He realised that at last, after the sombre pomp of the palace at Fez, he had settled down to modern life and refinement, and had attained " taste." It was his custom to arrive early in the morning and spend his days there, riding down from the Kasbah on a

fat saddle-mule caparisoned in purple or pale blue
or yellow, accompanied by men on horseback,
and with his black slaves running beside him.
Two old women—one a negress, the other a white
Berber woman—nearly always accompanied him,
poised upon fine saddle-mules and closely veiled.
The negress was his old nurse, the Berber woman
a soothsayer already mentioned. Arrived in the
garden, the usual series of mishaps began. One
of his old ladies would fall off her frisky mule,
or the key of the empty house was lost, and an
entry had to be made by forcing a window after
every one had fussed about pretending to look for
the key for half an hour or so. Then a carpenter
would be sent for to mend the broken window,
and a slave would suddenly remember that for
fear of losing the key he had tied it round his neck
on a string, where it still hung heavily on his
chest. Then breakfast would arrive, carried down
from the Kasbah on the heads of black slaves—
great trays of fresh bread, bowls of milk, sodden
half-warm cakes smothered in butter and honey,
excellent native crumpets, and a host of dishes of
fruits and pastry and sweets, and tea and coffee
on immense silver trays. It was a sort of pro-
miscuous meal, partaken of first of all by the
Sultan and his particular friends, then passed on
to the " courtiers," and finally handed out of the
windows to the slaves, gardeners, and retainers,
who completely finished what was left, however
great the quantity.

By this time the workmen had begun building

operations on the great palace a hundred yards
or so away, and the ex-Sultan would visit the site,
taking a very intelligent interest in every detail.
Then back to the villa, where native visitors would
be received and literary and religious questions
discussed. Mulai Hafid himself is no mean author,
and his Arabic verses would, if published at that
time, have gained him much praise and many
enemies. To-day there is no reason to remain
silent. Circumstances have changed. Was it not
he who wrote of Tangier ?—

" In the last day the people of Tangier came to
the judgment - seat of God; and the Supreme
Judge said, ' Surely you are the least and worst
of all people. Under what circumstances did you
live ? '
" And they replied, ' We have sinned; we have
sinned ; but our Government was international :
we were ruled by the representatives of Europe.'
" And the Supreme Judge said, ' Surely you have
been sufficiently punished : enter into Paradise.' "

By any one who knew and experienced the
international Government of Tangier these verses
cannot fail to be appreciated.
Did he not also write the following in his days
of contention with the French Government ?—

" Is not the wisdom of God manifest ?
Has He not given intelligence even to the dog ?
A little less, it is true, than to the elephant,
But a little more than He bestowed upon the
French Administration."

K

When Mulai Hafid purchased the property of
Ravensrock at Tangier, which had for many years
been the country residence of the late Sir John
Drummond-Hay, he began at once to fell the
beautiful trees for which the place was famous.
Most people of Arab race have a dislike for trees,
which is no doubt one of the reasons why Morocco
is so treeless. One after the other the great pines
and eucalyptus disappeared; but though numbers
of men were employed, the work did not progress
fast enough to satisfy his ex-Majesty.

One day some one proposed to him that dynamite would do the work more quickly, so he
promptly despatched one of the workmen to town
to buy dynamite cartridges from the Spanish
fishermen, who used them for killing fish at sea.
I was with the ex-Sultan when the messenger
returned. He stood before us, and, turning the
hood of his jelab inside out, let fall on the ground
at our feet a couple of dozen of these highly-
explosive cartridges. Fortunately none exploded.
A few minutes later the work had begun. Holes
were quickly drilled in the trees near the roots,
and the cartridges placed in position. Fuses were
lit, and one saw scurrying groups of men bolting
out of reach. Then there was a crash, and some
giant of the mountain came crumbling down to
earth, to the intense delight of Mulai Hafid. It
was reckless destruction of what had taken years
of care and attention to create, but nothing would
persuade the ex-Sultan to allow these beautiful
woods to remain. By dint of very special pleading

a few of the finest trees were spared, but only
a few. This wholesale destruction was carried
out principally because Mulai Hafid feared assassination, and wished to eliminate from his surroundings any covert in which the would-be assassin
could conceal himself.

The ex-Sultan took assiduously to bridge, and
played whenever he got the chance. One of
these chances was with his dentist. His relations with his own particular Spanish dentist
having been very strained on the question of the
price of a live lion, he was forced to apply elsewhere for such dental repairs as he required from
time to time ; and fortune favoured him, for he
discovered an excellent American dentist who had
lately arrived. A close friendship sprang up
between the ex-Sultan and the dentist, and, as
often as not, bridge took the place of dentistry.
The American would arrive with his timid lady-
assistant and all his implements of torture, only
to be invited to sit down at the table and play
cards. The lady-assistant was very young and
very shy, and was more accustomed to play
children's games than bridge. A fourth player
would be found, and the ill-assorted party completed. The ex-Sultan enjoyed himself immensely. He generally won, perhaps a little by
never permitting the trembling lady-assistant to be
his partner. In this manner the whole afternoon
would be passed, and Mulai Hafid in the evening
would show the few francs he had won with great
joy. The points were one franc a hundred, so no

very serious damage could be done; but rich as the Sultan was, he rejoiced more in his humble winnings at bridge than over his many thousands in the banks. Not a little of this enjoyment was owing to the fact that he felt that he was " doing " the dentist. " He comes," the ex-Sultan would say, " to mend my teeth and to take my gold, and in the end I win his francs." Weeks went by. Now and again there was an afternoon for real dentistry, but there were many more for bridge, and every time the Sultan won. But one day the climax came. The teeth were excellently repaired —the work was of the best,—there was no more to be done—but to pay the bill; and the bill very naturally and rightly included all the bridge hours—at so much per hour. It was the most expensive bridge Mulai Hafid ever played.

The ex-Sultan's bridge was peculiar. It would not for a moment be hinted that the irregularities that occurred in the game were due to anything but accident, but these little accidents were very frequent. The ex-Sultan, who all his life had been accustomed to sit cross-legged on a divan, soon tired of sitting upright on a chair. He would become restless, and tuck his legs underneath him. Now ordinary chairs are not intended to be sat in cross-legged, especially by bulky people; and as generally an arm-chair had been placed for His Majesty to sit in, he would constantly be changing his position, and wriggling to make himself more comfortable and to find more room for his capacious legs. These wriggles occasioned at times a decided movement to right or left, and if the players did not hold their cards well up it was their own fault. Sometimes he would drop his cards, and his long sleeve at the same time would sweep the tricks already won on to the floor, and there was confusion in sorting them. Once or twice an ace unexpectedly appeared for the second time in the game, picked up by accident from the floor, no doubt,—and as to revokes—but with a plaintive voice he would say, " I am only a beginner." When he won he was in the highest spirits ; when he lost he sulked—but he didn't very often lose.

It is a characteristic of the Moors that they hate to lose a game, no matter what they are playing. I have seen the most exciting games of chess, skilfully and quickly played, where the loser has insisted on going on playing game after game till sometimes in pure desperation his adversary allows him to win. Mulai Abdul Aziz, Mulai Hafid's predecessor on the throne, had a unique manner of scoring at cricket. When he was Sultan we used to play cricket in the palace at Fez, generally four on each side. The score was carefully kept, but no names were entered. When the game was finished the Sultan himself placed the names against the score, always, of course, putting his own in front of the largest. Then the name of the player he liked best on that particular afternoon had the second best score, and so on, and the lowest being reserved for the person most out of favour. The score-book was religiously kept, and often referred to by the Sultan, who would say, "That was a great afternoon. I made 61 runs and Harris made 48. X. played abominably, and only made 2." While as a matter of fact His Majesty himself had made 2 and Harris perhaps none; while the unfortunate man who was down in the book as having scored 2 was probably the excellent batsman who had made the 61 that the Sultan claimed. If one is an autocratic monarch one can do anything—even poach your neighbour's cricketing score. I remember well the first game of bridge I ever played with Mulai Abdul Aziz. It was in my own house after a dinner—the first European dinner the Sultan ever attended. There were present the British and French Ministers, and the staffs of the two Legations. It was all rather formal. The Sultan sat at the head of the table, and ate very little; he was then not at ease with knives and forks. After dinner we sat down to bridge. The Sultan and Sir Reginald Lister, who then represented Great Britain in Morocco, played against a member of the staff of the French Legation and myself. We cut for deal, and I drew the lowest card. The Sultan was seated on my left. I dealt, and declared "Hearts." "I can't play hearts," burst out His Majesty petulantly. "I haven't got any. You must give me your cards"; and I was obliged to pass him over the excellent "Heart" hand on which I had declared in exchange for his barren thirteen cards, containing only one small trump. But "Hearts" we had to play, and played, and my partner and I went down five tricks, much to the Sultan's delight. Luckily we were not playing for money.

That was not the only amusing episode that happened at that dinner. There had been a long diplomatic discussion as to the etiquette to be observed with the ex-Sultan, as this was the first European dinner he had ever attended and would form a precedent. It was decided that the guests should arrive at my house punctually at 8, and the Sultan at 8.15. I was to meet the Sultan at the door and conduct him into the drawing-room, where I was to present to him the Ministers of Great Britain and France, who in turn would present their suites. This was all very well on paper, but Mulai Abdul Aziz, taking an intelligent interest in dinner parties, thought he would like to see what went on before the guests came, and instead of arriving at 8.15 he came at 5 in the afternoon. He apologised for being a little before the time, and expressed his desire to see the preparations. Two minutes later he was in the kitchen, where his august and highly-saintly presence—for he was a direct descendant of the Prophet, and to his countrymen "the Commander of the Faithful"—somewhat upset the tranquillity of my native cooks and servants. But ovens had to be opened and saucepans uncovered, spoons introduced into them, and the contents exhibited; the ice-machine to be thoroughly explained, and a thousand and one questions answered. Then the pantry occupied for

some time His Majesty's attention. Nor was he
less interested in the floral decorations of the
table and the distribution of the plate. While I
dressed for dinner he sat and talked to my native
servants—the Sultan never losing his dignity nor
my men their respect—and all concerned were
completely at their ease. The Moor has nearly
always the perfect manners of a gentleman, no
matter what his position, and the sentiment of
the country is essentially democratic. It was a
common incident at the many dinners I have
since given for the two ex-Sultans, that they would
appeal to the men who served the table for confirmation of some statement, or for the generally
accepted opinion of the Moorish people on some
subject under discussion.

At 8 o'clock the guests arrived, and Mulai Abdul
Aziz, being already in the house, instead of arriving
at 8.15 as by the programme he should have done,
had to be concealed in a room upstairs. Punctually at 8.15 he descended the stairs, crossed the
hall, and entered the drawing-room. He was
dressed in his fine long white flowing garments,
and all my guests expressed to me afterwards
their appreciation of his dignity and carriage as
he made his formal entry and during the pre-
sentation of the guests. Nor were they less struck
by the undoubted charm of his manners, the
gentleness of his voice, and his intelligence, which
render Mulai Abdul Aziz perhaps the most attractive figure in Morocco of to-day.

When the moment arrived for the ex-Sultan to

take his departure, he called me aside and said that he had a kitchen-range in his palace, but had never used it. He was pleased to say that the excellence of my dinner had convinced him that his own range must be set to work at once—and had I a sack of coal, as he had none, for in his kitchens only wood and charcoal were burned ? In a few minutes my servants, in their smartest liveries, were filling a sack with coal in the back premises. When it was ready the Sultan left. The guests rose to their feet, the Sultan shook hands with them all, and I conducted him to the door. A magnificently caparisoned riding-mule awaited him, and mounted slaves were at the gate. On a second mule was an officer of his household, beautifully dressed in white clothes, struggling to balance across the front of his crimson saddle the almost bursting sack of coal.

It was always my great desire to bring about a reconciliation between the two ex-Sultans, Mulai Abdul Aziz and Mulai Hafid, but I never succeeded. Mulai Hafid had driven his brother, Mulai Abdul Aziz, from the throne, and naturally his brother had no reason to be grateful to him. At the same time, Mulai Hafid always blamed Mulai Abdul Aziz for having ruined Morocco, and of having sown the seed of the loss of Moroccan independence. There was also the question of precedence. Mulai Abdul Aziz had been Sultan *first*, and claimed the first place. Mulai Hafid equally claimed it, because he had been Sultan *last*. After many unsuccessful endeavours, I persuaded both to agree that if they met by chance on the road they would salute each other and embrace. For months they did not meet, but one day, turning a sudden corner, their riding-mules collided. So taken aback were their two Majesties that they entirely forgot their agreement, and rode away in opposite directions as fast as their mules could carry them.

Immediately after the reconciliation—if such it could be called—between Mulai Hafid and the French authorities, the ex-Sultan gave a dinner-party to the members of the French Legation and a number of other French officials, in a charming villa he had meanwhile taken on the Marshan, at Tangier. Not sure of whom he ought to invite to this solemn repast, Mulai Hafid had left the choice of his guests to the French Chargé d'Affaires, who had sent in a list. The hour of dinner arrived, and so did the guests, amongst whom was the very capable and excellent " Commissaire " of the French local police, whom His Majesty had not yet met. The presentations took place, and the Sultan called me aside—I was in attendance—and asked who certain of the guests, whom he didn't know by sight, were. When I informed him that one of them was the French Commissaire de Police, he became a little uneasy, and a shadow passed over his face. " What do you think he has come for ? " asked the ex-Sultan nervously.

Seeing an opportunity for a joke at His Majesty's expense, I hesitated a moment, and then, with many apologies, informed the Sultan that there had been stories current about his manner of playing bridge. No one, I said, believed them, but naturally the French authorities were most desirous that there should be an end to this false rumour, and had therefore decided, very privately of course, to bring the " Commissaire de Police " to watch his play on that particular evening. As soon as they were assured that His Majesty's play was above all suspicion, an official *démenti* could be given to these disturbing rumours. Mulai Hafid's face wore a look of unusual gravity during the long and sumptuous dinner.

After the guests had adjourned to the drawing-room we sat down to bridge. The " Commissaire," who was not a player, was purposely invited, without the Sultan's knowledge, to seat himself at Mulai Hafid's side. The game began. His Majesty was terribly nervous. Every time he wriggled in his chair and leant either to right or left, he would pull himself together and fix his eyes upon his own cards. Not once did he let his " hand " fall on the floor. Not once did his long sleeves sweep the tricks off the table. Not once did he revoke. He lost game after game, and his distress became painfully manifest.

Between two " deals " a guest approached and politely asked, " Is Your Majesty winning ? "

" Winning ! " cried the now thoroughly upset monarch, " winning ! How can I possibly win with this horror of a policeman watching every card I play ? " And the writer had to explain to the assembled company the whole plot.

Mulai Hafid was an excellent host, and was never happier than when entertaining. His dinners were well served and always amusing, and his guests, European and native, suitably chosen. On one occasion some charming and aristocratic French ladies were visiting Morocco. Amongst a series of fêtes given by the Diplomatic Corps and others for their entertainment was a banquet at the residence of the Moorish ex-Minister of War, Sid Mehdi el-Menebhi, G.C.M.G. At this banquet the ex-Sultan presided. The distinguished lady guests had been purchasing Moorish costumes, and it was arranged that they should come to this feast arrayed in all their recently-acquired magnificence. The result was charming—so charming that it was decided to send for a photographer and have the group taken. On his arrival the guests were posed, Mulai Hafid seated on a cushioned divan surrounded by the ladies in their Moorish dresses. The men stood behind.

The photograph was a great success, but its indirect results almost a tragedy, for Mulai Hafid placed a large copy of the group on the mantelpiece of the drawing-room of his villa. The ladies of his household never left the Kasbah, but on one occasion he sent an old Berber lady, before mentioned, and an aged slave, who had been his nurse, to visit the villa, and the eagle eyes of this venerable dame discovered the photograph. In their minds no clearer evidence of Mulai Hafid's wickedness could be imagined, for here was the ex-Sultan seated in a bevy of apparently very attractive native ladies, surrounded by European men. No combination of facts could to their eyes be more shocking. Not only was it clear that Mulai Hafid had been enjoying the society of ladies other than his wives, but he had even not hesitated to do so in the presence of "Christian" men. So the photograph was conveyed in their voluminous raiment to the Kasbah, where it was presented to the gaze of the Sultan's outraged wives. Mulai Hafid was out hunting that day, and it was he himself who recounted to the writer what occurred on his return. None of his ladies were in the courtyard to meet him ; no one, except a slave or two, was visible. Not a word of welcome, not a question as to the sport he had enjoyed ! Seeking the apartments of one of the royal wives, the Sultan had the mortification to see her go out of one door as he entered by the other. He called to her, but she paid no attention. He sought consolation elsewhere, with no better results. He was shunned and in exile—not one of the ladies would speak to him. He knew, of course, nothing of the reason, and could obtain no explanation. He slept in his little reception-room over the entrance of the Kasbah, and hoped for a brighter situation in the morning, but things were no better.

Then the two old women who had found the photograph and given it to the Sultan's ladies grew alarmed, and confessed, but the many wives were difficult to convince, and it was only when the writer was called in and explained to some invisible persons, concealed behind a thick curtain drawn across an archway, that peace and calm were restored in the Shereefian harem. As the Sultan said afterwards, " There are some institutions in Europe which are in a way preferable to ours. Monogamy has its advantage. When a man ever quarrels he has only one wife to quarrel with, whereas we—— ! "

The ex-Sultan had a very numerous family of young children, to whom he was really devoted, and with some of whom he would play for long hours together. They were—and are to-day—exceedingly well brought up, nice-mannered, and beautifully dressed, and now that they are a little older are being well educated. I sometimes was taken to see them in a garden in the Kasbah. There would be a few black slave women, and from ten to twenty children, all probably under seven years of age, and varying in colour from very dark to very fair. Once I mentioned to Mulai Hafid that they seemed to be many. He laughed, and replied that they were not all there : none of the younger ones were present, and that in all there were twenty-six under six or seven years of age. He was certainly a devoted father to his numerous offspring. During the whole period of the War he has been separated from them. In 1914 he went to Spain, where his relations with the German Embassy caused him to be suspected of instigating intrigues in Morocco. His pension was cancelled, and he remains to-day an exile. Any one who has

known him in his family life and witnessed his
devotion to his children cannot help desiring, if
his actions in Spain have not been more than
follies, that he may be permitted once more to
return to his home.

VII.

THE SULTAN IN FRANCE.

IT was on the quay at Rabat, that picturesque old town on the Atlantic coast of Morocco, that the Sultan Mulai Hafid finally handed to General Lyautey, the French Resident-General in Morocco, the documents of his abdication. It had been a long struggle to get them; for although His Majesty was decided that the only course open to him was to cede the throne and leave the country, still he was desirous, and made no concealment of his desire, to bargain to the very last moment. However, at length the question was settled, and as the Sultan stepped on board the launch to proceed to the French cruiser that was to take him as far as Gibraltar, *en route* to France, the official document of abdication was handed over. In return he received a cheque of £40,000, the last instalment of the agreed sum of money which the new Protectorate Government of Morocco had undertaken to pay him.

The following morning the cruiser, with the ex-Sultan on board, arrived at Gibraltar. I happened to be there, returning from Morocco to England, and was leaving the same day for Plymouth by steamer direct. Desirous, however, of seeing some personal friends who were amongst the ex-Sultan's suite, I proceeded on board the French cruiser to visit them. It was my desire, if possible, to avoid meeting the ex-Sultan, for a few months previously there had been a scene in Fez, in which the unchecked torrents of Sultanate wrath had been poured on my head for having given too much publicity to the barbarous atrocities which His Majesty had been committing, especially in the case of the torturing of the wife of the Governor of Fez, in order to discover an imaginary hidden fortune, and in the wholesale amputations of the feet and hands of certain rebel tribesmen. I had no desire that the discussion as to the necessity or advisability of perpetrating horrors should be continued on the deck of a French warship, and so I took every precaution not to be seen by His Majesty in order to avoid the outpourings of renewed wrath. But in vain. The ex-Sultan caught a glimpse of me as he stepped on board, and, hurrying to meet me, embraced me in the most cordial manner, and then stated that unless I would consent to join the suite and continue the journey with him to France, he (the ex-Sultan) would claim the right of being in British territorial waters, and refuse to proceed an inch farther. The situation was difficult. The Sultan, always neurasthenic, appeared, and undoubtedly was suffering under great nervous tension, evidently not

L

diminished by the sufferings he had undergone
during a particularly rough passage on a warship
that was renowned for its rolling.

A hurried consultation was held with the French
officials who were accompanying the ex-Sultan on
his journey to France. My plans were already
fixed : it was no easy matter to change them
at the last moment; but the Sultan insisted.
The French authorities, too, foreseeing real difficulties, begged me to alter these plans and to
proceed to France, to which I eventually con-
sented. The Sultan, appeased, offered no more
resistance to continuing his journey, and by midday
we were *en route* for Marseilles.

What had influenced the Sultan was this. He
was suffering from nerves, and once on board the
warship had become convinced that he was under
arrest, and was on his way to imprisonment in
France. He was particularly desirous of having,
therefore, as members of his suite one or two
persons of British origin, so that there might be
witnesses—or even objectors—in the case of his
incarceration. Of course such a thought had never
entered the minds of the French Government.
The Sultan had abdicated, and for political reasons
it was advisable that he should absent himself
from Morocco for a short period, so that the
proclamation and installation of the new Sovereign
might proceed without any hitch; for it was
always possible that so long as the ex-Sultan
remained in the country there might be some
opposition to the elevation of his successor to

the throne. Two days later Mulai Hafid landed
in Marseilles, where he was officially received.
The quay was hung with flags, there was a cavalry
escort, and military music enlivened the scene.

At Gibraltar the French cruiser had been
abandoned for the greater comforts and more
ample space of a P. & O. On board this steamer,
en route to Australia, was a music-hall troupe,
and it was their kind thought to give a performance in honour of the Sultan. The sea was calm,
the night warm, and after dinner the performance
took place—singing, dancing, and some juggling.
One item of the show took place in the saloon,
where a very attractive and skilful lady-conjurer
performed some most astonishing tricks. The
Sultan and his suite were much impressed, but
their astonishment reached its climax when the
charming young lady filled an apparently unlimited number of glasses with an apparently
unlimited variety of drinks out of a medium-sized
teapot.

As we threaded our way out of the saloon, one
of the more influential of the native suite whispered in my ear, " What do you think the lady
would take for the teapot ? " I naturally replied
that probably all the wealth of the world could
not purchase so unique a vessel. My friend was
disappointed ; he would clearly have liked to own
a teapot, and to have had it always beside him,
which would pour out any beverage he commanded. " It would have been," he added with
a sigh, " so useful when one was travelling."

His Majesty's stay at Marseilles was uneventful. Official visits, a gala at the theatre, and excursions to places of interest filled up his days. However, during the dinner—a semi-state ceremony—which was given to His Majesty at the hotel on the evening of his arrival, a little incident occurred. The manager of the hotel, looking very troubled, approached the high official of the police to whom the precautions for the personal security of the Sultan had been entrusted, and whispered in his ear. A few moments later I received a message asking me to leave the table for a moment's conversation in the next room. Here I was informed that, while dinner was proceeding, the Sultan's little black slave boys had found a big bag of five-franc pieces in His Majesty's bedroom, and were amusing themselves by throwing them one by one into the street, to be scrambled for by the crowd. The Cannebière was blocked, all traffic was at a standstill, and various wounded persons had already been taken to the hospital; but the black imps, delighted with their game, persistently refused to abandon so amusing an occupation unless they received the express orders of their lord and master to do so. These orders the writer hastily invented, and, personally visiting the scene, threatened such chastisement that the three or four little black demons slunk away to bed.

During this dinner the news had been published in the local evening papers of a serious battle in Morocco; for, although the French Protectorate had been proclaimed, yet there was still anarchy

existing in the remoter parts of the country.
Now the ex-Sultan had never been popular in
France, perhaps with some reason. He had
driven from the throne his brother, whose more
friendly feelings toward the French were known
and appreciated, and he had succeeded in so doing
by a frankly unfriendly programme toward French
policy. His tribes, and even his troops, had fought
them in the Chaouia Campaign of 1907-8, and
during the four years that he had held the throne
(1908-12) he had done his utmost to assist German
intervention in Morocco. It was therefore not to
be wondered at that the people of Marseilles
showed no enthusiasm for their guest, and complained of the honours that were being rendered
him and the cost the French Government was
incurring in his entertainment. Up till now, however, there had always been a show of interest
in his movements, and a little crowd to see him
wherever he went; and though his reception had
been by no means enthusiastic, no hostile demonstration had taken place. The receipt of the news,
however, of heavy French losses in this latest
Moorish battle, had stirred up some feeling against
him. The people felt it was ridiculous that while
their troops were being shot in Morocco the origi-
nator of the attacks of the tribes should be their
honoured guest in France. And so it was that
when, after the dinner, the ex-Sultan entered the
box that had been reserved and decorated for him
in one of the great music-halls of Marseilles, he was
met with hoots and whistling.

For a moment no one could explain this hostile demonstration, for the news of the battle had only just been published, and had not reached the dinner at which we had all been present. The manner in which the demonstration was suppressed, and a few moments later changed into a most friendly reception, was admirable, and spoke well for the capabilities of the " Commissaire de Police " attached to the ex-Sultan's suite. It was manœuvred in a way that was almost unnoticeable. A number of people seemed to be leaving the theatre, but discreetly, as if in the ordinary course of their affairs, and meanwhile their places and every vacant seat, and even the passage, were being filled up. In five minutes the building was full, and then suddenly the band burst out with the " Marseillaise " ; the Sultan stood up, and the whole audience, turning toward the royal box, shouted and cheered. It was well done, and had all the appearance of being a spontaneous demonstration.

Although Mulai Hafid was by no means popular in France, his visit received a good deal of attention, and the French public took considerable interest in his personality. He was, in fact, the man of the hour. His portrait appeared in every paper, and all his movements were closely reported and read.

His Majesty, who never minded how dangerously fast he travelled in motor-cars, had a horror of the train, and it had been a little difficult to persuade him to consent to proceed to Vichy by that means. The distance being great, the journey by motor, with his numerous suite of French officers and diplomats and all his native retinue, would have been a difficult one to have organised. So three days after his arrival at Marseilles he entered the carriages that had been specially added to the train that was to convey him to the fashionable health resort. He was unmistakably nervous as we left, and made no secret of it. As the pace increased he wanted the train stopped, and said he would *walk* to Vichy rather than continue; but the climax was reached when, with a shrill whistle, the train hurled itself into a long tunnel, and apparently into unending darkness.

The Sultan's fear was pitiful to behold. He literally clung to the French officer beside him, with terror staring from his eyes. All he could utter was, " Tell them to stop; why don't you tell them to stop ! " The fright of his native retainers was even more marked. They called out and clung to each other in abject fear, except the little black slave boys, who seemed intensely amused. Then the train whirled out of the tunnel into daylight again. The Sultan pulled himself together, and said, with an air of offended majesty, " You will kindly tell them not to do it again."

" I am afraid it will be difficult to avoid."

" Why ? "

" Because the line must pass under the hills."

" Then the train must stop and I will walk over the top and join it again on the other side."

" The distance . . ."

" I do not mind the distance. Anything is better than such suffering as it occasions me."

However, he was persuaded that his proposal was impracticable, and bore the few more tunnels that we passed through with commendable sang-froid and courage, though on each occasion His Majesty expressed his very distinct disapproval of railways and their builders, and more especially the folly of making tunnels.

At Vichy a villa, which formed an annexe to the well-known Hotel Majestic, was placed at his disposal. His Majesty was an early riser, and sometimes he would take an early morning prome-nade in the gardens and streets of the town. On one of these occasions he bought a little mongrel puppy, which an itinerant dog-seller was hawking at the end of a string. Returning to his villa with his purchase, the antics of the little puppy so amused the ex-Sultan that he called in his slaves, and ordered them to disperse over the town and buy more dogs. One of the dusky servitors ventured to ask how he was to know which dogs were for sale. The Sultan, fresh from his experience of purchasing the puppy, replied that every dog at the end of a string was for sale. As, of course, none of the slaves spoke anything but Arabic, they were ordered to bring dogs and sellers alike to the villa, where the bargains would be completed.

Now the municipal authorities of Vichy had recently issued an order that all dogs were either

to be led or muzzled, so when the fashionable
world went out to drink its early morning waters,
at least half of the ladies had little dogs at the
end of a string.

The writer was at breakfast when he was hurriedly summoned to the villa. At an open window
on the ground floor, sitting cross-legged on an
arm-chair, was His Majesty looking down with a
puzzled expression upon the little garden, crowded
with excited ladies and little dogs. Some were in
tears, others wore expressions of interested curi-
osity, and a few were evidently trying to look
their best, for no social distinctions had been
recognised by the slaves who had " rounded them
up " in the promenades of Vichy.

" I want to buy," said the ex-Sultan from his
window, " all these little dogs, but the sellers do
not seem to understand the first principles of
trade, and seem to be making a terrible fuss."

The situation was evident and acute. I explained it to the ex-Sultan, who politely apologised for having disturbed the ladies' early walks,
but still insisted, without success, in trying to
buy the dogs. It required all the writer's tact
and diplomacy to put an end to a difficult situation, and to restore equanimity to the indignant
ladies.

The ex-Sultan's purchases were often embarrassing. One evening at sunset he visited a farm a
few miles from the town, and insisted upon going
all over it. In an enclosure were collected from
twenty to thirty fine specimens of the beautiful

white cattle for which this part of France is so justly famous. The ex-Sultan decided to buy the lot, and gave the farmer his card, saying, "Send them round to-night to this address."

Now the address he gave was the Hotel Majestic, the most fashionable and magnificent of Vichy's palaces. About eleven o'clock that night, when life at the hotel was at its height, the manager sought the writer, and announced the unexpected arrival of twenty-seven enormous cows in the courtyard of the hotel. And there, sure enough, meandering in and out of smart motor-cars, lowing gently into the ground-floor windows, were the ex-Sultan's latest purchases. Where they passed the night the writer never knew, but the next day more suitable quarters were found for them.

The Sultan dined in the great dining-room of the Hotel Majestic. His table, a very large one, for there were constant guests, was raised on a dais at one end of the room, which gave him an excellent view of all the diners—and the diners at the Hotel Majestic at Vichy in the height of the season are worth seeing. One night the Sultan appeared " distrait " at dinner, and his eye roved over the crowded room with an anxious and sympathetic expression. He spoke little, and it was difficult to get him to talk. At last he asked to see the manager, and that most amiable and deservedly popular gentleman, the proprietor of the hotel, appeared at once. " These people," said the Sultan, waving his hand toward the crowd at dinner, " are badly distributed. Many

are not happy. Let us rearrange them. The old
gentleman with the long grey beard has no right
to be dining with the beautiful young lady in the
big black hat, wearing a pearl necklace. There
is a terrible disparity in their ages. She should
be dining with the charming young officer over
there "—he pointed to another table,—" and the
elderly lady, no doubt his mother, should be dining
with old greybeard. You should have "—and he
addressed the proprietor—" some thought for the
happiness of your guests. Now that lady there "
—and again he pointed in another direction—" is
terribly bored. She has been tapping the edge of
her plate with her fork for half an hour. She
evidently dislikes extremely the gentleman with
whom she is dining—probably her husband,—but
I have watched her, and she keeps looking at the
young man dining alone with the waxed mous-
taches. Go and introduce them. Her husband
hasn't spoken to her once this evening. He won't
miss her—and you will make two people happy ;
and if the husband is dull, invite that strange lady
with the red hair, who is just coming in, to sit
down beside him. She will keep him occupied, I
expect, to judge by her appearance."

But, alas ! interesting as such an experiment
would have been, it was impossible.

The first few days of the ex-Sultan's visit were
wet and cloudy, but one morning the August sun
asserted itself with uncompromising efficiency.
The villa reception-rooms faced south-east, and
by eight o'clock in the morning were insufferably

hot, for the Sultan refused to close the outside shutters, as he liked to see and to be seen. Half an hour later he decided to change his quarters. On the opposite side of the road was a charming villa, in the deepest shade, with a balcony on the first floor wreathed in flowering creepers. Ordering his slaves to follow him, the ex-Sultan strode across the road, entered the villa, and found his way to the upstairs room with the balcony. It was gorgeous but empty. An immense bed, which had evidently been slept in, stood with its head against the wall. A word from His Majesty and the bed was wheeled by the slaves into the window which opened on to the balcony, and, arranging the silk quilt and the lace-fringed pillows, the ex-Sultan seated himself cross-legged, gazing down into the street below.

Now the Russian lady of title who had occupied the bed had retired a few moments previously into her adjacent *cabinet de toilette* to take her morning bath. Her ablutions completed, but not clad for a reception, she entered her room to find a dusky oriental potentate, with his still more dusky slaves, in possession. The ex-Sultan's politeness was extreme. He bade her welcome, and invited her to sit down beside him.

An overflowing sense of humour on the part of the lady saved a situation which might otherwise have been embarrassing, and when the writer, hastily summoned, arrived, the lady, now more suitably arrayed, and her husband were thoroughly enjoying the novelty of the situation.

Mulai Hafid was often bored with such official functions as his position and his duty necessitated his attending. At a dinner given at a large provincial town within motoring distance of Vichy, he made his first public speech in France. He certainly had great fluency, and spoke well—in Arabic, of course, his words being immediately translated into French. When, with tears in his eyes, he explained his love and gratitude to France—whose policy in Morocco he had all his reign done his best to wreck—he was really immense. Never did words bear a more genuine ring; never was deep affection more apparent in a speaker's voice. But Mulai Hafid must not be misjudged. He had learnt much during his stay in France, and had probably realised long before this episode how much more successful a Sultan of Morocco he would have been had he followed more strictly and more sincerely the advice of his French advisers. But the Germans had been always at hand, with their intrigues and their incentives, with vague promises and much ready money, and with their recommendations to absolutism and to cruelty. On one occasion the Governments of Europe officially, through their Consuls at Fez, protested to Mulai Hafid their abhorrence of the barbarities he had been perpetrating. The German Consul was noticeable by his absence. Berlin deliberately refused to protest, and its representative at Fez was instructed to inform the Sultan that his Government considered that His Majesty had a perfect right to do what he

pleased, and advised him to pay no regard to the
protest of the Consuls of Great Britain, France,
and Spain speaking in the names of their respective
Governments and in the interests of civilisation.
But, happily, Germany has paid dearly in Morocco
for her sins in the past. It is a closed country for
her to-day, and her people are rightly looked upon
as outcasts and outlaws.

Successful as Mulai Hafid's first public utter-
ances were, these long and ceremonious dinners
profoundly bored him. As many as he could he
escaped, but some he had to attend. He took
the strongest dislike to the " Préfets "—a title
that, in the functions of the post, resembles our
" Mayor." He always had to sit on the Préfet's
right, and he complained that they were pompous
and dull.

When the programme of his journey to other
parts of France was being drawn up, he was asked
what towns he would like to visit. It was one of
his " off " days—he was silent and depressed.
He said he didn't care where, or when, or how he
travelled. No amount of pressing could get a direct
answer from him ; but the official of the French
Home Office could not return to Paris without a
reply. Urged finally to give some idea, however
vague, of where he would like to go, the ex-Sultan
answered wearily, " Anywhere—to any town that
has no ' Préfet.' " Many other distinguished
travellers must have often felt the same, but few
probably ever dared to avow it.

Mulai Hafid was by no means always in low

spirits. On one occasion we made a long motor trip to a famous watering-place, and after an official luncheon we ascended a neighbouring peak in a sort of funicular railway. In the railway carriage was a frock-coated and top-hatted gentleman of irreproachable get-up—a typical French *fonctionnaire* — polite, deferential, and with an official smile that must have taken a long time to acquire. Speaking through an interpreter, he informed Mulai Hafid that he was charged by the French Government to accompany and point out to His Majesty the beauties and spots of interest of the local scenery. Mulai Hafid, in an equally polite reply, thanked him, but hinted that he already had in his suite some one who knew the country extremely well, who would be only too pleased to assist in giving the required information, and he suddenly presented the writer to the French official. Needless to say, I had never been within a hundred miles of the place, and had no idea whatever of its beauties, its historical associations, and even less of its geological formation. I appreciated, however, one thing : that Mulai Hafid meant to play a practical joke on the suave and black-gloved functionary.

The train started and began the steep ascent. Mulai Hafid, innocently seated between the French official and the writer, asked, " What are those rocks ? " Before the authorised and official guide could reply, the writer had begun, " Those rocks are of the tertiary period, and contain many interesting remains : the skeletons of mammoths have been frequently found there, as well as the household utensils—a corkscrew amongst others—of primitive man." The poor functionary, too polite to protest, scarcely showed his astonishment, except in a furtive look in my direction. "And that wood ?" continued the ex-Sultan. "That wood," I went on, "was the scene of the eating by a bear of the children who mocked at Elisha." This time the functionary gave a little start. Farther up the line were the ruins of what had once probably been a wooden shed perched on a high rock. "And that ?" asked the Sultan. "That," replied the writer, "is all that remains of Noah's Ark, which came to rest here after the subsiding of the Flood." But the functionary was now only too palpably suffering tortures. He was on an official mission and terribly serious. He could not see that the episode was a joke, and seemed sincerely to believe that Mulai Hafid, the guest of the French Republic, was being purposely deceived. "It may have been," he began politely, " that local tradition at some period claimed this spot as the resting-place of the Ark— of that I know nothing—but historical facts have clearly proved that it was elsewhere that that interesting event took place."

A few nights later a gala performance of Meyer-beer's ' Roma ' was given in the ex-Sultan's honour at the Opera. Now, singing in Morocco is a nasal monotonous repetition of words, with little ex-pression and no gesture. The " basso " in the opera was an extremely corpulent gentleman, with

a voice like thunder, accompanied by wild gesticu-
lations. A few bars of recitative by the orchestra,
and his great voice burst out and filled the theatre.
To the Sultan the effect had nothing in common
with music, and all he could imagine was that the
performer was suffering intense unbearable pain,
more especially as the louder he sang the more
he waved his arms about and beat his capacious
stomach.

Springing to his feet, His Majesty cried, " Where
is Dr V—— ? " (Dr V—— was his English doctor,
who had accompanied him on his visit to France)
—" where is Dr V—— ? Find him quickly, some
one. He may be able to save his life " ; and with
an expression of terrible anxiety the ex-Sultan's
eyes alternately gazed fascinated at the singer
or sought for the doctor in the gloomy recesses
of the royal box. It was not without difficulty
that His Majesty was persuaded that the singer
was suffering no pain ; but that he was actually
supposed to be giving pleasure to the audience he
entirely refused to believe.

The ex-Sultan was bored, and left the theatre
before the end. The following morning he asked
me what had taken place in the last act, and on
being told of the terrible fate that almost all the
characters in the tragedy had suffered, he replied,
" I am sorry I did not stay. I should have sent for
the manager and insisted that the piece should
end happily. The young lady should have married
the soldier with the big sword. The blind woman
should have had her sight restored by an able

M

doctor, and no one should have been stabbed or built up in a tomb."

It was perhaps as well that he didn't stay till the end, for his amiable intervention might have disturbed the tragic climax of the opera.

RAISULI.

I.

Mulai Ahmed ben Mohammed er-Raisuli is to-day a man of about fifty years of age. He is by birth sprung from one of the most aristocratic families in Morocco, and is a Shereef, or direct descendant of the Prophet, through Mulai Idris, who founded the Mohammedan Empire of Morocco, and was the first sovereign of the Idrisite Dynasty. The children of Mulai Idris were established in various parts of the country, and it is from Mulai Abd es-Salam, whose tomb in the Beni Aros tribe is a place of great sanctity, that the famous brigand is directly descended—his family, and he himself, still holding a share in the lands, the rights and the privileges which were enjoyed by their renowned ancestor. A branch of the family settled in Tetuan, where a fine mosque forms a mausoleum for his more recent ancestors, and is venerated as a place of pilgrimage.

Possibly it was this holy ancestry that turned Raisuli from the paths of virtue, for after having received an excellent education in religion and religious law at Tetuan, he took to the adventurous, lucrative, and in Morocco by no means despised, profession of a cattle robber. It is a risky business, and requires courage. You may just as likely be shot yourself as shoot any one else; but prestige tells in favour of the head of the band, and a reign of terror of the young Raisuli ensued. He became celebrated. He was a youth of great courage, of the most prepossessing looks, and he and his followers earned money easily and fast—and spent it still faster. But cattle robberies led to other crimes. Murders followed, and it must be confessed that Raisuli's hands are none too clean in that respect; but murder in Morocco cannot be classed with murder in England. Life is cheap, and the dead are soon forgotten. By nature he was, and is, cruel, and the profession he had adopted gave him unlimited scope to exhibit his cruelty. On one occasion a Shereef who had married his sister proposed, according to Moslem custom, to take a second wife. Raisuli's sister, enraged, fled to her brother and complained. Nothing occurred till the night of the new marriage, when at the height of the festivities Raisuli and his men entered his brother-in-law's house and put to death the young bride and her mother.

At length his acts became insupportable. The whole country round lived in terror of his raids. The late Sultan ordered his arrest. His greatest friend betrayed him; he was seized, and sent to prison in the dreaded dungeons of Mogador. When, in 1903, I was Raisuli's prisoner at Zinat,

he narrated more than once to me the history of
those four or five years spent in prison. He
showed me the marks of the chains on his ankles,
wrists, and neck; he told me of the filth and the
cold; of the introduction of a file in a loaf of
bread; of five months' patient work at night;
and of a delayed flight. He escaped, but for a
very few hours. He did not know his way about
the town, and he had forgotten that the chains
would almost prevent his walking. He entered
a street that had no outlet, and was recaptured.
Fresh chains were heaped upon him, and it was
not till two years later that he was released on the
petition of Haj Mohammed Torres, the Sultan's
representative at Tangier. He came back to his
home, meaning to live a quiet and peaceful life,
but he found that his friend who had betrayed
him had become Governor of Tangier, and confiscated all his property. He applied for its
return, but could not obtain it. He threatened,
but they laughed at him—and then he took to his
old profession and became a brigand.

It was at this period that I first met him. I
was camping on a shooting expedition near Arzeila,
when he and his men paid me a visit and spent
the night at my camp. I confess that his personality was almost fascinating. Tall, remarkably
handsome, with the whitest of skins, a short dark
beard and moustache, and black eyes, with profile
Greek rather than Semitic, and eyebrows that
formed a straight line across his forehead, Mulai
Ahmed er-Raisuli was a typical and ideal bandit.

His manner was quiet, his voice soft and low, and his expression particularly sad. He smiled sometimes, but seldom, and even though I knew him much better later on, I never heard him laugh. With his followers he was cold and haughty, and they treated him with all the respect due to his birth.

When next I saw him I was his prisoner at his stronghold at Zinat, situated about twelve miles from Tangier—in June 1903. He had altered a little. His face had filled out, the mouth had become harder and a little more cruel, but he was still remarkably handsome. He had not changed for the better. Only a few months before my capture he had sold one of his prisoners to an enemy for $1500, and stood by to see the purchaser cut the victim's throat. As long as he had restricted his energies to cattle-lifting and to attacks upon natives no one paid very serious attention to him, though the Maghzen were trying to encompass his capture. On 16th June 1903 the Shereefian troops attacked and burnt Zinat; the same afternoon I was captured.

Hearing that a battle had taken place at that spot, situated some eight or nine miles away, I rode out toward the middle of the day in that direction, accompanied by my native groom, whose parents lived at Zinat, and who was most anxious as to the safety of his relations. Already the alarm had spread to the neighbouring villages, and we found the country round entirely deserted, the population having fled to the mountains of Anjera

with all their cattle and as much of their goods
as they could carry away. Although the attack
of the Government troops had been made with
the object of capturing Raisuli, the native cavalry
had wandered far afield after loot, and a considerable number of cattle, &c., had been carried off
from villages innocent of any rebellious intentions,
and in no way accessories to Raisuli's depredations.

I found it difficult on this account to obtain
any accurate information of what had occurred,
and a desire to do so, coupled with my groom's
anxiety, persuaded me to approach nearer than
was perhaps advisable to the scene of the morning's action. Skirting the stony hill on which
Zinat is situated, I entered the plain, crossed by
small gulleys, that lies to the south of the villages,
and until within two miles of the place met with
no incident worth recording. The whole country
was absolutely deserted. Not a single person,
not a head of cattle, was to be seen.

It was when we were crossing this plain that
suddenly a volley was fired at us from men concealed in the brushwood and rocks of a small hill
near by. The range was a long one, and though
we could hear the bullets whizzing over our heads,
I do not believe that any passed us very closely.
Setting spurs to our horses, we cantered away
out of range, and drew rein on an elevation in the
plain in the midst of a field of corn. Turning to
see what was happening, I perceived three or four
natives a considerable distance away, who had
taken off their cloaks and turbans, and were

waving to me to return. This waving of turbans
is always in Morocco a sign of " aman " or safety,
and I therefore waited for the men, who were
moving quickly in our direction. Two alone
approached us, both well known to me ; and having
arrived at the spot where we were stationed, they
apologised profusely for the mistake of their men
in having fired, and begged me to return with
them to Zinat to discuss the situation there.
They were Anjera men from the neighbouring
Roman hills, who had not been present at the
battle, but who had come down to Zinat, as the
irregular cavalry had carried off a considerable
number of their cattle. They stated that they
were desirous of knowing the intentions of the
Moorish Government with regard to their tribe.
If, they said, it was the Government's intention
to attack them, they were ready to resist ; but
if the Moorish forces had been ordered merely to
capture Raisuli and had looted their property
without authority, they demanded the return of
their cattle—a very reasonable demand. They
added that they were afraid to proceed to Tangier
to interview the authorities for fear of capture and
imprisonment there, and asked me accordingly to
take their message to the native officials, as on
such occasions I had often done before. Under a
promise of safety I proceeded with them in the
direction of Zinat, having agreed that I should
go to a spot near the hills where three or four
of the headmen of the tribe were to meet me.

It was when proceeding in that direction that I

was captured. We were crossing a small gully, thick with crimson-blossomed oleanders, when suddenly I discovered that I had fallen into an ambush. Flight was impossible, and as I was unarmed, resistance was out of the question. From every side sprung out tribesmen, and in a second or two I was a prisoner, surrounded by thirty or forty men, one and all armed with European rifles. I received no rough treatment at their hands, but was told that I was their prisoner and must proceed to Zinat. On arrival at the woods which surround the several villages which lie scattered on the Zinat hills, messengers were sent to inform Raisuli of my capture, and in a short time I was taken to him. He was seated under some olive-trees in a little gully, surrounded by his men and by the headmen of the neighbouring tribes, who had collected on learning what had taken place. Raisuli received me pleasantly enough. He was still a young man of handsome appearance, refined in feature and manner, and with a pleasant voice. He was dressed in the costume of the mountain tribes, a short brown cloak covering his white linen clothes and reaching only to the knees, with a turban of dark-blue cloth. His legs were bare, and he wore the usual yellow slippers of the country. After a short talk with Raisuli, who narrated to me all that had taken place, he led me to what remained of his house, the greater part of which had been burned by the troops. Up to this time I had nothing to complain of in the attitude of the tribesmen, but a great number had collected in the vicinity, all anxious to catch a glimpse of the Christian captive, and not a few inclined to wreak summary vengeance on me for the devastation the Government troops had committed in the place. There was a good deal of hooting and cursing, but Raisuli's influence was sufficient for him to be able to hurry me through the crowd, now very threatening, and his own followers closed round me and guarded me from the mountaineers. It was an unpleasant moment, for I soon perceived that no authority existed over this collection of tribesmen, who numbered at this time perhaps 2000—though by nightfall this number was probably doubled,—and that there would be no possibility of protection did they proceed to extremes. It was with no little relief that I saw the door of a small room in the remaining portion of Raisuli's house opened, through which I was pushed in. A moment later it was closed again, but it seemed as though the crowd without would break it down. But Raisuli and his men, and a score of personal friends amongst the tribesmen, formed up against the doorway outside, and were able to dissuade the rabble from their intention of dragging me out.

The room in which I found myself was very dark, light being admitted only by one small window near the roof, and it was some time before my eyes became accustomed to the gloom. When I was able to see more clearly, the first object that attracted my eyes was a body lying in the middle of the room. It was the corpse of

a man who had been killed there in the morning
by the troops, and formed a ghastly spectacle.
Stripped of all clothing and shockingly mutilated,
the body lay with extended arms. The head had
been roughly hacked off, and the floor all round
was swimming in blood. The soldiers had carried
off the head in triumph as a trophy of war, and
they had wiped their gory fingers on the white-
washed walls, leaving bloodstains everywhere.
However, I was not to suffer the company of the
corpse for long, for half a dozen men came in,
washed the body, sewed it up in its winding-sheet,
and carried it away for burial; and a little later
the floor was washed down, though no attempt
was made to move the bloody finger-marks from
the wall.

Here I remained alone for some hours, and it
was certainly an anxious time. I reviewed the
situation quietly, and came to the conclusion
that, in spite of the danger which I knew existed,
I had much in my favour. The fact that the
language of the people was almost the same to
me as my own tongue was a great assistance,
and amongst these mountain tribes I have a large
number of personal friends, who, I believed, and
rightly, would protect me as far as they were
able. Unfortunately, few of my influential
acquaintances amongst the mountaineers had
arrived, though to my joy I learned, from the
conversation of the guards outside the door, that
they were expected during the coming night. I
decided meanwhile to pretend absolute ignorance

of any danger, and to talk of my condition as only one of a series of adventures that I have undergone in Morocco and elsewhere.

At sundown Raisuli and some of his men brought me food, and I had a long conversation with them. Raisuli was polite, and made no secret that he intended to make use of me, though he had not yet decided in what way. He, however, kindly informed me that, should the attack of the troops be renewed, I should be immediately killed. His career, he said, was practically finished, and his sole desire was to cause the Moorish Government as much trouble and humiliation as possible, and he argued that there would be no easier way to do this than by causing my death. However, he promised me, at the same time, that provided no fresh attack was made upon the place, he would do his best to protect me. I was allowed to communicate with the British Legation, but was not aware till later that this letter never reached its destination, though the following morning I was in direct communication with His Majesty's Minister, and throughout my captivity no difficulties were put in my way in corresponding with the British Legation.

During the night a large contingent of the Anjera tribe arrived, amongst them several influential men on whose friendship I felt I might implicitly rely; and as a matter of fact I owe my release, and probably my life, largely to these men.

There is no need to give the details of the nine days that I spent at Zinat, sufficient to say that I suffered very considerable hardship. Though never actually roughly handled, except for a few insulting blows with slippers, &c., my discomforts were extreme. During those nine days I was never able to wash; I never took my clothes off, with the result that I was smothered with vermin. Once I went for thirty-six hours without any food, for none was procurable, as the village had been burnt, and during the whole time my life was threatened. My friends did what they could for me, but it was little they could do. There must have been some 4000 tribesmen present, and they obeyed no one, and no one had any authority over them. It was a trying time, but my only chance lay in pretending to place implicit confidence in them, and thus gain time while the negotiations for my release proceeded.

No words of praise are sufficient for the great tact displayed by Sir Arthur Nicolson, the British Minister, in conducting these negotiations. From the very beginning he realised the difficulties of success, and throughout, in every dealing that he had with the tribesmen, he showed the greatest tact and skill. He from the very commencement warned the Moorish Government not to take any steps to treat with the mountaineers, and conducted the entire proceedings himself, Mulai Ahmed, the young Shereef of Wazzan, being the means of communication between the British Government and the tribesmen. These negotiations were doubly difficult owing to the fact that the mountaineers had no recognised chiefs, and that many tribes were concerned. Yet in such a manner were the negotiations conducted, that throughout the whole proceedings the ignorant and fanatical tribesmen placed entire confidence in the Minister's word, and though delays occurred, as they always do in Morocco, there was never a serious hitch.

The first demand made to me for my release was the removal of all Englishmen from the Sultan's Court. I naturally treated this as preposterous, and persuaded the tribesmen that it was mere folly to mention it. This was followed by other equally impossible conditions, which were likewise abandoned; and by the time that the British Legation was in communication with the tribesmen they had lessened their demands to the release of a certain number of tribal prisoners confined in the prisons of Tangier and Laraiche.

At no time was a demand made for a ransom in money, and in this my capture differed entirely from those of Mr Perdicaris and Kaid Maclean, which took place later. I owe this immunity from a pecuniary ransom to an admirable trait in the character of these wild mountain tribesmen. My country-house at Tangier was situated about two and a half miles from the town, on the sea-coast, on the main track that passes between the Anjera tribe and Tangier. Just beyond my grounds, on the town side, is a tidal river, which then and now possesses no bridge, but it is fordable at low tide. Often the tribes-people found the tide too high to cross, and were obliged to wait long weary hours, in winter at times in darkness and rain. A large number were women and young girls carrying loads of charcoal to market. I had always made it a rule to give shelter to all such as asked for it, and had built a room or two for this purpose, and in winter-time it was seldom that some of the benighted peasants were not spending the night there. When it was cold and wet they had a fire, and as often as not a little supper. A very short time after my capture a proposal was made from Tangier that a very considerable sum of money should be paid for my immediate release. This was discussed by the tribesmen and refused. They decided that in the case of one who had shown such hospitality to their women and children, and often to themselves, there must be no question of money—and there was none.

There was one hitch which threatened to break down our negotiations, and which caused some delay to my release.

It had been agreed that twelve prisoners from the tribesmen, confined in various Moorish Government prisons, were to be released in exchange for myself; but after a very numerously-attended meeting, at which a large number of fresh mountaineers arrived, a demand was made for the release of over fifty. The British Legation was notified of this, and very rightly objected to this sudden and very large addition. Sir Arthur Nicolson wrote me to this effect. Before, however, making known the contents of his letter, I obtained the names of all the fifty tribesmen whose release was

demanded, and sent the list to Tangier, pretending
that it was to be submitted to the authorities,
in order that in the case of its acceptance, orders
for the release of the men might be given. Once
this letter well on its way, I made known to the
tribesmen that on no account more than the
original twelve prisoners would be released. At first
they tried persuasion, and then threats—but I felt
sure of my position. " You propose," I said, " to
kill me. Possibly you will do so, but you have
kindly given me a list of all your relations who
are in the Moorish prison—some fifty-six in all,
I think. This list is now in Tangier. You will
have the satisfaction of killing me, but remember
this—on fifty-six consecutive days one of your
sons or brothers or nephews will be executed—
one each morning ; and more—their bodies will
be burnt and the ashes scattered to the wind.
You will see the smoke from here "—for Tangier
was visible from where we were. Now, the Moors
believe in a corporeal resurrection, and the burning of a body means the depriving of the soul of
resurrection. It was a splendid bluff, and I felt
the greatest delight in using it. I was there alone,
seated in the centre of a great circle of the tribesmen, who swore and cursed and threatened ; but
to no avail. I even explained that it was a matter
of no importance in the Christian religion what
became of one body—and pointed out the consequent loss of fifty-six good Moslem souls, deprived
of going to heaven. I was successful. The tribesmen returned to their original demand.

In all my dealings with the Moors I have found this, that the intelligent European, provided he has a complete and absolute knowledge of the language, holds a very distinct advantage over the Moor. He has, in fact, two advantages—hereditary training of thought, and education. The Moor is generally, by his environment and isolation, a slow thinker, and in the many difficult situations in which I at times found myself I have always had confidence in my own mental superiority over the average native. I have been able to turn threats into ridicule, or to raise a laugh, or to persuade by the mere superiority of the power of thinking and of giving utterance to one's thoughts. The Moor is very susceptible to sarcasm and ridicule, and often I have turned what looked like becoming a stormy incident into the pleasantest of channels. I have, almost without exception, carried no arms, which are often more a source of danger than of security.

The only time that I left my quarters at Zinat for more than a few minutes together was on one occasion, a few days after my arrival, when I was taken down to a gully below the village to be shown the corpse of a Moorish cavalry soldier who had been killed during the engagement. In revenge for the beheading of the Zinat man who had been killed, the tribesmen had mutilated the soldier's body. It was a ghastly sight. The summer heat had already caused the corpse to discolour and swell. An apple had been stuck in the man's mouth, and both his eyes had been gouged out.

N

The naked body was shockingly mutilated, and the finger-tips had been cut off, to be worn, the tribesmen told me, as charms by their women. The hands were pegged to the ground by sticks driven through the palms, about a yard in length, bearing little flags. A wreath of wild flowers was twined round the miserable man's head, and the village dogs had already gnawed away a portion of the flesh of one of the legs. I was jokingly informed that that was probably what I should look like during the course of the next few days.

During the entire nine days that I was at Zinat I was no doubt always in danger, and certainly always in great discomfort ; but I had used every opportunity to bring the friendly tribe of Anjera over to my side, and on the night of the ninth day my friends rose nobly to the occasion. They surrounded Raisuli's house and village with perhaps a thousand men, all armed and prepared, and demanded that I should be handed over to them, threatening that, if this were not immediately carried out, they would shoot or arrest Raisuli. It was a little *coup-d'état*, and it was successful. In the middle of the night I was hustled out of the small room which I shared with a dozen guards, placed on the back of a mule, and carried off into the Anjera mountains by my friends of that tribe. For six hours we proceeded through mountain passes and thick brushwood, arriving soon after sunrise at the village of Sheikh Duas, one of the most influential of the Anjera tribesmen. It was a journey I will never forget—the dark-

ness of the moonless night, the rough mountain
tracks, the silence of the hundreds of armed men
who accompanied me, and the intense relief that,
even if my captivity was long protracted, I was
amongst men who would, at any rate, protect my
life. I was tired and weak. Nine days of constant
strain, in great heat, on a diet of inferior dry bread
and water, with the necessity the whole time of
pretending rather to enjoy the situation than
otherwise, had worn me out. But from the friendly
tribe of Anjera I received nothing but kindness—
every word, every act of theirs was cheering and
thoughtful; and though life among them was
rough enough in its way, I owe them a debt of
gratitude that it will be difficult ever to repay.
I remained twelve days at Sheikh Duas's village
in the Anjera mountains, and throughout that
period I never suffered an indignity or an insult
from him or his people. A little room in his house
was put at my disposal, and infinite pains were
taken to render it clean and habitable. The best
of such food as was procurable was given me—
milk and cream-cheese, and a rough porridge of
sour milk and millet. His followers—for Duas is
not above being a cattle robber on a large scale
—helped me to pass my time pleasantly enough,
and with them I explored the neighbouring mountains, and sat in the shade of the fruit trees of
their little gardens listening to their local musicians
or watching the ungraceful movements of their
dancing-girls. I made friends there whose friendship I shall always value. I was treated as one of

the tribe. I wore their dress, shaved my head, and conformed to all their customs; but above and beyond all, my anxiety was at an end—I knew that I was out of grave danger.

Meanwhile the British Minister, ably assisted by the Shereef of Wazzan, was carrying on the negotiations. Although I was now amongst friends, these negotiations were delicate and difficult, for the Anjera tribe had given their word to the other tribes concerned not to release me until their prisoners were set free, and these other tribes were constantly desirous of changing their conditions, and, owing to the distances which separated them, this necessarily meant delay. The very fact that I was now some twenty-seven miles—a day's journey—from Tangier protracted the negotiations. Several times I seemed on the point of release, but some small hitch, unimportant, it is true, would arise and a delay occur.

Except for this, time passed pleasantly; the scenery was delightful, and although it was the middle of summer the air was cool at this altitude. Little streams of water ran in every direction, and I was able to bathe and be clean once more. To all intents and purposes I was free to go where I pleased, and though always accompanied by guards, so thoughtful and kind were they that one forgot that they were there to prevent my escape, and we all became the best of friends. Meanwhile the Shereef of Wazzan spared himself no trouble. No sun was too hot for him to travel, no journey too tiring for him to undertake. He

attended the tribal meetings and made known
to the headman the British Minister's intentions
with regard to the tribal prisoners, orders for whose
release had meanwhile been received from the
Sultan. His Majesty's readiness to comply with
Sir Arthur Nicolson's request was deserving of all
praise, for it must be remembered that the action
of the rebels throughout was intended to humiliate
the Sultan and his Government. What rendered
the situation during my captivity, especially during
the first part of it, doubly insecure was the fact
that the tribes were in active communication with
the Pretender to the Moorish Throne—the leader
of the rebellion in the Rif,—and it was proposed
over and over again to send me to him as a useful
hostage; and, had it not been for my friendship
with the Anjera tribe—a friendship of long standing—I have no doubt this proposal would have
been carried out.

On Saturday, 4th July, a large tribal meeting
was held near Sheikh Duas's village, and during
the usual wrangling which occurred on these
occasions the Shereef of Wazzan arrived, having
travelled the twenty-seven miles from Tangier
that day, in spite of the heat of the July sun.
His opportune presence settled my fate, and the
negotiations were brought to a conclusion, not
without considerable opposition. The following
day a large contingent of tribesmen, the Shereef,
and I set out for Tangier, spending the night some
twelve miles from that place. Even here a last
attempt was made—an attempt that nearly led

to bloodshed—to prevent my release, but happily
unsuccessfully. The next morning we moved
down towards my own house, which stands alone,
some two and a half miles from the town. In a
ruined fort a quarter of a mile from my villa a
halt was made, and messengers were despatched
to town with letters to the British Minister to
release the tribal prisoners, who for the last week
or so had been comfortably housed in the basement
of the British Consulate, having been brought up
from Laraiche in specially-chartered steamers.
Within an hour we saw the sixteen prisoners
arriving, and very shortly afterwards they were
being welcomed by their friends. Lord Cranley,
Mr Wyldbore-Smith, Mr Kirby Green, and Mr
Carleton accompanied the prisoners on behalf of
the British Legation, but no formal exchange
took place. The moment the prisoners arrived I
was free to depart, though the many adieux that
I had to make with my mountain friends took
some little time. We parted on the best of terms,
and, wild and savage as the two hundred tribesmen
looked, I could not but feel how great a debt of
gratitude I owed them for having released me from
the dangers and discomforts of my first days of
captivity.

For a year after this adventure Raisuli remained
tolerably quiet, but the following spring he carried
out a *coup* even more daring. He surrounded the
villa of Mr Perdicaris at night, and carried off both
the proprietor and his son-in-law. The American
Government sent a fleet to Tangier, and the whole

world watched the ensuing negotiations. Mr Perdicaris and Mr Varley were restored to liberty ; but at what a price ! Raisuli demanded and obtained from the Sultan the following terms. That he should be appointed the Governor of all the districts in the neighbourhood of Tangier ; that the existing Governor—his former friend, who had betrayed him—should be deposed ; a ransom of $70,000, the imprisonment of all his enemies, and the release from prison of all his friends— and other concessions of less importance. The Sultan surrendered, and the terms were carried out. Raisuli found himself all-powerful—a hero in the eyes of the Moors, a menace in those of Europe.

His first acts were good. He put down the effervescence which Bou Hamara's rebellion had caused in the neighbourhood, and he opened the roads to caravan traffic, and since he was made Governor not a single caravan had been robbed within the limits of his jurisdiction. He brought about, in fact, a period of greater security than had existed during the previous year or two—but a security that depended upon Raisuli was naturally a doubtful one.

As his influence increased he became a despot. He squeezed the people under him, and extorted money from even the very poorest of the poor. The Maghzen lived in terror of him, and let him know it, with the result that he ignored their orders and commands, and even the treaties with Europe. He threatened and blackmailed even the

Maghzen authorities, who openly acknowledged
their incapacity to deal with him, and he became
at the same time the protector and the scourge
of Tangier and the surrounding districts. He
enforced his authority up to the very gates of the
town, and his armed followers even entered and
dragged out of prison men who were not in his
jurisdiction. His representatives administered justice (!) in the market-place, and beat people to death
within a few yards of the French and German Legations. In 1906 Raisuli had reached the zenith of
his power. At Zinat it was sufficient to tell a man
that he was a prisoner, and he would never attempt
to escape. There was no need to lock him up—he
knew that his master's arm was long enough to
reach him wherever he fled to,—and the strange
sight of dozens of prisoners at liberty could be
seen there on any day. Raisuli showed all the
qualities required by a strong Governor in Morocco,
but unfortunately he overdid it. For him there
existed no treaties. His and his representatives'
actions at this period are well known. The flogging of protected natives, the cutting off of the
electric light, the blackmailing of Europeans, the
destruction of property—a long list of acts of
unbearable tyranny.

At length the representatives of the European
Powers could endure it no longer. They addressed
a collective Note to the Moorish Minister of
Foreign Affairs at Fez, demanding that an end be
made to the impossible state of affairs existing
in the Tangier districts. It was almost an ulti-

matum, for the bay was full of the warships of
France and Spain, present to protect European
interests until the introduction of the new police.
The Sultan and his viziers could not misunderstand
the purport of this Note. The Minister of War
was ordered to proceed to Tangier with all available forces.

Early in January 1907 the troops that had
arrived from Fez were camped not many miles
from Raisuli's stronghold, waiting for orders to
attack. News was brought to me that this attack
would take place two days later, on Saturday,
6th January; and it was still dark when that
morning, at a very early hour, I left Tangier on
horseback with three trusted Moors to see what I
could of it. I had clothed myself in the flowing
dress of a trooper of Moorish irregular cavalry, as
I knew that orders had been issued to prevent
Europeans approaching the spot, and also so as
to be able to move about the scene of action without attracting notice. Before we had emerged
into the open country we had passed no less than
six outposts of some twenty-five men each, for
the Maghzen authorities had been taking great
precautions to protect the town; but even the
clattering of our horses' shoes upon the paved
roads failed to wake a single man from the deep
slumber in which they were lying inside their
tents. At dawn we were a good many miles away,
but we had time to spare, and rode slowly,
realising that a long day lay before us; and it
was seven o'clock before, from the point of a low

hill, the camp of the Shereefian troops was visible in the plain below us. A mile to our left was the famous hill of Zinat, with its rocky crests and precipices, and its steep lower slopes stretching down to the plain, at places dotted with olive groves. Set in the midst of this background stood Raisuli's stronghold, a large rambling building, half-fort, half-house, with windows dotted irregularly about its front, and here and there a battlemented tower rising above the rest of the roof, a strong building in a very strong position. Away behind Zinat and in front of us rose the higher peaks of the Beni Msaour Mountains, range beyond range, until, bounding the eastern horizon, they were overtopped by the snow-clad summits of Beni Hassan. There were no signs of the coming struggle at that moment. Cattle were feeding near the little villages on the plain, and thin white smoke, hanging heavily in the bright air, issued from the thatched roofs and tents of the plains-people as they cooked their breakfasts. In the Shereefian camp there was some movement, and near Raisuli's stronghold his followers could be seen strolling about, while the smoking chimneys of his house bespoke the fact that they too were preparing their breakfasts.

It was nine o'clock before the scene changed. Clear in the still air a bugle rang out in the camp. They must have heard it away at Zinat, for suddenly from the summit of the rocks above Raisuli's fortress a long thin column of white smoke arose, then another and another, and then from peak to peak, as far as the eye could reach, the fires were answered. The mountaineers were signalling to one another that the great battle was imminent. Down in the camp below us the infantry were "falling in" and the cavalrymen mounting their horses, and it was only a few minutes later when amongst the beating of drums and the blowing of bugles, the neighing of horses and the fluttering of coloured banners and flags, the Shereefian troops marched out on to the plain. A hoarse shout arose from every throat, "Ah! salih en-Nebi, Rasoul Allah!" an invocation to the Prophet, repeated again and again, and answered by a far-away and fainter cry of the same words from the fortress and rocks of Zinat.

Once all the troops are out on the plain they are drawn up in formation for the attack. On the right were the artillery, two field-guns, and a couple of Maxims, carried by mules. Near them, amidst a panoply of banners, rode the Commander-in-Chief and his staff, a group of a hundred or so persons well mounted and gaily dressed, with their bright saddles of every shade of coloured cloth and silk adding to a scene already brilliantly picturesque. In the centre were some 800 infantry with a strong support of tribal cavalry, while on the left a somewhat smaller force formed the flank. The contingent of loyal mountaineers in their short black cloaks could be seen already scaling some low hills away on the extreme right. Then slowly the whole army advances.

It was a moment of thrilling excitement. From

the rocky hill where I had taken up my point of vantage the whole scene was passing at my very feet. On my left the fortress and rocks ; on my right the slowly advancing forces—the left flank within a hundred yards or so of where I stood. At Zinat there was not a sign of life, though with my glasses I could see the glint of rifle-barrels in the embrasures of the house, and now and then amongst the precipices and rocks above it. The troops are within 1200 yards now, and in the open, but still advancing slowly, for the most part in close formation, and offering even at that range—a long one for the Moors, who are proverbial bad shots—an excellent target. The sunlit air is so still that every little sound rises unbroken from the plain below : a word of command here, a bugle-call there. Then suddenly the firing opens from Zinat —the quick nervous spitting of the Mauser rifles,— rendered the more impressive from the fact that nothing can be seen, for there is not a single man there who does not use smokeless powder. A few Askaris are seen to fall, killed or wounded, and the advance ceases. The whole army replies, firing at an impossible range into a solid fort and still more solid precipice with rifles that have only reached Morocco after they have long been discarded as useless in Europe, and with powder that issues, evil-looking and evil-smelling, from the barrels of their weapons. After all, it made little difference where they fired, for few or none had ever handled a rifle before, and there was nothing to shoot at. Meanwhile the cavalry galloped to and fro in every direction, except to advance, waving flags and firing their rifles, apparently at the green plover that swept over in flocks, disturbed by the unusual racket.

Inane impotent warfare, carried on by undisciplined and uncourageous men, whose uniforms alone bespoke them as soldiers.

A curl of thin yellow smoke, widening as it ascended, rises from the rocks far above the house —the first shell fired by the artillery, followed by another and another, which, although aimed at the house itself, fall in widely different directions, more than once nearer the Maghzen troops than the enemy. During the entire action of this Saturday, although the range was only about 1000 metres, the house was only struck twice, and even the explosion of these two shells did not force the defenders to abandon the flat roof and windows, though they cannot have failed to be effective. Meanwhile the troops on the left, under the cover of the rocks, had entered and burned a village out of Raisuli's line of fire, and were returning toward the camp laden with loot, under the impression that their duty for the day was over. Nor did any one attempt to persuade them to re-enter the fight, and I watched them disappear, staggering under huge mattresses, chests of painted wood—the dowry of every Moorish bride,—and a thousand other household articles. For a background—the burning village, the flames of which rose lurid and roaring into the still air, to pass away in great rolls of heavy white smoke.

From one to two o'clock the firing slackened, but at the latter hour another attempt was made to advance. The whole line pushed forward, but 700 or 800 yards from Zinat they broke, and— well, if they did not exactly run, they certainly returned very quickly. It was at this moment that two picturesque incidents occurred. From Raisuli's house emerged a woman, who, crossing the open ground under a heavy fire, mounted upon a rock and thence cursed the troops. She threw back her thick "haik," and, tearing her hair, waved her arms towards heaven, but the firing drowned her voice. Then slowly and majestically she drew her veil around her and retired. A few seconds later eight men, no doubt encouraged by her bravery, rushed into the open grounds, shouting and jeering at the retiring forces, and firing the while with their Mausers. It was then that the Commander-in-Chief fell wounded in the neck. A mule was brought, and, supported by his retinue, he was hurriedly taken back to the camp. By this time the army had used up all their shells and nearly all their cartridges. Even a reserve force, hidden in a river-bed a mile in the rear, had been firing at that range at the mountain ever since the morning, to the imminent danger of their advancing comrades.

The army was now retiring in good order, followed by Raisuli's eight men, who every now and then sped a parting shot at them. The battle at Zinat was over. The great effort of the Maghzen had failed, and the stronghold and village, except

for a few holes made by the shells, stood as placid
and peaceful in appearance as it had been in the
morning. The great Shereefian army had proved
itself to be—like everything else in Morocco,
except perhaps Raisuli himself—a gigantic bluff.

It was well on in the afternoon now, and the
scene of the fight was deserted. I crept up a little
gully to within 400 or 500 yards of the house, and,
peeping from between the rocks, I took a long
view with my glasses. On the green sward in
front of the house stood a man holding a pair of
glasses to his eyes. On either side of him were
a few retainers. He stood silent and still, watching
the retreating army. It was Raisuli.

At dawn on Sunday morning I was back again
in the hills near Zinat. Never did the sun rise
over a more peaceful scene or one more serenely
beautiful. Peak after peak, many touched with
snow, turned pink and gold as the first rays of the
rising sun touched their summits. At Zinat itself
all was quiet. A little blue smoke, the smoke of
wood fire, arose from the chimneys of Raisuli's
house, in front of which half a dozen mountaineers
were warming themselves over a small bonfire.

It was nine o'clock before the troops left the
camp, and, deploying in much the same formation
as the day before, advanced across the plain.
But their numbers were increased, for reinforce-
ments had been hurriedly sent by night from
Tangier, and fresh contingents of loyal mountaineers had turned up in force. But what was
still more important was the addition of one man,

an Algerian artillery officer attached to the Sultan's
service by the French Government, whose shooting
with the field-guns at Taza and Oujda had largely
saved the situation at both places. It had been
the intention of the Maghzen to send him on
Saturday, but owing to his being a French subject
they decided not to do so, as in their own consideration any one to do with France was at this
period a person to be avoided. Their folly lost
them the day. Had Si Abderrahman ben Sedira
been behind the guns on Saturday, Raisuli's house,
and probably Raisuli and most of his followers,
would have been destroyed. The proof, if one
were needed, is this. He accomplished more
destruction with the two shells he fired at the
fortress on Sunday morning than in the 130 shots
fired on Saturday. A general advance toward
Zinat was commenced a little before two, and the
two shells above mentioned were fired from the
field-guns. There was no reply from the house
or from the rocks above it. Already the troops
were considerably nearer than they had ever got
the previous day. A little hesitation was visible,
for no doubt the soldiers imagined that they were
being allowed to approach to within an easy and
certain range. The left were well ahead, led by
Raisuli's late Calipha, more royalist than the
King nowadays, who was followed close by his
contingent of the Fahs tribe. Three hundred
yards only now separated them from the village.
With a wild shout and a volley from their rifles
the cavalry charged. Over the rising ground they

passed, a brilliant flash of colour, and never drew
rein till they were at Raisuli's door.

The house and village were empty. Then began
a scene of pandemonium. Askaris, horsemen,
and tribal contingents rushed upon the castle,
and the wildest looting commenced. Other bands,
intent upon pillage, ransacked the neighbouring
houses. In a few minutes flames burst forth
from the thatched roofs of the surrounding huts.
The flames spread, and in as short a space of time
as it takes to write it the whole village was ablaze.
The strong wind drove the heavy smoke in huge
clouds across the face of the mountain, and in
half an hour all that was left of Zinat were the
burning houses from above which Raisuli's fortress towered, as yet but slightly damaged. Then
smoke burst out from its windows. The roof,
already half blown off by the shells, fell with a
crash ; a wall toppled over in clouds of dust, and
little by little the stronghold became a useless
ruin. Not a shot was fired from the mountain,
for there was no one to fire one. Silently in the
night Raisuli and his followers, and the inhabitants
of the neighbouring villages, with all their old
people, their women and children, and their flocks
and herds, had crept away into the darkness over
the plain and on into the mountains. Not a guard
had been posted to keep watch, not a blow had been
struck to prevent them escaping. Under the rocks
upon which I was seated the soldiers, laden with
loot, were returning. Carpets, mattresses, boxes,
vases of artificial flowers, tea-trays and tea-cups,

sacks of flour and grain, rolls of matting—all the belongings and appurtenances of Moorish houses formed their burdens. One soldier, a cheery kindly-looking giant, was whistling to a canary in a cage, which he had brought away in preference to more valuable loot.

As I rode over the brow of the hill on my way back to Tangier I drew rein for a moment and looked back. The army was leaving Zinat, and the burning houses were little more than heaps of smouldering ashes. Beyond lay the high mountains of Beni Msaour, whence Raisuli and the inhabitants of his villages must have been looking upon the ruins of their homes.

II.

RAISULI was now completely outlawed. He lived in the fastness of his mountains, where the Sultan's troops could never even attempt to penetrate. Thence he spread alarm right and left, causing constant fears and panics, even to the Europeans at Tangier.

The whole situation in Morocco was seething. The tribes had become to all intents and purposes independent, and many threw off all pretence of obeying the orders of their Governors or of paying taxes. Such as were more vulnerable, either from their geographical position or by their numerical weakness, were persecuted and squeezed to make up for the delinquencies of the others. The rapacity of the viziers was greater than ever, and the Sultan's extravagances seemed to have increased by the fresh supply of money that an ill-advised foreign loan had a year or two before brought into his spending power. Bou Hamara, the Pretender, in the Rif, and Raisuli amongst the mountain tribes, were the two principal thorns in the Maghzen's side. With Bou Hamara, who stated that he was the eldest brother of the Sultan, nothing could be done. He remained in the inaccessible Rif tribe-lands, where he governed as a petty Sultan; and even the Spanish authorities, who waited long to see him driven out, were at last obliged to enter into relation with him, in order to ensure the security of their "Presidios." That Bou Hamara and Raisuli were in communication is certain, but there was little respect and little confidence between them, and except for the passage of letters no compact of real or practical importance seems to have existed between them. Yet that their relations were cordial is clear, from the original document in my possession sealed by Bou Hamara with his great seal of State, by which he appoints Raisuli Governor of certain of the mountain tribes. On this seal of State, Bou Hamara uses the style "Mohammed ben Hassen"—claiming thereby to be Mulai Mohammed, the eldest son of Mulai Hassen, and therefore the elder brother of the reigning Sultan.

Raisuli had no pretensions to the Sultanate, though in the eyes of Europe he played a more important part, for his principal activities were employed in the districts of Tangier, the diplomatic capital of the country.

In 1906 that futile Conference of Algeciras— futile, that is to say, in so far as it had any beneficial effect in Morocco—had met, discussed, signed, and separated. It had for Europe, no doubt, cleared the situation, and was a check to Germany; but poor Morocco gained little—in fact, it marked one more step on its road to ruin. Never probably did such a collection of diplomatists, whose high-

sounding titles fill the first few pages of that
insignificant little yellow - book which contains
the results of their insignificant labours, give
themselves airs of such importance. For days
together they discussed the questions of the import
of sporting-guns and the rifling of gun-barrels with
all the pomposity of affairs of the gravest moment
—to pass to the rules for the distribution of parcels
post. Three or four men were playing a great
stake—representatives of England and France,
and of Germany—and it was well played. The
victory remained with the two former. The rest
were puppets, but didn't realise it. They really
thought, or seemed to think, that their endeavours
were being of service to the country which few
of them knew anything about, beyond the distant
view they could obtain of it from the hills above
Algeciras.

Northern Morocco was at its worst the year after
the Algeciras Act had been signed, and even the
pleasure-loving Mulai Abdul Aziz perceived that
affairs were becoming serious. He decided to
open negotiations with Raisuli. For this purpose
Kaid Maclean had an interview with the brigand
chief in April (1907). Raisuli listened to the
Kaid's proposals, but refused to accompany him
to Fez, where the Sultan was then residing.
However, a step had been made toward a possible
arrangement. A month later, armed with the
authority of the Sultan, Kaid Maclean returned
to Alcazar, a town on the Tangier-Fez road,
situated about sixty miles from the former. But

meanwhile it has leaked out that Raisuli would attempt the capture of this important functionary. Every effort was made by the Sultan, who had also received the news, and by the British Legation, to cancel the interview, and the British Consular Agent at Alcazar was instructed to this effect to continue the negotiations. An interview with Raisuli was secretly arranged, to be held on the borders of the Ahlserif tribe-lands, some few miles from Alcazar. There these two personages met. The Sultan's propositions were made known to Raisuli, who pretended to accept them, and to be disposed to return to Fez with the Kaid. He would, he said, start at once, and if the Kaid would accompany him to the village where his camp was pitched they would set out the next day. The Kaid agreed, and entered the mountains with his host—only there was no setting out the next day, for he found himself a prisoner, and remained in captivity for some seven months, suffering considerable hardships.

Of all the negotiations for the obtaining of the liberty of Raisuli's prisoners, these were the most difficult. The terms demanded by Raisuli were preposterous, and a score of people seemed negotiating on their own account, while the Kaid himself was doing his utmost, and very naturally, to obtain his release. The result was confusion and misunderstanding, and the distance from Tangier at which Raisuli kept his captive increased the difficulties. Had the whole affair been left in the hands of Sir Gerard Lowther, who at this period ably represented England in Morocco, it is probable that Kaid Maclean's release would have been more quickly obtained. But on every occasion on which a solution seemed near some perfectly new proposition, emanating from unauthorised sources, would frustrate the official plans. In the end Raisuli obtained £20,000, and he was made a British protected subject; and there were other minor terms. Kaid Maclean was released. The only pleasing aspect of all these brigandage cases was the absolute confidence that Raisuli always placed in the word of the British Government, the British authorities, and in fact that of all Britishers.

Some years after this event, when the ex-Sultan Mulai Abdul Aziz, who had just abdicated, was visiting my villa at Tangier, I showed him two Arabic documents. One was his original " Dahir " for the nomination of Raisuli as Governor of the tribes, which the brigand had extorted as part of the ransom of Perdicaris; and the other was Raisuli's appointment as Governor of the same tribes, bearing another great seal of State, that of the Pretender, Bou Hamara. Mulai Abdul Aziz asked me how I had become possessed of these two documents. I told him. The " Dahir " of the Pretender I had found, during my imprisonment, in a secret cupboard in a room of Raisuli's house at Zinat. I had carried it, sewn up in my clothing, with other equally interesting correspondence, during the whole period of my captivity. The firman of the Sultan himself I

had obtained the day Raisuli's house was looted
by the Maghzen troops, at which picturesque
incident I had been present.

The ex-Sultan smiled. " There seems," he said
rather cynically, " to be nothing of interest in
Morocco which hasn't reached either your knowledge or your hands; nothing that you haven't
had given you—acquired ? "

" The most valuable of all things was given me,"
I replied.

" And that was ? "

" Your Majesty's friendship."

It was at this period, while an outlaw in the
mountains, that Raisuli nearly made his most
important capture. It was an incident that was
kept very quiet at the time, but leaked out in
the French Press a little later. The truth was, we
Europeans who played a part—and we very
nearly played a very serious part—in the story
had no desire for publicity.

The facts were these. The ruins of Raisuli's
stronghold at Zinat were only distant from Tangier
about fourteen miles, and formed a tempting
excursion, but one which no one undertook, as
it was notoriously unsafe. However, as time went
on and nothing occurred in the neighbourhood of
Tangier to disturb the tranquillity, and as Raisuli
and his band seemed permanently to have taken
up their residence in the mountains at a considerable distance from the scene of their former
activities, a picnic at Zinat was decided upon,
and I was invited. The other members of our

party consisted of Sir Gerard Lowther, then British Minister to Morocco, Monsieur and Madame de Beaumarchais of the French Legation, and Mr Christopher Lowther, the son of the Speaker of the House of Commons. I formed the fifth member of the party.

One hot summer morning we rode out, having sent our lunch on in advance. On nearing Zinat we were hailed by a countryman who was ploughing his fields. I rode to see what he wanted, and was informed that Raisuli's band was back at Zinat, apparently having come to take away some treasure which had, by being buried, escaped the looting of the soldiery at the time of the destruction of the castle. He advised us not to proceed. We discussed this news, and in the folly of an enjoyable excursion, decided, *as the lunch was on ahead*, to proceed. Nothing could surpass the tranquillity of the scene on our arrival, and we were soon lunching under the shade of the olive-trees. I confess that the pleasure of the *foie-gras* was mingled, in my case, with a certain nervous apprehension from which the others appeared immune. We did not believe, or had pretended not to believe, the story of the return of Raisuli's brigands.

Lunch was nearly over when the glint of a rifle-barrel in the thick brushwood caught my eye, and another and yet another in the rocks, for the hill at Zinat is a wild precipitous slope of broken masses of rock and scrub. A minute later we were surrounded. The men were perfectly polite, and

to all intents and purposes appeared merely to
have come to wish us good-day. At their head
was the good-looking young Ahmed el-Aoufi,
Raisuli's second-in-command, a personal friend of
my own, who had shown me considerable kindness
during my captivity with the brigands in 1903.
He shook us warmly by the hand, and, his rifle
between his knees, sat down to spend the time
of day. A few yards away, in a complete circle
round us, were thirty or forty of his men.

I confess that situations like this exhilarate me.
I hate bloodshed and noisy encounters, but a
delicate situation has a zest that is unique, and,
heavens! it *was* a delicate situation. The British
Minister and the French Chargé d'Affaires—what
a coup! I was the only member of the party who
spoke Arabic, and the suspense the others must
have suffered during the next hour or two must
have been extreme. Yet no one made a sign.
I have often seen great examples of self-restraint,
but never, I think, greater than on this occasion.
Remember, my friends understood nothing of
what I was saying, except that every now and
again I referred to them for confirmation of my
assertions. For me the situation was very exciting.
If I was taken after all, it was only what had
happened before, and I was used to adventure and
hardship—but for the others! and I could not
help thinking of the terms—probably impossible
terms—that Raisuli would demand for their release—and of the possible consequences! I have
found on occasions like these—for this was by

no means the only tight place of the kind that I have been in—that not only is there a kind of exhilaration, but also that one's power of concentration of thought is accentuated. However inauspicious the actual surroundings may be, one feels and knows that the mental superiority rests with the European, and that hereditary training of thought and education stand one in good stead. The Moor is no fool, he is cunning and astute, but his mind is untrained—and he is confiding when dealing with Europeans. In the first moments of our encounter at Zinat I knew that our safety depended upon the game that I was determined to play—and which I played successfully.

I began with an enormous untruth. Holding El-Aoufi's hand, I told him I was delighted to see him, and that his visit was most opportune —nothing, in fact, could have been better. Then I sat him down, and talked to him and to his chief companions seriously. It was at this moment that Madame de Beaumarchais, with the admirable sangfroid of a talented and courageous Frenchwoman, took a photograph. The man to whom I was talking was Ould el-Aoufi; the European seated just behind me was the late Sir Gerard Lowther.

The story that I told them was this. I reminded them that Raisuli had been driven from the Governorship of Tangier and the surrounding tribes at the demand of the European Powers. They had acted unwisely and realised it, and now they regretted their action. " Do you know," I asked, " who these people are who are here to-day ? "

" We are not sure," they replied.

" Then I will tell you," and I did. Instead of, as would seem natural, trying to conceal the identity of my distinguished friends, I launched out into exaggerated statements as to their importance. I saw I had made an impression. My audience were now thoroughly puzzled.

" And why are they here ? " I asked. " Listen, and I will tell you. The Powers of Europe regret Raisuli's departure and disgrace. They desire him to be reinstated, but the Sultan has refused. The Powers insist, and as the Maghzen still holds out, the Governments of England and France have telegraphed to their representatives—the gentlemen you see here to-day—instructing them to visit the scene of the depredations on Raisuli's castle, and to make all the necessary arrangements for its reconstruction as quickly as possible, so that Raisuli can be restored to his own, and once more introduce law and order into the region. For this purpose we are come to-day—against the advice of all our friends—so that the work can be undertaken at once. Meanwhile the letter recalling Raisuli from the mountains is being drawn up." I then added, " We were warned on the way that we should find you here, and advised to turn back, but I told the people who warned us that Raisuli's men would perfectly understand our mission, and nice trouble they would get into with their chief if they captured the very men who are insisting on restoring him to his former grandeur, and obtaining the return of all his confiscated property—and even rebuilding his castle at the expense of the Governments they represent. " I should like to see your face, friend Ahmed el-Aoufi, after Raisuli had discovered the ' gaffe ' that you had made; and if I know your chief, friend and confidant as you are, I can imagine the stripes he could lay upon your bare back. Do you think that, unless we had been really his benefactors, we should ever have been such fools to have ventured into this hornets' nest ? Now up with you," I cried, rising, " and we will see what we can do with these ruins."

I led the way down to the ruins, and for the next hour measured walls, took notes of the local price of masons and carpenters and the possibilities of obtaining bricks on the spot, proposed a new water-supply which the laws of gravitation rendered quite impossible, and even whispered in El-Aoufi's ear that there would be money to build him a little house adjoining his chief's. We came to the conclusion that for between £12,000 and £15,000, taking into consideration that Raisuli could obtain a plentiful supply of forced labour, and as much material as he liked, the house could be restored to more than its pristine glories.

Another photograph taken by Madame de Beaumarchais pictures us pacing out the length of the walls of the house.

My note-book full of figures, I sat down again and dictated to El-Aoufi the following letter, which he wrote: "To the trusted and well-beloved Shereef, the learned Mulai Ahmed er-Raisuli, peace and the mercy of God be upon you; and acting on the instructions of their Governments, of which the letter I sent you yesterday will have given you full particulars, the British Minister and the French Chargé d'Affaires have paid a visit to the ruins of your Kasbah. They have grieved much to see its piteous state. As you will have learned by the contents of my letter, it is the intention of their Governments not only to restore you to power but also to reconstruct your castle. To-day we are at Zinat, and we had the good fortune to find your faithful and intelligent deputy, my lord Ahmed el-Aoufi, and your followers, who have been of great use to us, and have shown us many things that have helped us, and have guarded us in security and peace from any bad people who may have been about. We are grateful. And my lord Ahmed el-Aoufi will tell you of many things which in our friendship for you we have confided to him. We will await at Tangier a reply to the letter I sent you yesterday, explaining fully those things, and immediately on receiving the reply measures will be taken to commence the restoration of your Kasbah; but it is trusted that you will not wait its completion before returning to your former position, for any delay will only protract the unsatisfactory state of affairs existing at present, and continue the nervousness of the population of Tangier and the oppression of the poor country people. My lord El-Aoufi will tell you all. May peace be with you."

To this epistle I put my signature, and not one pang of conscience did I feel, nor have felt since. Raisuli and I had played many games—only this one was a little bigger than the rest. To tell the truth, so far from feeling guilty, I literally revelled in my deception.

It was time to return to Tangier, and I confess I was nervous. I proposed to El-Aoufi that the others should start first, and that I should remain for a while and catch them up on the road. I wanted to spend, I said, a little while longer in his company—it was a pleasure so rare and so valued.

With a sigh of relief I saw the rest of our party mount. El-Aoufi shook hands with all of them and thanked them for their visit—and they rode slowly away. My fears were at an end.

I sat for half an hour, and explained to El-Aoufi that Raisuli would have already received my (perfectly imaginary) letter of yesterday which explained the whole situation, and that on his return to his chief in the mountains, some six or eight hours' journey farther on, he would find him fully informed. He (El-Aoufi) must, I added, have crossed my letter en route. Had he not met the messenger, whose name I gave? No! Well, then, he must have taken another track. My friends were now no more than little black specks far away in the plain. I rose and embraced El-

Aoufi, and in the manner of the country we kissed each other's shoulders. My horse was brought, and, cantering slowly down the slope, I rode away toward Tangier.

In spite of the deliberate series of falsehoods of which I had been guilty during those few hours, I never felt less conscience-stricken—and perhaps never happier—in my life.

I have seen Raisuli many times since the incident. He referred to El-Aoufi, after a trial fight, as a lion of courage.

"There was no finer creature in God's world," I replied, "than the lion, but sometimes the wily jackal deceives him."

I noticed a little flash in Raisuli's eye, but he answered languidly, "Verily the jackal is an unclean beast."

Sir Gerard Lowther, the Beaumarchais, Christopher Lowther, and I all dined together the night of our adventure, but we didn't talk very much about it. Our thankfulness for our escape was only equalled by our appreciation of our immense folly in having undertaken the expedition. We agreed that, if possible, the incident was to be kept a secret, but a few weeks later the 'Temps' contained the whole story, which had leaked out from native sources and got to Paris.

I should have liked to have seen the interview of Raisuli and El-Aoufi when the latter related the incident and gave him my letter. He fell from favour for a time, as might be expected, but he came to see me in Tangier a few months later. We did not mention the visit to Zinat, but discussed more general subjects. Talking of the good and bad qualities of mankind, El-Aoufi said, " The most degrading thing in the world is deceit," and he said it quite nastily.

" In my opinion there is something even more humiliating," I replied.

" That is ? "

" To be made a fool of."

But we parted the best of friends.

RAISULI

III.

ALTHOUGH, as will have been appreciated, my relations with Raisuli were varied and adventuresome, I bear him no grudge; and I think he always considered me as a friend, and I hope does so now. He has, on his visits to Tangier, often spent hours at a time in my house, discussing the many situations in the country and the varying attitudes of the mountain tribes. He had lost much of his former handsome appearance, having become heavy and stout, and his expression perhaps more cruel. He was always courteous and generally amusing, often in a very sarcastic cynical manner. He was full of his own importance, and seemed to realise that he was unique—which, perhaps happily, he certainly was.

On one occasion while at my house, he saw in a glass case an illuminated Koran of considerable artistic value, both on account of its antiquity and of its beauty. Now, the Moors cannot bear to see their religious books in the possession of Europeans, and Raisuli, without more ado, extracted the book from the *vitrine*, kissed it reverently, carefully wrapped it in a silk handkerchief, and placed it in the hands of one of his slaves.

He gave no explanation of his action, which, after all, needed no explanation. The conversation flowed on in other channels, and he never so much as mentioned the book. A little later he left—and so did my Koran.

I had two of these Korans, but the one which Raisuli had taken was much the finest, from the collector's point of view. The second copy was, however, newer and more brilliant in colour, and certainly would appear in the eyes of a Moor a more desirable acquisition, for to them antiquity is of no great account. This second copy Raisuli had not seen.

The next day I sent one of my Moors with it, wrapped in silk, to ask Raisuli whether he would be willing to restore me the one he had taken in exchange for this newer and far better preserved volume. The first copy, I informed him, perhaps not quite truly, had a very great personal interest to me, and I begged him to accept the second and restore me the older one. I hinted that the second was a much superior book. My man returned crestfallen and sad. His mission had failed. He brought me many friendly messages from Raisuli but no book, neither the first nor the second, for Raisuli had kept both. It was exasperating, but there was nothing to be done but to swear to be equal with him at some future time.

One morning, about a month later, I sent to him asking him to lend me two riding-mules with their saddles, for some friends of mine to ride on to a picnic—good pacing mules, as my friends were not accustomed to riding. Half an hour later two very fine mules, caparisoned in rich red saddles, arrived, led by Raisuli's slaves. I myself put them in my stable and turned the key. I then sent to Raisuli to say that when I had my books he could have his mules. One of his secretaries returned with my messenger, and after the usual compliments informed me that his master had instructed him to say that the books were invaluable, and that he could not restore them. The mules were mine, he added; in fact everything Raisuli possessed was mine—except, of course, the books—and if I required more mules or horses he could send me as many as I wished. He could easily have done so : he possessed dozens and dozens, if not hundreds, nearly all confiscated or extorted from the people of the country. They had cost him nothing to get, then they would therefore cost little to give.

My conscience smote me. My little trick appeared so mean beside this dignified magnificence and generosity of Raisuli. I offered to restore the mules, but he would not hear of it. They continued in my stables, and my friendship with their former owner flowed on undiminished and unchanged. I saw him often. Since the episode of the Koran, books have never been mentioned between us ; now mules were also placed upon the Index. Never directly or indirectly in his conversations did we ever refer to the subject. Nor was my capture ever spoken of. Only once a tactless

European broached in the brigand chief's presence
of my having been for some time at his stronghold
at Zinat. With a pleasant smile Raisuli interposed :
" My house is always at the disposal of my friends."
Hospitality is innate in the Moorish character.

The giving and taking of presents was practised
a great deal in the " old " Morocco, but it is now
happily disappearing. It was always a great
nuisance. One often gave away something one
really wanted—and it was so difficult to replace
anything—and got in return some perfectly useless
acquisition. I have arrived back in Tangier after
a long journey in the interior with half a dozen
new horses, most of them neither good nor bad.
I couldn't possibly ride them all, and they were
only a very irksome expense and luxury. At
first, and for a long time, I hesitated to adopt the
custom of the country, and hand them on as
presents to some one else. A feeling possessed me
that gifts were " sacrosanct," and must be kept
at all costs, and that the giver would be hurt in
his feelings to learn that his present had been
passed on. But in time I found that the donor
didn't care the least what became of his presents,
or ever give them a second thought.

One of the viziers once gave me an amber necklace of transparent cut beads. He said the Sultan
had given it to him, and that His Majesty had
received it from a high official from the southern
capital. A few years afterwards I gave it to a
young European lady about to be married, as a
wedding present, to find out that it had been her

father who had brought it to Morocco—as looking much more expensive than it really was—and had given it to one of the tribal Governors in return for something else. It had travelled all over Morocco, but got home at last to where it had started from, to meet with no appreciation. We laughed over the history of the necklace, and the damsel got another present in exchange. My amber beads now deck the fair throat—if she ever wears them—of a beautiful and distinguished lady far away from Morocco.

My stables were often full to overflowing, and were a very great strain upon my resources, until I steeled my heart and gave the horses away as they came in. But unfortunately it was not horses the Moorish authorities wanted : they had already too many. No, it was one's watch or one's shot-gun, or a sporting-rifle, or a barometer or field-glasses that they always set their hearts upon—something rare and impossible to procure or replace in the country. Nor were one's troubles over when the exchange of presents was accomplished, for there were the numberless tips that had to be given. A horse would be brought, led by a slave and accompanied by the chief of the stables and two grooms—and they had to be satisfied. Then probably the son of the donor would pay a visit to my camp and express a sudden and intense desire to be possessed of my shot-gun or my watch-chain ; and when he had left, satisfied perhaps with a less costly present from a box of objects brought for the purpose, the secretary of his father would arrive to apologise for the son's rudeness, and to say that he would be punished by his father for having ventured to ask for anything. He would sing the praises of my recently-acquired horse. Then a tone of sadness would be adopted. He was a poor man ; he had had troubles. He wouldn't have breathed of it to another, not if lions' teeth were tearing his entrails ; but he felt that the bond of sympathy between us was so close that—and then came out a long story, perfectly untrue of course, of the meanness of his employer, and of his unpaid salary, &c. He could keep his secret no longer, he must tell it, and with tears in his eyes he would beg for a sum of money, generally modest enough. However, there was always scope for bargaining, and his demands would diminish, till eventually he would go away with a few coins in ecstasy of pretended gratitude.

Accepting the hospitality of the great chiefs was only a little less costly, and a night's entertainment by some dignitary or governor of a tribe was often both tiring and expensive. It meant a succession of visits to one's camp on the part of a host of inquisitive people, most of whom wanted something. There were the guards too, who were specially given one to keep away these inquisitive people, but who, in fact, only added to their number. These guards expected payment for the duties they so signally failed in accomplishing. Then great quantities of food were sent by the high official—living fowls, a live sheep, loaves of sugar, packets of tea, barley for the horses, and these commodities, supplied in abundance that was as extravagant as it was irksome, necessitated unending tips in exchange. It took three men, for instance, to lead the sheep, and a slave to carry each fowl—and one and all waited their *pourboires* before departing. Then at dinner-time—generally it was so late that it was nearly midnight—great dishes of cooked food would arrive—and very excellent they were—and probably the great man himself and some of his household would invite themselves to the dinner they had so amply provided. It was nearly always very tiring, and always very late before sleep could be obtained. Once in a way it was pleasant enough, and I can look back upon many and many a night spent in this way in feasting with the great men of the land, the memory of which is very pleasant. No food was wasted, for the sheep and chickens were killed and the retainers and slaves came and helped in the camp-kitchen, and brought great earthen pots and pans for the cooking—and sat and sang and ate the whole night through. On the outskirts of the camp would collect the poor, and these were never forgotten.

I have travelled in China and Japan, in Persia, Arabia, and Abyssinia, and in many parts of North Africa, Turkey in Asia and Syria, but "old" Morocco was by far the most expensive to travel in. There were absolutely no facilities —no caravanserais to put up in, and all food and sometimes fodder and fuel had to be carried with one. Nothing but a sheep and chickens could be bought on the road, even one's bread had to be transported or cooked in camp. The purchase or hire of caravan animals was always heavy, and sometimes exorbitant. Tips were excessive. Only at the towns at long distances apart could any stores be replenished, and in the inland cities, beyond tea, sugar, and candles, nothing else was procurable. In spring-time butter could be bought, but even if it was procurable at other periods of the year it was always the preserved " smin " with its strong taste and smell. I have never yet discovered the reason that rendered travel so difficult and so expensive. The bad Government no doubt had much to do with it, for there was actually not only no incentive to the people to pros-per and breed animals, but on the contrary to be rich or even fairly well-to-do rendered the native liable to arrest, confiscation of his property, and perhaps total disappearance. Yet the Moor has been always thrifty, ready to turn his hand to work, and still more ready to earn money. In spite of this, it was often difficult even in the big centres to collect caravan mules for a journey, and then hire was often exorbitant.

I am writing of journeys in which I travelled as a European with a large camp, often alone, sometimes in the company of friends, when all the rigid etiquette and formality of visits to the Kaids and local authorities had to be paid. But there were other journeys when, with half a dozen mules of my own, and my own men with me, a few good horses, and tents of less pretensions and native in character, I wandered through the country alone and in native clothes, for months and months together. Those were the great days: long almost objectless journeys, wandering whither the desire led me—now to the cities of Wazzan, Fez, or Marrakesh, now on the borders of the snows of the Great Atlas. Unless actually exploring, as on my Tafilet journey, I never, of course, pretended to pass as a native; but the fact of the Moorish dress kept away the inquisitive people, and even reduced the constant demands that were made upon one's purse. It rendered life much more pleasant. Instead of pitching one's camp outside the great men's castles, I was invited to stay within, generally in a little guest apartment of two or three rooms, and the masses of unnecessary food were reduced to pleasant meals with one's host. To the Moor " Christian " clothes and a hat on one's head meant the most formal of relations, while once these were discarded I was accepted in intimacy.

The latest visit that I have paid to Raisuli is about eight years ago, when he was building his palace at Arzeila. I was accompanied by a young niece, who had come on a short visit to Tangier, and by a girl friend of hers. I thought nothing could be more amusing for two English girls than to pay a visit to the famous brigand at the little old walled town of Arzeila, with the remains of its old Portuguese castle and bastions. A zest was added to this visit by the disapproval it occasioned amongst my friends. It was late at

night when we reached Raisuli's camp, for he had
come some way to meet us. A tidal river had
delayed us, and we had sat on its banks waiting
for the water to descend, until after dark. It
was with a sigh of relief that I saw the lights and
fires of the camp, for the night was pitch dark,
and our horses—stallions, of course, for no one
rides anything else in Morocco—had become very
excited from the proximity of numerous mares,
invisible in the blackness of the night.

We found Raisuli in his great tent, a circular
canvas pavilion some twenty-five feet in diameter,
with high walls and a lofty roof. An immense
square pillar, rather than a pole, supported the
great weight, for the whole tent was lined throughout with heavy and very expensive dark-green
cloth. The outside of the tent was of white
canvas decorated in designs of indigo blue material,
appliquéd to the canvas.

While our tents were being pitched we dined in
Raisuli's pavilion. The famous brigand was accompanied by a certain number of his friends and
secretaries, while an ex-high native official had
also arrived on a visit the same day, to take part
in the hunting we were to be offered. My niece,
her friend, and myself were, of course, the only
Europeans. Tall highly-polished brass candle-
sticks, bearing large candles, stood on trays of the
same material, and sufficed to light the tent and
to illumine the faces of the guards of mountaineers
and the black slaves who stood or squatted in
groups without the door, ready to do their master's

bidding. A number of smaller tents were pitched in a great semicircle, of which the apex was formed by Raisuli's pavilion.

Seated on luxurious mattresses, which were arranged all round the walls of the great tent, we were served with dishes of cooked meats, green tea, with its flavouring mint and herbs, and coffee.

The following day we rode on to Arzeila. Raisuli's retinue, a couple of hundred of mountaineers, spread themselves out in a long line and hunted as they went, with horse and gun and greyhound, and sticks and even stones—singing and shouting the whole time.

On our arrival we were invited by our host either to take up our residence in a house in the little town which had been furnished and prepared for us, or in a vast camp that had been pitched for our reception near the sea-shore, and within two hundred yards of the Atlantic breakers. We chose the latter, for the outskirts of Arzeila form one of the most delightful camping-grounds in Morocco.

On our left lay the old town, with its frowning towers and battlements rising above the olive- and orange-trees of the surrounding gardens. In front the soft green grass sloped gently to the yellow sands and the great expanse of ocean, while behind us rose undulating grassy hills. The camp buzzed with life: soldiers in uniform, slaves and servants passed and repassed, and a long line of some forty horses, tethered by their feet in the custom

of the country, were at our disposal should we
want to ride other horses than our own. Food,
dead and alive, poured into the camp—it seemed
one perpetual procession of great cooked dishes
and flocks of sheep and crates of chickens and
pigeons. A native band discoursed shrill music
at all the most inconvenient hours of day and
night.

Raisuli was the best of hosts, and in excellent
spirits. Amongst other entertainments that he
offered us was a luncheon to my niece, her friend,
and myself, served in an upper room on one of
the high towers that overhung the sea. With the
sweetest of smiles, and in a most successful en-
deavour to interest his young lady guests, if not
to amuse them, he pointed out one of the windows
of the room—an old embrasure in the walls—
through which at the point of the bayonet he and
his men had driven the late Governor of the town,
the Kaid Khalkhali, to fall forty feet on to the
rocks beneath, only a short time before. The past
history of one's hosts at Moorish entertainments
added a piquant flavour to the repasts. In
Morocco one mustn't be too critical, and it was
seldom one dined with any great native authority
in the country who had not a record behind him
that would have outdone Newgate's historic annals.
Thank God, those days are over. The advent of
the French has put an end to the period that was
really terrible. Yet when one lived amongst these
great crimes—the sudden appearances and dis-
appearances, the midnight burials in desert places,

the carrying off of women; hate, love, revenge, and now and again some great unselfishness—the exaggeration, in fact, of all qualities and all sentiments good and bad,—one ceased to wonder. Whole families would fall—in wealth and luxury to-day, and gone to-morrow—to rise again perhaps a generation later, and carry on the blood-feud of revenge and hate—or perhaps, generally unwisely, to forgive.

IV.

As has already been stated, one of the terms for the release of Kaid Maclean demanded by Raisuli and complied with by the British Government was his being made a British protected subject, which status put him outside the jurisdiction of the Sultan, and rendered him amenable to British law. It was a humiliating sacrifice for His Majesty's Government to have to make, but there was no way out of it. Raisuli might have perhaps been persuaded to abandon the £20,000 that he received in cash, but never this other clause of the terms. Freed thus from fear of arrest by the Sultan, he took to a more regular life, and began the construction of his great residence at Arzeila. It must be added, that pending the period during which he enjoyed British protection he committed no crimes that we know of more than those of extortion from the tribes—and no doubt certain cruelties. It was fortunate that the suffering tribesmen did not complain to the British authorities, as it would have been difficult even to summon Raisuli to appear in the Tangier Consular Court—and still more difficult to have got him there.

While Raisuli was living quietly at Arzeila, if

being visited by all the neighbouring tribesmen and living in a turmoil of building can be so described, affairs elsewhere in Morocco were seething. In 1908 Mulai Abdul Aziz, defeated with his army in the south, abdicated, and Mulai Hafid seized the throne. After a long and dangerous journey the new Sultan installed himself at Fez.

Raisuli felt that his chance had come. He had helped in the overthrow of Mulai Abdul Aziz, and had been one of the first to proclaim Mulai Hafid in the north; and, ambitious by nature, he wished once more to play a part, and a great one, in the new régime. Secret negotiations were opened between him and Mulai Hafid, which ended in a visit to the Court at Fez. The tussle that ensued was most interesting. I was in Fez, and in constant touch with both the parties interested, during the negotiations. Of the two, Mulai Hafid was the shrewdest. He had more patience and more cunning than Raisuli, though he too was by no means lacking in this latter useful oriental characteristic. The brigand chief had come to Fez full of the importance of his power and influence, but he did not realise that at the educated and civilised Court he was looked upon as little more than a very successful robber, who nevertheless was recognised as a danger and a thorn in the Sultan's side. His reception by Mulai Hafid was not cordial, in fact he was kept waiting for some time before he could obtain an audience. The viziers were polite—and barely that. Raisuli, installed in a very palatial residence in the city, was bored. He longed to get back to the north, where he reigned supreme, and to be quit of Fez, where he was suspicious of lurking danger, and considered as a person of no great consequence. But Mulai Hafid purposely let the negotiations drag on, and Raisuli had great difficulty in obtaining audiences of his Sovereign—and even when arranged they were continually postponed. At last, weary of so much delay, he began to act, and to Mulai Hafid's annoyance, affairs in the northern tribes began to go badly. There were rumours of a likelihood of Mulai Abdul Aziz being proclaimed again, and the tribes were getting out of hand. Raisuli was the only man who could exert real influence in those regions, and both the Sultan and he knew it. I was consulted by both, and as the peace of the country was more important than these local quarrels in Fez, I strongly advised both to come to terms. They did. Raisuli was appointed Governor over practically all the tribes of North-West Morocco, with the exception of Tangier and its surrounding district; but before receiving this appointment he was forced to abandon his British protection, for by the law of the land no " protected subject " could hold a Maghzen appointment. He was also called upon to refund the £20,000 which the British Government had paid him for Kaid Maclean's release.

So far Mulai Hafid had scored, for the British Government was pressing him, as Sultan, for the repayment of Maclean's ransom, which had been advanced to the impecunious Maghzen, unable to raise the sum. At the same time, in abandoning his British protection, Raisuli became amenable once more to Moorish law and jurisdiction; and Mulai Hafid, who hoped to be able to consolidate his sovereignty in the north, foresaw the possibilities of being able some day to rid himself of this chieftain if he became too troublesome. Raisuli, on the contrary, knew that within a few months he could easily repay himself the £20,000 out of the tribes he was now appointed to govern, and he was sufficiently sure of his own influence and power to fear no possible reprisals on the part of the Sultan. He promised devoted loyalty, but had already determined on absolute independence. Having satisfied the Sultan and given considerable presents in money to the viziers, he left Fez for the north—and has never returned to the capital since.

It must be acknowledged that during the four years that Raisuli was Governor of these northern tribes he maintained order in the region. The roads were open to caravan traffic, and robberies were rare. But it was a government of terror and extortion. His prestige was enormous, and he exerted it to its full. The tribes brought everything that he demanded—and he demanded much. Money poured into his coffers; labour they supplied free. Caravans of lime and building material came in endless array to Arzeila, and the great house rose tier above tier over the sea-walls of the town. He built residences, too, at Zinat and at Tazerout, in the Beni Aros tribe.

His stables were filled with horses and mules, for
which he paid little or nothing. He entertained
hospitably—in fact, kept open house, as is the
custom of the country. But behind all was the
cruel iron will and the heavy hand, and thousands
who might have been free obeyed him as if hypno-
tised, and brought their little all to him, generally
to be told to go back and bring more. Half revered,
half feared ; a little loved and perhaps entirely
unhated—for no one dared to hate him,—Raisuli
ruled the tribes of North-West Morocco, and treated
them as slaves. His principal enemy at this time
was the Kaid er-Remiki, who had offered his services to Spain, and had organised the pretended
attack on Alcazar, which gave the Spaniards the
excuse for occupying that town in 1911. Remiki
was a German agent, even in those days, and he
and his family's actions had long been suspect.
His relations with Raisuli were strained, for the
mountain brigand saw in this leader of the plains
—for Remiki was Kaid of the Khlot tribe—a possible rival. His presence, too, with the Spaniards,
and the aid he was openly giving them, drove
Raisuli still further into a spirit of independence
and opposition ; but as time went on and the
Spanish troops occupied the plains round Alcazar,
Raisuli saw his position—or at least his property
—threatened, for he owns very considerable estates
in those regions. Spanish attempts at opening
negotiations with him failed for a considerable
time, but at last a *modus vivendi* was arrived at,
which at first seemed successful. A permanent

understanding between Raisuli and the Spanish
authorities was, however, more than could be
hoped for—both were overwhelmed by an exaggerated sense of *amour propre*, and neither understood, nor desired to understand, the mentality
of the other. Raisuli was ready to be friendly so
long as his independence was not interfered with ;
the Spaniards were also prepared to be friendly so
long as Raisuli did not exert this very independence
that he claimed and insisted upon. The result was
constant friction. Nor was the situation rendered
easier by the fact that the methods being adopted
by the Spanish civil authorities were completely
at variance with those of the military chiefs, for
neither consulted the other. A good deal of the
correspondence which passed between the Spaniards
and Raisuli at this date came into my hands. It
is of no very particular interest except in showing
the totally opposed objects and ends of the Spanish
military and civil authorities. Things even went
so far that measures were taken by certain military
authorities to bring about the " disappearance "
of Raisuli. The accident was to have taken place
while he was *en route* to pay a visit to the Spanish
civil authorities at Tangier with the idea of arranging a visit to Madrid. The Spanish Legation at
Tangier was, of course, completely ignorant of this
plot, and had given a safe-conduct to Raisuli.
It only reached the ears of the Spanish Chargé
d'Affaires at almost the last moment. There was
just time to send a native runner to Raisuli to
warn him not to start on this journey, which

would certainly not have passed without a probably fatal incident. The Spanish authorities at Tangier behaved, as might have been expected, with great promptitude and correctness. The fact was that the jealousy existing between the Spanish military authorities at Laraiche and the Spanish representative at Tangier was such that neither knew what the other was doing or proposing to do. While General Silvestre, who commanded the Spanish troops at Laraiche, was pursuing an energetic policy, and foresaw, rightly, the difficulties that Raisuli's presence and attitude would cause Spain in the future, the Spanish Legation at Tangier was, on the contrary, in favour of making terms with the brigand, and using him in furtherance of Spanish aims and ambitions. Either policy, if skilfully applied, would probably have been successful, but both put into action at the same moment did not tend to allay Raisuli's suspicions. Eventually he came to Tangier, where at least this time his life was safe ; and while he was actually negotiating with Madrid, the military authorities at Laraiche, exasperated by the difficulties put in their way by his intrigues, confiscated his properties and broke off all relations with him.

Raisuli was once more an outlaw, and took to the mountains. His one object—his one desire— became to make the Spaniards restore his property and to have revenge. It was not long before his schemes took form, and the Spanish troops and military " posts " received no rest. There was constant murder, and constant theft and " sniping,"

and attacks and alarms at night. Civilians, too,
suffered, for any and every Spaniard was an object
of Raisuli's wrath and vengeance.

The brigand's attitude with regard to Spaniards
had never been a secret. He may have cordially
disliked subjects of the other Powers of Europe,
but the inhabitants of the Peninsula he despised.
During the latter period of his outlawry, when he
was threatened with attack by the Sultan's troops,
he had ordered his followers to " capture a Christian " as a hostage. It was no easy matter, for
precaution had been taken at Tangier ; but one
day a band of his men chanced upon a little
caravan of Spanish workmen *en route* from Tetuan
to Tangier. They were promptly seized, and a
messenger was hurriedly sent to Raisuli to announce
that some " Christians " had been taken. The
brigand chief was at this moment in the Beni
Msaour Mountains, and thither the captives were
despatched. When he saw them he waxed exceed-
ing wroth, and turning to his men, he shouted,
" I ordered you to capture me ' Christians ' and you
bring me Spaniards "—and promptly let them go.
He knew by experience that the terms he could
extract from Spain for the ransom of half a dozen
poor Spaniards would be small indeed. In a
former case in which two Spaniards, a boy and a
girl, had been captured from Arzeila, they had both
been killed by the brigands owing to the unfortunate manner in which the negotiations had been
opened by the authorities. In later years, however,
since the occupation of Tetuan by the Spaniards,

the mountain tribes have engaged profitably in local brigandage. They know the exact value of a Spanish soldier or non-commissioned officer, and a Spanish civilian, man or woman, and the price that they can extort without apparently running any risk of eventual punishment. There were several cases of such brigandage in 1919-20, in some cases accompanied by murder.

Raisuli's attitude toward the Spanish authorities and troops caused great anxiety in Spain. The public fretted at the continual loss of life which his resistance to the Spanish occupation of the country occasioned, and General Silvestre, who commanded the troops at Laraiche, was recalled. Negotiations were once more entered into with Raisuli. The terms he demanded and received were extortionate; but Spanish public opinion and the Madrid press demanded a termination to the constant and often heavy losses that the troops were suffering. His terms had to be accepted. He received a little native army of his own, to be paid and armed by Spain, a large monthly stipend, and a host of minor favours. He became practically dictator of the north-western part of the Spanish zone, governing Spaniard and Moor alike. His own " zone " was clearly demarcated, and woe betide any Spaniard who attempted to pass his frontier and enter the country under his jurisdiction. The roads were closed, and there was insecurity under the very walls of Ceuta and Tetuan.

Raisuli was an agent of the Germans long before

the war. He had made contracts with the famous Mannesmann Brothers with reference to mining in the mountain districts, which practically closed those regions to other nationalities and other companies. When war broke out he continued his friendly relations with the German Consuls at Tetuan and Laraiche, and with the many German secret agents that the Spanish zone harboured. Under their guidance he gave active assistance to German criminal intrigue and propaganda, and was in direct relations with the German Embassy at Madrid. The 'Times' of 3rd September 1918 published a translation of a letter from the German Embassy to Raisuli, which contained amongst other things a definite promise of arms and ammunition.

To those who have no personal knowledge of the mountain tribes of Morocco, the perpetual state of anarchy in which they live, the oppression by their lawful and unlawful chiefs, the revenge and murder must seem incredible.

In the Anjera tribe in the early years of this century there were two great families, the Deilans and the Duas. Both were amongst my intimate friends. I had been—always dressed as a native and always received as a welcome guest—at the weddings of several of the Sheikh Deilan's sons in their village on the mountain-tops, where hundreds of the tribesmen would be collected spending the moonlight nights in feasting and singing, for the time of full moon, and generally late spring, summer, or early autumn were chosen for these festivities. What wonderful nights they were ! On the most level spot that could be found in the neighbourhood of the village the mountaineers would congregate, leaving an open circular space in their centre, with vacant " aisles " in the closely-gathered throng radiating into the crowd. To the music of shrill pipes and drums —wild exhilarating music to those who have learned to appreciate it—the dancers, trained boys, would take up their stand in the centre and slowly at first, then faster, begin to dance. These mountain dances have nothing in common with the ordinary oriental dance that is witnessed in the towns and in the plains. There is none of the inartistic and suggestive wriggling that to the European point of view is so ungraceful. Dressed in long loose white garments, almost reaching to their feet, with flowing sleeves held back by cords of coloured silk, and with a small scarf thrown over the head so as to half veil the face, the youths moved gracefully in and out, each dancing alone, and yet fitting his dance into a plan of concerted movement.

The mountain dancing begins by the performers standing motionless for a few moments, the head thrown back, and the arms loosely falling to the side. Then, to the time of the music, there is a sudden quick movement of the feet—a little soft stamping—but without the least motion of the body. As the musicians increase their energy the dancer's body takes life. The movement of the feet is accentuated, and suddenly he glides forward toward his audience, with outstretched arms, raising the scarf from the face for a moment, and then once more the body becomes motionless. But, as if against his will, the music conquers him. The movements become more general. The feet are raised higher from the ground, and the dancer gyrates and falls on one knee, rises again and glides, holding the body almost motionless, up the empty aisles that lie open between the sections of the crowd. Never is the graceful posing abandoned; the veil, now half raised, now drawn down again, the little tremble of the shoulders and the gliding movement of the feet—all has a charm and artistic merit. Every now and again, with a quick turning movement of the body, which sends the loose folds of the long white garment floating round him, the dancer falls on one knee before one of the guests, and, removing the veil, awaits the pressing of a silver coin upon his forehead, and to receive the exaggerated and poetical compliments of the donor.

There is one movement in these dances which is admirable, though there are few who can accomplish it, for it means a complete subjection and training of the muscles. The dancer suddenly stands erect with outstretched arms, the head thrown back. Then from his feet up a little trembling—a little shudder, as it were—passes up the body, to die away in the tips of the fingers of the outstretched hands. In its upward movement each portion of the limbs and body trembles alone; the rest is motionless, and even the trembling is so delicate that it might pass almost unperceived. The rigidity of the body is undisturbed, and one feels rather than sees this ascending "nervous thrill" which illumines the figure, as though giving life to a statue.

But I digress. The Deilans and the Duas were the great families of the Anjera tribe. Of the two the Deilans were the most powerful, for the old Sheikh had many sons and nephews and kinsfolk. Naturally the eternal jealousy arose, and ended in an open quarrel. For a time the two families lived apart, but in the end a reconciliation was arranged. Deilan and his family visited Duas to partake of a great feast to celebrate the termination of their quarrel. While seated over the steaming savoury dishes in the courtyard of Duas's house a signal was given, and Deilan and his sons were shot, many of his retainers also falling victims to the carefully-prepared treachery. For a time Duas was undisputed chief of the tribe in his stronghold on the very summit of a mountain. I had been a prisoner in this house not long before for a few days—during the latter part of the time when I was taken by Raisuli—and my recollection of Duas, whom I knew well, and of his household is a pleasant one. I was treated not only with respect but also with great friendliness, and my time of captivity was rendered as easy and as pleasant as possible.

Then, a little later, the Duas family began to pay the penalty of their treachery and murder. One by one they were " sniped " and died. Sometimes it was by day, sometimes by night, but always a well-directed and unfailing bullet from a Mauser rifle, fired from the rocks or brushwood. Then came the turn of Duas himself. He was riding a mule on his way to a local market surrounded by his retainers. The bullet seemed to avoid his men, and found its mark in their chief. He fell dead. And so the blood-feud went on, carried out by one man alone. He was a nephew of the Sheikh Deilan, by name Ben Ahmed, who had escaped the massacre at Duas's house. I knew him well —a handsome young man, not knowing what fear meant and sworn to revenge. He was shot at last, but he had killed Duas and eleven members of his family. The names of Duas and Deilan are already almost forgotten in the Anjera. If any members of the families still live they have fallen to the unimportance of ordinary tribesmen, and others have arisen in their place.

Of one other Anjera chief a few words must be said. Of all my friends amongst the mountaineers he was the one whose friendship I most valued and appreciated. Sid El Arbi bel Aysh was a member of an important Shereefian family of the Anjera, and a direct descendant of the Prophet Mohammed, and a brigand as well—the two professions so often go together in Morocco! Of undoubted courage—the Spaniards gave him the name of " Valiénte "—he had taken part in many tribal fights, and once, with a handful of his followers, had held his mountain fastness against several hundred tribesmen. His aim was unerring, and woe betide the man at whom he shot. Up

to the end of his short life—he was killed in 1915
—he was a constant visitor of my house, coming
regularly from his mountain home to spend a
week or so at Tangier. He won the heart of
every one he met—a brigand perhaps, but a
brigand against whom no accusation of cruelty
was ever made. With the hereditary manner of
a chief whose family originated 1300 years ago
with the Prophet Mohammed, with a presence
of much grace and manly beauty, with a voice
that charmed and a personality that attracted,
Sid El Arbi bel Aysh was the perfect type of
Moroccan mountaineer gentleman. His open smile,
his good-natured wit, rendered him a *persona grata*
everywhere, and nowhere was he more welcome
than in my house.

Sid El Arbi's moral courage was as great as his
physical courage, for he held himself aloof from
all his tribe when in 1913 they declared war on
the Spaniards. For a long time he refused to
fight, though thereby endangering his own life,
for his fellow-tribesmen at one moment meditated
his assassination on this account. Unfortunately,
however, the Spaniards did not appreciate his
action, nor know how to turn it to their benefit ;
and yet he was perhaps the only loyal friend upon
whom they could have counted in the Anjera.
In the question of a sale of some of his lands,
with the accompanying water rights, to the Spanish
authorities of Ceuta, he was treated in a manner
that is best left undescribed. Briefly, he never
received but a small portion of the purchase price.

Every advantage had been taken of his goodwill
to bargain over the transaction till the sum agreed
upon was preposterously small, and even most of
that he never got. Exasperated at this treatment,
and urged by the gibes of his tribesmen, he eventually took up arms against the Spaniards. A very
few weeks later he was killed in battle, struck down
by a fragment of a shell.

Shortly before his death I had arranged an
interview between him and a high Spanish authority, in the hopes of bringing about a reconciliation
and of obtaining Sid El Arbi bel Aysh's influence
in the interests of peace. Unfortunately the
Spanish official did not realise that he was dealing
not only with a powerful young chieftain but also
with a member of one of the oldest families in
Morocco—and, moreover, a gentleman. With a
want of tact that amounted almost to insult, the
Spaniard asked Sid El Arbi whether the real reason
of his taking up arms against them was because his
wives had stigmatised him as a coward and had
rendered his life unbearable at home. In Moslem
countries one does not talk to a man of his women,
but Sid El Arbi laughed and replied, " No, that
was scarcely the reason."

" I suppose they called you a ' coward ' and a
' Christian ' for not taking up arms against us ? "
continued the unfortunate Spaniard.

I tried my best to change the conversation into
other channels, but it was too late. Again Sid El
Arbi laughed.

" No," he replied again, " it was not that. All

the world knows I am not a coward, and some of
my best friends are Christians."

" Then what made you fight us ? "

" I will tell you," said Sid El Arbi, still smiling,
but very angry. " I bore all the gibes till one day,
in desperation, I was called a ' Spaniard.' That
insult was more than human nature could bear.
From that moment I have been at war with you."
Still smiling, Sid El Arbi rose, and, breaking off
his interview before its object had been reached,
bade adieu to our host and left the house. *

It was the final straw. He returned to the
Anjera, and died fighting a short time after. //

The occupation of Tetuan by the Spaniards in
1912 put an end to all travel in the mountains
of North-West Morocco, where in the past I had
spent so many pleasant months, fishing for trout
and shooting. A few months before the Spanish
troops entered the town the roads were still safe,
and English ladies rode alone over the forty-two-
mile track that led from that town to Tangier.
But nowadays the tribes have completely changed
in character, for they have become distrust-
ful, and are always at war. As late as the
spring of 1912 Sir Reginald Lister, who was
British Minister to Morocco—he died, alas ! in
November the same year—and I made several
excursions overland to Tetuan unaccompanied by
any one except our grooms. Often a mounted
soldier of the police would start with us, but we
always left him far behind, and no doubt he would
turn back. Sir Reginald had bought and restored

a delightful little Moorish house in Tetuan, and
there we spent our week-ends. We would leave
Tangier at eight in the morning, and arrive at
Tetuan at three in the afternoon, with an hour
for lunch *en route* : not bad going, for the distance
is forty-two miles, and the road in many places a
mere stony track. Sometimes, if the going was
heavy, we changed horses half - way, but as a
rule I rode one horse right through. From Tetuan,
delightfully situated overlooking the wide valley,
with its background of rugged peaks, we would
make excursions to the country round, with merely
a man who knew the country as a guide and our
grooms. Leaving early in the mornings, we rode
to the mountain villages, to meet everywhere
with the kindest of welcomes from the people.
Some of these villages had seldom—and perhaps
never—been visited by Europeans, and our coming
caused much interest. At times the tracks were
too rough for our horses, and we would leave them
in charge of our men, and scramble up the rocks
to the little groups of thatched huts that seemed
to hang to the mountain-side. The views were
always beautiful, often extending over the whole
Straits of Gibraltar, which seemed but a narrow
stream dividing the rugged mountains of Africa
from Europe.

Then came the Spanish occupation, and the
closing of all this country. With all the troops at
their disposal, it took several years before these
villages were reached. The mountains, where
many Europeans used to camp and shoot in

perfect security, are as difficult of access to-day as the wildest regions of Central Africa, and far more unsafe. While in the French Protectorate immense regions, unexplored until the advent of the French, can be travelled in perfect security —often by train or motor — the advent of the Spaniards has, on the contrary, tended to close the greater part of the zone which lies under their influence, many parts of which were formerly open to travellers and sportsmen.

It need not have been so. At first things went tolerably well, but want of knowledge of the natives and their ways, want of tact, and want of generosity quickly brought about mis-understandings, with the result which exists to-day —a total absence of security, constant aggression, and little accomplished.

Throughout the whole period of the war Raisuli maintained this pro-German attitude. He pos-sessed at the same time the absolute confidence of the Spanish Government, which supplied him with almost unlimited sums of money, with rifles and ammunition, and with uniforms for his native troops and foodstuffs to feed them. Any one who, from knowledge of the situation or of the man, ven-tured to express an opinion that Raisuli's sentiments toward Spain might be open to doubt, was assailed by official denunciations and press attacks from Madrid. Yet the situation was perfectly clear. Raisuli was gaining time. He was increasing his wealth and his means of resistance—if the situation should require resistance—and gave little or no

R

thought to any one or anything except himself and
his own future.   I sent to him once during the war
and asked him whether it was true he was taking
German money.   He evaded my question in his
answer.   He replied, " If the British or French,
or any other nation have money to give away, I
will willingly accept it—the more the better."

He worked in the interests of Germany because
he was paid to do so, just as he would have worked
in the interests of any other country under similar
circumstances.   When Raisuli realised the results
of the war, and the rejoicings for the signature of
peace were being held at Tangier — it was on
14th July 1919, — Raisuli sent to me to say
that he too was keeping the peace by having
massacred a few hundred Spaniards.   He congratulated France and England, he said, on having got
rid of Germany, and would himself rid the Allies
" of another enemy, Spain."   So much for his
German proclivities.

At the end of the war the condition of affairs
in the Spanish zone was frankly impossible, from
every one's point of view.   The Spaniards had put
their money on the wrong horse; the Allies had
won, and Madrid had to explain away the evil
purposes to which the Spanish Government had
allowed its zone in Morocco to be put—and it was
not an easy explanation.   Too late they began to
expel the German spies and to put down the
intrigue that had been allowed practically free
scope up to then.   Nor was Spain's own position
in her zone a pleasant one.   Even the Spanish

High Commissioner was to all intents and purposes under Raisuli's orders, and no Spaniard could travel in a great part of their zone without a special passport from the brigand chief. One or two who ventured to do so disappeared, and nothing more was heard of them.

At last public opinion in Spain revolted. Raisuli had received millions of pesetas of good Spanish money for which he had rendered no services, unless the prevention of Spanish occupation of the country can be considered as a service. General Jordana, the Spanish High Commissioner, died suddenly in Tetuan, and the Spanish Government decided upon taking action. What amounted to an ultimatum was sent to Raisuli—and disregarded—and a crisis arose. General Berenguer, an able Spanish general with considerable knowledge of Morocco, was appointed Spanish High Commissioner, and successfully inaugurated his period of office by winning over the large and important Anjera tribe to the side of Spain. But even he made too sure of success, and a few days after he had made a declaration to the " Press " stating that there would be no more fighting in Morocco, the Spanish forces received a very severe check at the hands of Raisuli. The series of combats of Wad Ras, began on 11th July, and lasted till 13th July 1919. The Spanish authorities made every attempt to hide the truth of what had occurred, but failed. All the assistance, all the money, and all the arms the Spaniards had for five years been giving to Raisuli were now turned against the donors, as any one who really knew the situation had long realised must ultimately be the case. The small Spanish force operating on the north crests of the Wad Ras hills, about twenty miles from Tangier, was practically cut to pieces. The losses have never been published, but I have every reason to believe that they were about 300 killed and probably 1000 wounded. There were no prisoners, and the Spanish wounded were massacred to a man. Not only were Raisuli's forces, thanks to the generosity of the very people he was attacking, well armed, but they were also possessed of Spanish uniforms, disguised in which they were able to massacre a column of over 170 soldiers. To add to the horrors of this episode, Raisuli's tribesmen came provided with hand-grenades and asphyxiating bombs. This disaster —for, whatever the Spaniards may assert, it was a disaster—led to fresh revelations. The hospitals were reported to be in a shocking state of neglect ; there were no beds for the wounded, and complete disorganisation in every department.

The Spanish Government at last realised that something must be done, or a continuance of the policy hitherto pursued would soon prove fatal to Spanish prestige, not only in Morocco but also in Europe. The general responsible for the fateful incidents of July was dismissed, and General Silvestre, a well-known enemy of Raisuli, was sent from Spain to take command. Vast quantities of material were shipped to Africa, including aeroplanes, tanks, artillery, rifles and ammunition, and, happily, hospital necessaries in sufficient quantities. In two months from the critical days of July the Spanish army in Morocco was prepared once more to advance and to drive Raisuli from his mountain strongholds.

The new campaign began on 27th September 1919. Twelve thousand Spanish troops were collected to form the principal columns which were to encircle the Fondak of Wad Ras, whence Raisuli held the road leading from Tangier to Tetuan. In former days this road was open to traffic, and parties of lady tourists often rode from Tangier to Tetuan accompanied only by a native guide. Since the occupation of Tetuan by the Spaniards, Raisuli had closed this track to all but natives. Its importance to the Spaniards was paramount, for it forms the one direct means of communication between the district of Tetuan and of Laraiche on the Atlantic coast. As long as Raisuli held the Fondak no communication was possible, and to proceed from one town to another in the Spanish zone the only means was by sea. The Spanish forces advanced with caution. Raisuli's tribesmen offered no great resistance. They were powerless in the presence of the immense war material the Spaniards had lately brought to the scene of action. Artillery and aeroplanes harassed them. Shells and bombs burnt their villages, and killed their women and children. The odds were too great. For a moment the operations were checked by a small revolt of native troops behind the Spanish lines. Spanish officers and men were massacred; but the mutiny was suppressed, and the columns, attacking from three directions, drew near the Fondak.

On Saturday, 4th October, there remained only a very few kilometres, and the Spanish troops had already begun the ascent of the slopes leading up to the Fondak. On Sunday morning the surrounding brush-covered hills were heavily bombarded, and the troops advanced on the last stage of their march, burning everything that would burn *en route*. From the hills above Tangier I could see the bursting shells, the explosions of falling bombs, the ruthless destruction of villages by fire—in fact, the ruining of hundreds of families and the rendering desolate dozens of homes, which marks the introduction of civilisation into this part of Morocco.

And somewhere on those mountain-tops Raisuli saw it too, and as he never forgot or forgave the destruction of his castle at Zinat, so he will never forget or forgive this last campaign. He may be impotent to fight a force numerically more than twice his own, and armed with every modern and hideous appliance of war, but, if I know his character and his warfare, he will wage a guerilla campaign of midnight attack and murder that will last long and prove costly in its toll of lives amongst the invaders of his country.

The solution rests with the Spaniards. If they bring prosperity and justice to the natives of their zone they will be left in peace. At present they have brought neither, but much may be hoped

from the Spanish Government, which realises that
the manner of their occupation of Morocco is as
important for the good name of Spain as is their
conduct of affairs in the Peninsula itself. They
must not forget that Raisuli still lives, and that he
is, in his way, the biggest man in Morocco.

There are few countries that could produce a
Raisuli. It necessitates an environment which
exists, perhaps happily, only in such countries as
Morocco. Yet during the last few years of his
career he has made himself famous, and a real
touch of romance surrounds the brigand, who,
born of an aristocratic family, has terrorised and
yet in a way protected Tangier, a city of 40,000
inhabitants, the seat of a dozen legations. In
spite of his celebrity, very few Europeans have
ever seen him. He has seldom, if ever, been
photographed, and never written his name in the
autograph collector's album. He has been throughout a sort of mysterious personage, half-saint, half-
blackguard, whom every courageous male tourist
has volunteered to capture, and many a still
more courageous female tourist to marry. Mulai
Ahmed er-Raisuli is unique—and perhaps, after
all, one of his kind is enough.

SAINTS, SHEREEFS, AND SINNERS

THE political influence that the Moslem " con-fraternities " possess in Morocco is not easy to estimate. In ordinary times of peace and prosperity it is probably very small, but the germ of fanaticism which can never be entirely absent from such cults, might under certain circumstances become a dangerous factor in the situation.

In Morocco reside a large number of Shereefian families, descendants of the Prophet—foremost amongst them that of the reigning Sultan. As Shereefs they claimed in the past, and were permitted, great privileges. They were universally respected, not only as forming a superior and religious nobility, but also on account of their great local influence, which they used as a means of mediation between the secular authorities and the tribesmen. Considered, through their possession of the holy " Báraka "—the birthright of all descendants of the Prophet—as men to whom ordinary laws were not applicable, these great families, especially certain selected representatives of them, possessed extraordinary influence and power. Their advice was sought, and followed, by the country people on every question, and their decisions were accepted as final in all points in dispute, even though at times their judgments might be contrary to the unalterable laws of Islam. Not only did these Shereefs live beyond the reach of the ordinary civil and criminal laws, they were also considered as meriting no punishment for their sins. This immunity from the laws of God and man gave them unlimited opportunity—of which they were usually not slow to take advantage—to practise extortion and tyranny, "frailties" which were accepted in silence by the people, who saw, or imagined they saw, in every act and deed of their Shereefs the guidance of the hand of God.

Existing largely on offerings brought to them, or to the tombs of their ancestors, by pious pilgrims, and upon a system of religious taxation, the Shereefian families formed a class entirely apart, and though often enough thoroughly bad, they not unseldom were of great use in settling intertribal disputes and preventing bloodshed.

To such a class European invasion, or any form of stable and just government, meant ruin, and it is not surprising that it was the Shereefian families who have in the past always been averse to any kind of reform in Morocco.

The arrival of the French in the country was the deathblow to the irregular influence of these families—not, be it understood, that any repression took place, but from the fact that once peace and security existed in the country there was no longer any necessity for them. Intertribal disputes ceased with the advent of good government, and the intervention of the Shereefs ceased with it. The system of general and just taxation put a stop to much of the revenues of these families, for there was no longer any necessity for the tribesmen to pay large sums to an influential Shereef in order to avoid having to pay still larger ones to the Moorish Government. Although it has been the policy of the French to uphold rather than to suppress the great influential families of Morocco, circumstances have nevertheless lessened their repute and prestige. The native himself has " found them out." The spiritual benefits they promised or bestowed—paid for at a rather high price—were not as valuable as the temporal benefits which accrue from a just and reasonable Government. He has found that he can claim as his right, and not as a privilege to be purchased by money, the justice and assistance which he previously had to buy, often without tangible results. The famous Shereefian families of Wazzan, Bou Jad, and Tamshlat are becoming year by year more dependent upon their agricultural estates for their wellbeing, owing to the falling-off in the offerings of the " faithful." The Moor who formerly put a portion of his fortune into unproductive religious investments in the form of offerings to Shereefs, now puts it into real estate. He still respects the Shereefs, he still kisses the hem of their robes, but he keeps his money for himself.

This gradual disappearance of reverence toward the living descendants of the Prophet has not to any great extent diminished the veneration that

is paid to the tombs of deceased saints. Of the
two this veneration of the deceased is preferable
to that of the living, for at all events the buried
Shereef is dead and unable to stir up strife and
rebellion. The French policy has been extremely
able with regard to the "holy places" and
"tombs"—for which the authorities demand the
greatest respect, and which they themselves treat
with respect, even so far as assisting by influence
and gifts the prestige of the tomb or mosque as
the case may be. It is this respect for the person
and tradition of dead saints and scholars that has
given so strong an impetus to the "confraternities"
or sects of Moslem Morocco.

The study of the introduction of these "confraternities" is beyond the scope of this work.
It is sufficient to state that many of them had
their origin in the early days of Islam, some even
before the time of the Baghdad Khalifs, whose
literary tastes and erudition introduced the ideas
of Indian and Greek philosophy into a religion the
principal attribute of which is its simplicity and lack
of imagination. It may almost be said that the
only want of judgment exhibited by Mohammed
in originating the faith of Islam was in depriving
his followers of what is so necessary to all oriental
character, an environment of mysticism. But the
want supplied itself, for so prosaic a religion as
Islam in its crude form was irreconcilable with
the traditions and characteristics of the Arab
nature. One of the first innovations was the
invention of the "Báraka"—or holy birthright

pertaining to descendants of the Prophet—which doctrine helped not a little to cause the first great split in Islam, the separation of the Sunni and the Sheiya. By the close of the second century A.H. the traditions of Pantheism and the learning of India and Greece had so permeated the Moslem world that there arose an old cult under a new name—Sufism—the traces of which exist to-day in every one of the sects and " confraternities " of Morocco.

More than the briefest survey of Sufism is impossible here, but brief as it is, it will be sufficient to show how entirely the doctrine stands apart from orthodox Islam.

To the Sufi the world is an illusion. It is merely a collection and massing together of the shapes and forms of things which have no real existence, being but the lights and shadows of the reflection and " essence " of the Deity. Given this theory, the Sufi considers that the highest ideal of life, and its ultimate aim, is the merging of all individuality in this vague " essence " of the Deity. It can well be imagined how a doctrine of such a character can be misunderstood and misconstrued amongst an ignorant people, and to-day, in the place of pure Sufism, with its seeking after ideals, we find a number of sects, one and all founded on Sufism, but most of them erring far from its primitive aim. Yet the very incomprehensibleness of these doctrines to the larger part of the people who have adopted them has given a great impetus to the success of these " confraternities." The real philosophy has been lost, and its place has been taken by a belief, the more attractive in that it is inexplicable, that the repetition of certain prayers and extracts from the Koran has mystical powers tending to accomplish the aim in view, the effacement of individuality. It is curious that no cabalistic forms are used in this " dikr " —or formulæ—and that even to the most strict Moslem it would be difficult to find fault with the outward and visible form of the tenets of the " confraternities." Yet though in all North Africa the greater part of the population adheres to the orthodox Maleki school of Islam, these sects are so impregnated with Sufism, and even with Neo-Platonism, as to be, one and all, completely unorthodox.

In order that the importance of these sects may be realised, a few words are necessary as to their organisation, for they owe their strength principally to the system by which the various centres are kept in touch with one another, and obedience to supreme orders guaranteed.

Each " confraternity " has its central " zaouia " or sanctuary, where either the chief of the sect resides or its founder is buried. From these centres their policy is promulgated, and by means of subordinate " zaouias," each under the charge of a spiritual " Sheikh " or " mokaddem," orders are passed on to the devotees. The larger " zaouias " consist usually of a group of buildings containing a mosque and quarters for pilgrims, and for the education of the " tholba," or scholars, all of whom are kept supplied with food from the funds at the disposal of the local officials. It is at these "zaouias" that the initiation of the devotees takes place, and that the followers of each sect gather together from time to time for religious intercourse and services. Scarcely a town exists in Morocco that has not "zaouias" of at least half a dozen saints. All over the country districts, too, they are found, often consisting of only a thatch hut in the vicinity of some revered tomb, but none the less a spot for the concentration of the devotees, and the object of many a long and weary pilgrimage.

It is not necessary that the "Sheikhs" of the sects, or even the founder, should be a descendant of the Prophet, though such is often the case. In some sects the choice of the supreme chief is elective, in some it is hereditary, as in the Wazzan family. In others, again, it is neither elective nor hereditary, it being left to divine agency to disclose who the heaven-appointed "Sheikh" may be. In this latter case, on the death of a "Sheikh," no move is made to name or discover his successor. In due time it "becomes known" that a certain adept at a certain spot is the new chief, and he is at once accepted as the spiritual leader. He need perform no miracle; he need possess no mark or sign to disclose his calling; he may be, and generally is, of extreme poverty; and it is not apparently necessary that he should have any great personal qualifications. There can be no doubt that this curious system of nominating their religious "Sheikhs," though not always put into practice and becoming rarer, is but an example of the secrecy with which their plans are made and carried out, and that the man is really chosen by a secret council without even the knowledge of the individual himself. Word is surreptitiously sent to the heads of all the "zaouias," and upon a given day it is announced to the faithful that a new "Sheikh" has "appeared" in such and such a spot. The frequenters of "zaouias," hundreds of miles apart, obtain the information upon the same day, and the credulous people consider it a revelation from God. The "Derkaoua" are the principal sect that follow this course.

In the hands of the supreme chief lies the selection of the minor "Sheikhs," who in turn possess certain limited powers in the nominating of the "mokaddems," or lesser officials, all of whom have the right, as a rule, of initiating devotees, and all of whom are agents for the collection of funds.

The general and public tenets of the sects are good enough: chastity, patience, poverty, obedience, and prayer are the principal teachings, though the "derouich," who abandons the ways of the world, and the "khoddam," who is merely an adherent, follow different rules of life and conduct.

The importance of these Moroccan confraternities depends entirely upon the political influence that they are able to exert. When left to themselves, in ordinary times, they consist of

little more than religious institutions and brother-
hoods, of which the concealed energies, such as
they are, are not called forth by circumstances.
It is only when they come directly into contact
with Europe and Europeans that their essentially
religious features might become impregnated with
anti-Christian policy. A " Jehad " or " Holy War,"
accepted and furthered by the united sects of
Morocco, might be very dangerous, but, happily,
it is also very improbable.

Perhaps the most renowned of all the Shereefian
families of Morocco is that of Wazzan (Ouezzan).
Descended from the Prophet, the Shorfa of Wazzan
can boast of an unbroken lineage for thirteen
centuries, though it was not until a couple of
hundred years ago that they became of great
account. Up to that period they had apparently
lived the ordinary devout lives of people of holy
descent, no doubt looked up to and probably the
recipients of many offerings. The last few genera-
tions have, however, enjoyed a great renown
throughout Morocco—Mulai Abdullah Shereef, Sid
el Haj el-Arbi, and Sid el-Haj Abdesalam. The
last named, who died some twenty-five years ago,
married an English lady, still residing at Tangier,
who carries on there many good and charitable
works amongst the Moors. It was she who introduced vaccination into the country, and herself
has vaccinated many thousands of the people.
She is much loved by the Moors and respected by
the Europeans. Her husband, Sid el-Haj Abdesalam, had, by previous marriages with native

s

women, three sons, who at the time of which I write—the end of the 'eighties and the early 'nineties of the last century—resided in Wazzan. In my early journeys I often visited this fanatical and difficult district, and became great friends of the two elder brothers. In 1889-90 I spent many months at their little religious Court, the only European in any of those regions.

It was a life of great interest: there were constant relays of pilgrims, who came to pray at the tombs of the ancestors of the family and to bring offerings to its living members. They would arrive by dozens, and sometimes by hundreds—men, women, and children, with caravans of mules, ponies, and camels, laden with grain and other products of the country as an offering to the " House of Surety," as it was called by the natives. These pilgrims, who were lodged and fed by the Shereefs, were generally received in audience the day after their arrival. The Shereefs, Mulai el-Arbi and Sidi Mohamed, received them separately, either in their little walled gardens, full of running water and flowers, or else in one of the courtyards of the " zaouia " or sanctuary. Often Mulai el-Arbi would be seated just inside an open window, through which the passing pilgrims could bend to kiss his holy raiment, while an offering in money was laid upon the window-sill, to be dropped into a basket by the Shereef as each pilgrim proceeded on his way. When the entire string of visitors had passed, Mulai el-Arbi would count his newly-acquired wealth. Although the sums were never great—for the population of Morocco was in its worst days of oppression—the total received during the autumn and winter pilgrim season was no mean one.

The two brothers, Mulai el-Arbi and Mulai Mohamed, were of entirely different characters. The elder was religious and timid, while his brother, Mulai Mohamed, was a hunter and a man of courage and action, whose influence over the surrounding wild mountain tribes was very great. He did not hesitate to use force when he considered it necessary. During the period of my stay at Wazzan the town was constantly attacked. The Shereefs had organised a garrison for its defence, consisting of their followers and slaves, who were well armed and well supplied with ammunition. Sometimes these attacks were really serious, though the casualties were never very great. On one occasion the enemy lost a dozen killed, but, as far as I know, this was the largest number of losses on any one day.

I was present on one occasion when an attempt was made to assassinate Mulai Mohamed. He was seated in a room which was built over an archway across a street. Opening on to the street at either end of this room were two large windows. The ground below sloped upwards, so that any one higher up the street could see right through the room. It was here that Mulai Mohamed often sat, surrounded by particular friends and retainers. We were there one afternoon drinking green tea, the favourite beverage of Morocco,

while a relation of the Shereefs was reading aloud
from an old Arabic manuscript. Suddenly the
glass of the windows at both ends of the room
was broken, and simultaneously we heard the report of a rifle. There was a little panic amongst
the guests, but Mulai Mohamed, without a
moment's hesitation, ordered his cousin to continue the reading. The bullet had passed through
the room, just missing the Shereef. The would-be
assassin was never discovered. The shot had been
fired from the upper end of the street a hundred
yards or so away, and no clue was ever obtained
as to who fired it.

Wazzan was the home of tragedy. Except for
the paramount influence of the Shereefian family
there was no Government of any kind. The
Sultans had at various periods attempted to en-
force their jurisdiction, but had never succeeded.
Although ostensibly on good terms with the
Shereefs, the jealousy between the reigning family
and Wazzan was intense. The followers of the
Shereefs, and such tribal villages which were
counted as special devotees of the " zaouia,"
paid no taxes, and were outside the jurisdiction
of the Sultan's governors. The result was constant
friction; but the Wazzanis' religious influence
was so strong, and in such fear was their name
held, that on the whole the Shereefs were able to
set the Sultan's word at nought.

Both Mulai el-Arbi and Mulai Mohamed are
long since dead. The elder brother was insane
for some years before his death, and the last time

I saw him his mind was completely deranged. He was seated in a chair in the centre of a semicircle of his women, who were, of course, closely veiled, though it was contrary to all tradition that they should be there at all. Besides his ladies, the room contained several live sheep and a host of fowls, ducks, and pigeons. He had changed but little in appearance. I noticed that his retainers, who introduced me, paid perhaps more deference to the mad Shereef than they had done in the days of his health; but oriental people have a strange reverence for insanity. Mulai el-Arbi made no sign of recognition, and sat immovable. I recalled to him the months I had spent as his guest and incidents of my many visits, but to no avail. He listened, but made no reply, though from time to time I noticed a puzzled look on his face. I made a move to go, but with his hand he beckoned me to be seated again, and once more I continued trying to recall the wandering memory of my host. At last a gleam stole into his eyes, and he said very slowly, " Yes, and greyhounds ; lots of greyhounds." He had remembered ; for, hunting often, I had kept quite a number of native " slougis " in the days of my stay at Wazzan. It was all he said. He died a few months later.

Some idea of the sanctity of this man even in his own household can be gathered from an incident which occurred during one of my visits. A china teacup of considerable value was missing after tea had been served. The slaves were summoned, and one was accused by the Shereef—it must be confessed on no evidence—of having stolen it. He was severely beaten: when I say severely beaten, he received a flogging that would probably have killed a European. That night, after the Shereef had retired into his house, I went to see the slave, who, considering the terrible punishment he had received, was bearing up very well. I asked him if he was guilty of the theft. His reply was pathetic. " I have no recollection of having stolen the teacup, but I must have done so, for my lord the Shereef has divine knowledge, and could not have made a mistake." The cup was found and the slave proved guiltless, but he received a severe reprimand for not having been able to prove his innocence from the first.

Mulai Mohamed, the younger of the two brothers, predeceased Mulai el-Arbi. He died of a lingering and painful malady. He was by far the most attractive of the two—a sportsman, energetic and witty. I accompanied him on many a great hunt in the Wazzan districts, when wild boar, jackals, hares, and partridges were slain galore—driven from their covert by hundreds of tribesmen. Often these hunts lasted several days, and the evenings and nights were spent under canvas in feasting and revelry: great days and great nights !

The third brother, Mulai Thami, had also a tragic end. He had served as a youth in the French Army in Algeria, and had learnt to read and write French, but he had fallen a victim to

intemperance. He was a good deal younger than
his two brothers, and the son of another wife,
and considerable jealousy existed between them.
He complained that his share of the revenues did
not reach him, and that he was often sorely in
need of money. When drunk he at times became
very violent ; on other occasions he was charming,
an excellent conversationalist, and he had received a good education. Drink at length affected
his brain, and a series of incidents led to his
imprisonment. I was at Wazzan at the time. In
a fit of madness he fired from a window of his
house upon people passing to the mosque to
prayer. Several were killed, but his sanctity
rendered him immune from any punishment. The
townspeople stated it was the " Will of God,"
manifested through the holy Shereef, and some
even envied the people who had found death at
his hands. All that was done was to post a soldier
in front of his house to warn the passers-by that
there was a risk of being shot ! The same night
Mulai Thami wrote me a letter. It is undated—
it was December 1889—and is written in French :—

" Mon cher Ami,—Je vous prie de dire à mes
frères que je les remercie beaucoup de m'avoir
envoyer encore un soldat pour me tuer, parceque
aujourd'hui j'ai monté dans mon ' couba ' pour
prendre un peu d'air. Comme je regardai par la
fenêtre je voyai un soldat armé de sa carabine.
J'avais peur, alors j'ai armé sur lui ma carabine,
mais comme il m'a dit qu'il ne me fera rien je
l'ai laissé passé tranquilement. Aussitôt est allé

dire à mes frères que j'ai voulu le tuer. Je vous jure par la tête de notre Prophète Mohamet si je voudrai faire ça j'ai d'autres endroits où je pourrai tuer tout ce qui passe, mais seulement je ne suis pas fou. J'ai tué ces hommes parceque j'étais ivre, et puis en colère, à cause du voyage et à cause d'une histoire entre moi et un chérif. Je vous jure, mon cher ami, que je n'avais pas la tête à moi.

"Maintenant, cher ami, dites à Muley el-Arbi qu'il me rend mon mulet et qu'il m'envoie de l'argent, car je crève de faim, moi et ma famille.

"Je vous prie de faire votre possible avec mes frères pour me sauver la vie à moi et ma pauvre mère. Le coup de fusil qu'il m'a donné le soldat ne m'a attrapé.

"C'est comme ça qu'on doit être les frères ?

MULEY TOUHAMI."

(Translation.)

"MY DEAR FRIEND,—I beg you to tell my brothers that I thank them very much for having sent still another soldier to kill me, for to-day I went up to my couba (upper room) for a little air. As I looked out of the window I saw a soldier armed with his rifle. I was afraid, and I aimed my rifle at him, but as he told me he would do nothing I let him pass quietly. He at once went to my brothers to say that I had wished to kill him. I swear to you on the head of our Prophet Mohamed that if I had wished to do so I have other places from which I could kill every one who passes, only I am not mad. I killed those men because I was drunk, and also angry on account of a journey and on account of a story between me and a Shereef. I swear to you, my dear friend, that I was ' off my head.'

" Now, dear friend, ask Mulai el-Arbi to return me my mule, and that he send me some money, for my family and I are starving.

" I beg you to do your utmost with my brothers, so as to save my life and that of my poor mother. The shot that the solider fired missed me.

" Is it thus that brothers should be ?

MULEY TOUHAMI."

He omitted to state in this letter that he had, as well as killing the people he speaks of, attempted to murder the two sons of his brother Mulai Mohamed, by firing on them inside the mosque !

On Christmas night, a few weeks after these incidents, I went to see Mulai Thami, who had been sober and in his right mind for some time. We were to go hunting the next day at dawn, and a few details of our excursion still remained to be settled. I had supper with him, but on leaving the supper-room in which we had spent the evening I was treacherously attacked by the Shereef and his slaves. In the struggle I fell down the steep flight of stairs. My call for help had alarmed some passers-by, and the Shereef's retainers heard voices in the street. They fled, and their master disappeared into the inner part of the house. After a short period of unconsciousness I was able to open the door and get out into the street—a pitiful figure, my clothes torn to rags and stained with blood from a wound on the head, happily only skin-deep, and much bruised.

Mulai Thami was imprisoned. After a period of incarceration at Wazzan he was taken to Tangier, but he had become quite insane, and on being brought into the presence of his father, Sid el-Haj Abdesalam, who still lived at Tangier, he wanted to assassinate him. He was confined at Tangier, and some little time later was sent to a lunatic asylum in France, where he lived for several years, suffering from the strange delusion for a Mohammedan—that he was Jesus Christ.

Wazzan was at this period the most lawless place in Morocco. Many murders of important personages took place. The almost total immunity of the Shereefs from punishment—for it was only this head of the family who had the right to imprison them, a right dangerous to exercise for fear of reprisals—increased crime. One instance will be sufficient to demonstrate the absolute anarchy which existed.

A Fez merchant, who was residing at Wazzan at this time, possessed a daughter who was reputed to be of great beauty. A Shereef asked the father for his daughter's hand in marriage, and was refused. The Fez merchant desired her to marry a young man of his own native town, and the Shereef in question was quite undesirable. In time the wedding of the young Fezzi and the girl took place. It was night, and the bridegroom rode at the head of the procession, which had proceeded to fetch the bride from her father's house. In the gaily-decorated " Amaría "—a sort of box carried on a mule's back—was the bride, surrounded by her relations. Many of the crowd carried lanterns, and the air rang with the gay music of drums and fifes. Suddenly the procession was attacked by a group of men emerging from a side street. It was the disappointed Shereef and his retainers. The bridegroom was shot, the guests dispersed, and the bride carried off to the house of the Shereef, who forthwith married her.

Wazzan, surrounded by its gardens and olive groves, is one of the most picturesque towns in Morocco. It is situated on the eastern slopes of a double-peaked mountain, with an extensive view over range after range of wild hills to the highlands, often snow-covered, of the Sheshouan district. Snow often falls, and lies for two or three days together, in Wazzan itself. The result is inconvenient, for as fast as it accumulates on the flat roofs of the houses the inhabitants shovel it off into the streets, which at times are completely blocked. Situated on the borders of the " Jibala " —" mountaineer "—country there is no district more turbulent, and Wazzan has been for several years unvisited by Europeans. It falls in the French sphere of influence, and its occupation by the Protectorate troops has lately been spoken of as imminent.[1] The town has lost much of its religious prestige. All over Morocco the reverence for the many Shereefian families is disappearing, the native finding that the spiritual return in blessings is scarcely worth the financial sacrifice that is entailed to obtain them. In fact, the days

[1] Wazzan was occupied by the French Protectorate troops in October 1920.

of the " Holy Shereefs " are nearing an end, though there is still a new rôle for them to play in Morocco. Their influence, if exerted for good, may yet be very beneficial to the country, and the sons and grandsons of the English wife of Sid el-Haj Abdesalam are setting a good example. Her eldest grandson, who speaks French and English perfectly, is to-day a brilliant young cadet of the Protectorate army in the new military school for the sons of " Nobles " at Meknés. His younger brothers are to enter various professions, in which they can look for every success in the future.

The following sects are the most influential and numerous in Morocco :—

Derkaoua.—Followers of Mulai el-Arbi ben Ahmed el-Derkaoui, who was born about 1730, and is buried in the tribe-lands of the Beni Zerual tribe, in the mountains of North-West Morocco, to the north of Fez. He was a Shereef, or descendant of the Prophet, and a renowned scholar. He himself practised the cult of the Chedili sect, a branch of the better-known Kaderia, or followers of Mulai Abdul Kader el-Ghrailani of Baghdad.

The order of the " Derkaoua " is certainly the most powerful in Morocco. It is, as a rule, entirely religious, but would be capable of speedy secret organisation and combined political action. It is a " socialistic " and " ascetic " sect, depreciating all temporal rulers, and only accepting the Sultans of Morocco on the grounds of their Shereefian descent. They accentuate the great doctrine of Islam, the Unity of God, and consider the

Prophet and all other holy men of secondary importance, though they reverence them. They may perhaps best be described as the Unitarians of Morocco. Besides counting a very large number of devotees amongst the middle classes, the sect boasts many professional adherents, for the most part beggars, who can be recognised by their rosaries of exaggeratedly large beads.

The political influence—at present non-existing, but capable of almost instantaneous appearance, should circumstances bring it to life—of this sect is important. Exerted in the interests of peace and order, it might prove invaluable in a time of trouble, for not only is the sect very numerous, but it could also bring much pressure to bear on the people, and other sects. On the contrary, should the Derkaoua proclaim a campaign against Europeans and European influence, their power would be equally strong in the interests of evil, especially in stirring up other religious sects of more fanatical tenets, such as the Aissaoua and Hamacha.

The Derkaoua seem to be the only confraternity in Morocco that still maintains intact their secret organisation.

Aissaoua.—Followers of Sidi ben Aissa. A sect dating from the seventeenth century A.D.; the founder is buried at Meknés, where the great annual festival in his honour is held, on the Mouloud, or Prophet's birthday. The adherents of this sect are principally people of the lower classes. They resemble more the " dervishes " of the East than the generality of the other Moroccan sects, for they dance, and work themselves into a state of wild frenzy, in which they devour live sheep, glass, burning coals, the leaves of the "prickly pear," and other equally indigestible food. A number of fables, of little interest, are stated as being the origin of these very unorthodox proceedings, which are looked on askance by the educated Moor. Sidi ben Aissa is also the patron saint of the snake-charmers.

Although when excited to a state of frenzy the "Aissaoua" are capable of acts of fanaticism, they are in their ordinary lives, as a rule, peaceful law-abiding people. There are "zaouias" of the sect all over Morocco, presided over by "Sheikhs" and "mokaddems"; but their organisation appears to be almost entirely localised, and therefore capable of no sudden political combination—nor need such be looked for in any case. There are a certain number of professional adherents, musicians, reciters, snake-charmers, who travel from town to town, and live on charity.

Hamacha.—Followers of Sidi Ali ben Hamdouch, who is buried on the slopes of the Zarhoun Mountains, near Meknés. Like the Aissaoua, whom they much resemble, they are principally people of the lower classes. When worked into a state of religious frenzy, they cut their heads with hatchets and throw up heavy cannon-balls which they let fall on their skulls. They are capable of fanaticism when in a frenzical state, but peaceful citizens in ordinary life.   There are a few professional Hama-cha, who perform in the towns and country markets for money.

Taibiya.—Followers of Mulai Taiyeb, son of Mulai Abdullah Shereef, of Wazzan.   Mulai Taiyeb lived in the early nineteenth century, and is buried at Wazzan.   The adherents of this sect are, as a rule, respectable middle-class people.   A member of this Shereefian family is always the chief of this order.

Ulad Sidi Ahmed ou Mousa.—"Sons of Sidi Ahmed ou Mousa."   The patron saint of all the acrobats.   This Shereef was a descendant of Mulai Idris, and died early in the thirteenth century.   No political importance of any kind.

Tijania.—Followers of Sidi Ahmed el-Tijani. The adherents of this sect are few in Morocco, though strong in Algeria.   Essentially religious.

Shingata.—Followers of the Shereef M'al-Ainin of Shingit, in the far south of Morocco.   The sect was founded by this Shereef, who only died five years ago.   He was of very holy reputation, and was always veiled.   The Sultans Mulai Hassen and Mulai Abdul Aziz paid him the greatest respect, and loaded him with presents on his periodical visits to the Court.   On his death he was succeeded by his son, Mohamed Hiba, who took advantage of the disturbed period of 1912 to declare himself Sultan.   He even entered Marra-kesh, the southern capital, but fled on the approach of the French forces.

Mohamed Hiba was always in revolt, but never venturing out of the southern Sus districts, where an expeditionary force attacked him in 1917, defeating his followers, who were dispersed. He died in 1919.

Kaderia.—Followers of Mulai Abdul Kader el-Ghrailáni, of Baghdad, where he is buried. This " confraternity " has numerous adherents in Morocco, which Mulai Abdul Kader is supposed to have visited. He died in the twelfth century A.D.

It is a strictly religious sect, differing from others solely in the form of prayer used, and in the position taken up when at prayer, and " in the absorbing of the individual in the essence of the Deity " by repetitions of the name of God. This sect shows more traces of Sufism, being of Persian origin, than any other cult in Morocco, but its original practices seem to have become adapted to Moroccan thought and sentiment. It is strictly religious, and it is difficult to say whether it could play any political rôle.

Nasaria.—Followers of Sidi ben Nasr, who is buried at Tamgrout, on the Wad Draa. An essentially religious and innocuous sect.

Kittaniin.—Followers of Sidi Mohamed el-Kittani, who was beaten to death by order of the Sultan Mulai Hafid in 1909. His martyrdom appears to have given a great impetus to his followers, who are increasing in numbers, especially in Fez. A religious sect.

There are, in addition to the " zaouias " of

the " confraternities," a large number of tombs
which are visited as places of pilgrimage. It is
usual for one day in the year to be set aside for
the festival at each of these tombs, and great
crowds proceed to these " mousim." A general
holiday is kept in the surrounding districts, and
pilgrims arrive from far and near. Often if the
tomb is situated in the country a whole town of
tents springs up around it.

The following is a list of the principal tombs,
given in the order of their relative importance :—

The tomb of Mulai Idris I., in the mountains of
  Zarhoun (died 790 A.D.)

The tomb of Mulai Idris II., at Fez (died 828(?)
  A.D.)

The tomb of Mulai Abdesalam ben Mashish
  (died twelfth century A.D.), in the mountains of the Beni Aros in North-West
  Morocco.

The tomb of Mulai Brahim in the Ghergaya district, on the northern slopes of the great
  Atlas, to the south of Marrakesh.

The tomb of Mulai Ali Shereef at Tafilet) died
  1590 A.D.)

The tomb of Mulai Busseta el-Khammar in
  Fichtala, to the north of Fez (twelfth century A.D.)

The tombs of Sebat er-Rejal, " the Seven
  Men " (i.e., the seven patron saints of
  Marrakesh).

The tomb of Mulai Bou Shaib at Azimour.

T

The tomb of Sidi Ben Daoud at Bu Jad, on the plains of Central Morocco.

The tomb of Mulai Bouselham, on the sea-shore of the Gharb province, not far from Laraiche.

The tomb and hot springs of Mulai Yakoub, near Fez.

CHANGES AND CHANCES

THE change that is taking place, and will still for a long time be taking place, in Morocco must be gradual. The deep conservatism of the people— the spirit that kept the country closed for century after century to Europe—has not yet disappeared. It is, except in the case of the more remote tribes, less an open opposition to reform than an unceasing disinclination to any alteration in their status. In many ways it is better it should be so —old bottles cannot stand too much new wine— and little by little the Moor and the tribesman is imbibing the new state of things without appreciating, or at least without fully realising, the great change that is already coming about.

There is no doubt that effectively it is easier to organise civilisation, primitive though it may at first have to be, amongst the savage tribes of Central Africa than to try and adapt, and necessarily to some extent to destroy, what has previously existed. The state of civilisation of Morocco has for centuries been a high one compared to most of Africa. It has been, it is true, for a long period in its decadence, but none the less possessing certain admirable features. The institutions of the country, the architecture and art, the remnants of learning, the water-supplies of Fez and Marrakesh, the manners of the people and their capacity as merchants, traders, and agriculturists, all bespeak evidences of an attainment of civilisation, uninfluenced for many centuries past by Europe, that can only be considered as admirable. There has been little or no progress. The Moors lived on the mere echo of the past, but were proud both of that past and of the spirit that they had inherited from it—a spirit of closing the door of their country to all aggression, and the door of their hearts to all external influence.

When it does come—the beginning of the great change, as it has come in Morocco—the new system must expect to be met with suspicion and unpopularity. In course of time the benefits will be fully recognised, and some gratitude will be shown, but it may be a very long time. Few people in the world really appreciate radical change, especially if radical change is forced upon them by foreigners in race, in language, and in religion. Yet, on the whole, the Moor of Morocco is meeting it in the same stolid spirit of disinterest as he bore the former persecutions of his own Sultans and Government. He accepts all as the will of God, but finds that he has now for the first time —I am speaking of the French Protectorate of Morocco—security of life and property. He dislikes all foreigners, but he acknowledges the improvement in his situation. He is richer, happier than

he was. This he puts down to the merciful provi-
dence of God. In return he has to pay regular
taxation, which he particularly dislikes; and
that he puts down to the intervention of the
French. He eases his conscience, and takes advantage of the situation.

Yet gradual as the change is, much has already
been accomplished. Only those who knew the
country before and who know it now can realise
the extent of what has been done. When the
French bombarded Casablanca and thus opened
the road to their occupation of the greater part
of Morocco, they entered a closed house, tenanted
by suspicion, fanaticism, and distrust. The country
considered itself impregnable, and the people
looked upon the "Christians" as a despised
race, condemned by their religion, unwarlike by
nature, and ridiculous in appearance. The Moor
imagined that with a small Moslem army, aided
by divine assistance, he could easily defeat all the
"Christian" forces of the world. "Your shells
and bullets will turn to water," they said, "for
the saints and holy men who protect us will never
allow the infidel to invade our land. Storms will
wreck your ships, and even should your soldiers
land, a handful of our horsemen would suffice to
drive them back into the sea." They really
believed it.

What a change has come about since then—
and it is only thirteen years ago that the bombardment of Casablanca took place! From time to
time I accompanied the expedition that invaded

the Chaouia and the highlands beyond it, when
one by one the tribes gave way and acknowledged
that those two French columns, advancing and
ever advancing, were stronger than all the saints
in their tombs and than all the Holy Men with
their promises of victory. The Moor had to realise
a fact. It was very difficult at first. It changed
his whole aspect of life, his whole mentality. A few
thousand Christians were conquering his country !
And the two columns were as irresistible as the
fact itself. He took refuge in the supreme solace
of his religion—cried, " It is the will of God " ;
laid his rifle aside, and either went back to the
fields or enlisted in the French Army.

Behind the show of force there was another
and still more important factor at work. As
district after district was occupied and the troops
passed on, there sprung up a new organisation, a
new administration that safeguarded the interests
of the people, their lives and their properties.
They experienced, for the first time for centuries,
security. The ever-present fear of death, confiscation, and imprisonment, under the shadow of
which they had passed their whole lives, as had
their parents and their ancestors before them,
disappeared. The extortion of the " Kaids "
ceased, or was greatly curtailed, and justice was
obtainable.

In the introduction of civilisation the French
have shown admirable tact. Their every act and
thought has been influenced by a desire to amelio-
rate the condition of the people and to render them

prosperous. They have built endless roads. They have opened hospitals and dispensaries, and everything has been avoided that could wound the religious susceptibilities of the people. They had the experience of Algeria and Tunis. They studied our action in Egypt. They have known what to adopt and what to avoid. They have maintained upon the throne a descendant of the ancient line of Sultans, and, governing in his name, they have been able to obtain an elasticity of administration which the codified laws of France could never have given, had a system of direct government been adopted. They have met with far less opposition than might have been expected. In fact, the introduction of civilisation into Morocco, in times of great difficulty during the war, has been a fine example of the true spirit of pacification and progress. I, who have known Morocco for over thirty years, can bear witness that in the parts of the country occupied by France the improvement in the welfare of its people is immense. There is yet much to be done. Decades must pass before the work is completed, but I am convinced that the great policy inaugurated by General Lyautey in Morocco will be accepted as the basis of government—to the mutual benefit of the " Protecting " and the " Protected."

Yet there are those who still talk of the " good old days " of Morocco before the French came to the country ! That any one can regret that time is incredible. Only those who failed to see beneath the surface—and how little surface there was to hide the facts—can possible compare the two periods. The most that can be said against the French régime is that the native finds the introduction of regulations annoying. He has regular taxes to pay instead of suffering the extortion of his own authorities, as he did in the past. He dislikes regularity, and some Moors would probably prefer the uncertainty and gambling chances of the past to the uneventful prosperity of the present. It is true there was the risk of death, of confiscation, of imprisonment; but there was also the chance of loot and robbery, of acquiring a position by force or by bribery, and of being able, in tolerable security, to confiscate the property of others and put others in prison; and if in the end one died in prison oneself—well, it was God's will. The Moor is a gambler. He staked under that old régime not only his fortune but his life. Often he lost both; but sometimes he won, and it was the lives of others that were sacrificed and their properties that accrued till a great estate was built up, till palaces were built in all the capitals, till his slaves were legion and his women buzzed like a swarm of bees—and then one day the end came. If fate was kind he died in possession of his estates—and they were confiscated on the day of his death; but more often he died in prison while his family starved. Meanwhile nothing could be imagined more pitiable than was the lot of the country people, victims of robbery of every kind, for, from the Sultan to the village sheikh, the whole Maghzen pillaged and lived on the poor. No man could call his soul his own. Thank God, the " good old days " are gone and done with!

I sometimes wonder whether, in spite of all that has been written on the subject, the state of affairs existing in Morocco up to the date of the introduction of the French Protectorate in 1912 is fully realised.

While Mulai Hafid was Sultan, from 1908 to 1912, in which year he abdicated, the palace was the constant scene of barbarity and torture. The Sultan himself, neurasthenic, and addicted, it is said, to drugs, had his good and his bad days. There was no doubt that at first he meant to reform his country—or perhaps, more correctly, to save it from the encroaching intervention of France. He was possessed of a certain cunning intelligence, and had some idea of government, but disappointment met him. Things had gone too far. Morocco was doomed. Finding all his attempts to preserve his country's independence futile, he gave way to temptations, and became cruel and avaricious.

Rebels taken in the war—many, no doubt, were harmless tribesmen—had their hands and feet cut off. Twenty-six were thus tortured at Fez in one day. Twenty-five succumbed, mostly to gangrene ; for though the European doctors in Fez implored the Sultan to be allowed to attend them, Mulai Hafid refused. Publicly the butchers cut and hacked from each of these unfortunate men a hand and a foot, treating the stumps with pitch. The one survivor of that particular batch is living to-day.

Earlier in his reign—in 1909—Mulai Hafid became jealous of a young Shereef, Sid Mohamed el-Kittani, a member of a great family, who, having taken to a religious life, had gathered round him a group of cultured men and founded a sect. People spoke much of him ; his popularity and reputation were great. From the precincts of the palace the Sultan followed his every move-ment, and spies reported his every word, but no excuse could be found for his arrest. But Mulai Hafid was determined that he must be got rid of. He let the young Shereef understand that he was in danger, that the Sultan meant to arrest him, and, influenced by a spy, the young man was per-suaded to abandon Fez. He fled by night—straight into the trap. He was allowed to reach the Beni Mtir tribe-lands, and there he was arrested. Mean-while the report was spread that he had tried to get himself proclaimed Sultan, and evidence to this effect was easily produced. He was brought back to Fez—I saw him brought a prisoner into the palace—and in the presence of Mulai Hafid he was flogged. Blow after blow from knotted leathern cords was rained upon his back and legs, till, life almost extinct, he was carried away and thrown into a prison in the palace. He was not even allowed to have his wounds tended. He lived for a few days only, and the slaves who washed his dead body for burial told me that the linen of his shirt had been beaten so deeply into his flesh, which had closed in hideous sores over it, that they had merely cut the more exposed parts of the evil blood-stained rags away and left the rest.

Perhaps the most tragic of the tortures perpetrated by Mulai Hafid were upon the family of the Basha Haj ben Aissa, the Governor of Fez, a man whose reputation was certainly no worse than that of the majority of Moorish officials, and very much better than that of many.

Believing that he was very rich, Mulai Hafid had the Governor arrested and thrown into prison, with several members of his family. The usual floggings and privations took place, and Haj ben Aissa surrendered all his properties to the Sultan. But Mulai Hafid was not satisfied. He believed in the existence of a great fortune in money. As a matter of fact, the Governor of Fez had been a keen agriculturist, and had invested all his gains—licit and illicit—in land, but nothing could persuade the Sultan that this was the fact. He gave orders that the fortune was to be found; and thus fresh privations and more floggings ensued, but all to no avail. Then the women were arrested, amongst them the aristocratic wife of the Governor of Fez, a lady of good family and high position. It was thought that she would know, and disclose the hidden treasure. She was tortured, but disclosed nothing, because there was nothing to disclose.

The whole of this story came to my knowledge, and the barbarity of the Sultan's proceedings determined me to let the world know what was passing. The 'Times' opened its columns unreservedly to these wrongs, as that great paper has never failed to do whenever there has been a wrong to redress. It was not so much the torturing of the wife of the Governor of Fez—terrible though that was—as the fact that these things were still happening in Morocco—and must cease. The evidence I had was legally slight, but I determined to see it through. The Sultan denied, threatened, and denied again, but the repeated efforts of the 'Times' were sufficient even to move the Foreign Office, and it was decided that some action must be taken. The late Sir Reginald Lister was British Minister at that time, and his encouragement and help assisted me in my campaign. At long length the British Government decided to ask the Sultan to produce the lady, as no other proof would be sufficient to persuade them that great cruelties had not been perpetrated. The French Government stood side by side with our own in the interests of humanity. The Sultan agreed willingly, but failed to produce the lady. The energy of Mr McLeod, the British Consul at Fez, was untiring. He was determined to see the matter through. At length, driven by the force of circumstances, the Sultan allowed the Basha's wife to be visited by two English lady medical missionaries, accompanied by the wife of a French doctor. They saw her in the recesses of the palace, and, in spite of protestations and threats on the part of the slaves, they insisted on examining her.

Her crippled body, and the terrible scars of recent
wounds, amply justified the 'Times' action. The
Sultan had lied throughout. The woman had
been cruelly tortured.

With that humane spirit which he has shown
throughout his whole life, Sid el Haj Mohamed
el-Mokri, who was Grand Vizier then, and to-day
so ably fills the same post, took the injured wife
of the Governor of Fez into his own house, where
she received all the medical assistance of which
she stood in need, and all the kindness of the
vizier's womenkind.

I have two letters referring to this incident
which I value. One is from Mr J. M. McLeod,
C.M.G., then British Consul at Fez, dated 28th July
1910, in which he writes to me to tell me that the
surviving members of Haj Ben Aissa's family had
been to see him for the purpose of asking him to
let me know how grateful they were for the " great
efforts I had made on their behalf, which had been
an immense solace to them." The second is a
letter from the British Minister, Sir Reginald
Lister, dated 22nd February, from the Dolomites,
in which he says, " I write first and above all to
congratulate you on your triumph in the matter
of the tortures." After all, my part had been
small. It was the publicity that the ' Times '
gave to my telegrams and messages that obtained
the success. Two years afterwards, when circumstances had brought Mulai Hafid and myself
together again, I asked him to explain his action.
He told me that he knew the woman had been

tortured—she was not the only one—but that he personally had not intended it. He said that when he had been informed that Haj ben Aissa's fortune could not be found, he had ordered the arrest of his womenkind. A little later he was told the women " wouldn't speak," and he acknowledged that he had replied, " They must be made to speak." Such words from such a source were taken to mean one thing, and one thing alone—torture ; and they were tortured.

Of the end of Bou Hamara I have written elsewhere : his long confinement in a small cage, his being thrown to the lions in the presence of the Sultan's women, and eventually his being shot after the savage beasts had mangled and torn his arms.

Those were the " good old days " !

It was not only in the palace that there was cruelty. In every governor's Kasba, deep in damp dungeons—as often as not holes scooped in the earth for storing grain—there lay and pined those who had committed, or not committed, as the case might be, some crime ; and still more often, those who were rich enough to be squeezed. In such suffering, and in darkness, receiving just sufficient nourishment to support life, men were known to have existed for years, to emerge again long after their relations had given up all hope of seeing them. But there was always a chance— a chance that the Governor might die or fall into disgrace ; and then the dungeons in his castle would be opened and the wrecks of his prisoners

be released. And what prisons! what horrors of
prisons they were, even those above ground and
reserved for the ordinary class of criminal. Chained
neck to neck, with heavy shackles on their legs,
they sat or lay in filth, and often the cruel iron
collars were only undone to take away a corpse.
The prisons in the towns were bad enough, but
those of the country Kasbas were far worse.
Mulai Abdul Aziz, who reigned from 1894 till
1908, and who still lives at Tangier, deserves at
least some credit, for at one period of his reign he
put the prisons of Fez in order. They were largely
restored, a water-supply was added, and they
became less hideous than they had been before;
but gradually the old system crept back again,
and the improvements lasted only a little while.
With all the good intentions in the world, a Sultan
of those days could not break down the traditions
and corruption of his surroundings.

Amongst the great Berber chieftains of the
Atlas, life was even harder; but at all events there
was not the same persecution and squeezing as
existed in the plains and richer districts. The
more than semi-independence of the Berbers freed
them from the perpetual exactions of the Maghzen,
though by no means from the extortion of their
own chiefs. Yet the very climate, the hardships
of life in those inhospitable peaks, the constant
warfare in which the tribes were engaged with one
another, made men of them, and all the traditions
of their race were democratic. But if the same
oppression for the sake of extorting money did not

exist, their treatment of prisoners taken in war whose lives were not forfeited, or of those held as hostages, was harsh enough. They, too, the great Berber Kaids, had their castles and their dungeons, and the latter were seldom empty. The whole life in those great Atlas fortified Kasbas was one of warfare and of gloom. Every tribe had its enemies, every family had its blood-feuds, and every man his would-be murderer. Since quite my early years in Morocco I have visited these far-away castles, and with many of the Berber Kaids I enjoy to-day a friendship that has lasted over many years. With the family of the Kaids of Glaoua I have long been on intimate terms. When I first knew them, Sid Madani Glaoui was merely the Governor of the Glaoua tribe, and his younger brother, Sid Thami—a youth then—held no official position. Remarkable for their skill in warfare and for their ability in tribal diplomacy, the members of the Glaoua family seldom left the high mountain peaks, except to pay periodical visits to Marrakesh, three days' journey from their home. Their Kasba at Teluet, the grandest of all the Atlas fortresses, is situated over 7000 feet above the level of the sea. Such ability did these young brothers possess, that it was not difficult to foresee that they must be destined to play a rôle in the history of Morocco. They began by consolidating their power in the Atlas, both by diplomacy and by a series of little wars, in which they surpassed themselves in feats of arms, and in which both were repeatedly wounded. As Commander-

in-Chief of the Shereefian forces the elder was
employed by Mulai Abdul Aziz in his wars against
the Rif tribes. Meanwhile the Glaoua faction in
the south was becoming all-powerful, and when
Mulai Hafid in 1908 unfurled the standard of revolt
against his brother, the Glaoui chiefs supported
him. Without them his cause must have failed
at once. Madani became his Minister of War and
later his Grand Vizier ; his brother, Haj Thami,
was appointed Governor of Marrakesh and the
surrounding tribes. Capable in the art of native
government, they were equally capable in the
management of their own affairs. Their estates,
the most extensive of any except, perhaps, the
Sultan's Maghzen properties, were admirably
worked and conducted, and vast revenues flowed
in. At the moment when the French Protectorate
was declared, both these able men threw in their
lot with France, and have served her loyally.
Intelligent, realising for years past that the end
of the independence of Morocco might be staved
off for a short period, but was eventually inevitable,
the Glaoui brothers had never disguised their
preference for reform and their desire for the
opening up of Morocco's wealth. The Berber race
possesses not only a keenness of intellect, but
also an activity that is wanting in the other inhabitants of Morocco. Roads, railways, machinery
pleases them, and they are eager for their introduction. Their mentality is European and not
African.

Madani Glaoui died two years ago, a man who

U

was really regretted, not only by the French, to whom he rendered great services, but also by the natives. He was one of the greatest, the richest, and the most generous of Berber chiefs, a man of delightful manners and much learning. His brother, Haj Thami, still a comparatively young man, is to-day Basha of Marrakesh. He lives a simple life in the midst of much splendour, and spends all the hours that he can spare from his official duties in visiting his estates or in handling and reading his wonderful collection of Arabic manuscripts. On one of my visits to their Kasba at Teluet, I think in the year 1901, I allowed myself to be persuaded to stay on and on, though I ought already to have been on my way toward the coast. First it had been Kaid Madani who had asked me to remain another day, then one or other of his brothers or cousins, and so on. Every morning I prepared to start, and every time I was begged to stay. At last I really expected to be allowed to leave, but I was led out into a great court-yard, overlooked by the frowning walls of the Kasba. On the terraced roofs were gathered a multitude of veiled women. My host, bidding me look up, said, " To-day it is our womenfolk who beg you to stay," and with a loud cry the women uttered their welcome. The Berbers are less strict about womenkind, and I often conversed with elderly ladies of the Glaoua family. On asking one of these personages—she was a very near relation to Sid Madani—why it was the women of the Kasba desired me to prolong my stay, she replied, " Because since you have been here there has been a truce to war and to feud. Our sons and our sons' sons are in safety. Before you came no one ever laughed in the Kasba, for the men think only of war, and we women only of death ; but for a fortnight now we have laughed and sung, having no fear. But when you go the truce will end, and all our laughter will cease." It made one realise life in the Kasba of Teluet.

When Sid Madani Glaoui was at Fez as Grand Vizier during the reign of Mulai Hafid, he had only a few of his very numerous children with him. Amongst these few was a favourite son by a black slave woman. He was about twelve years of age, very dark, but of a remarkable vivacity and intelligence, and most amusing. Unfortunately this temperament had its disadvantages, and his conduct for his age was disgraceful. He had already indulged in the wildest life. His father had sent him to the French school, but it was only on the rarest occasions that he ever turned up there. No matter how many of the Vizier's retainers took him to the door, he invariably by some means or other escaped, and spent his days in far less eligible society elsewhere. At last things became so bad that the schoolmaster insisted on complaining personally to his father. The boy was summoned into his presence, and was asked why he played truant. He denied it, to the surprise of both. He insisted that he attended school regularly, and that it was only because the schoolmaster disliked him that this accusation was made against him. The schoolmaster continued naturally to contradict the boy, who at last said, " Well, I can prove it. If I hadn't attended school I couldn't speak French. Examine me." Hurriedly one of the Vizier's Algerian retinue was called and asked to address the boy in French. He did so, and the black imp replied with the facility almost of a Parisian, but it wasn't the French that schoolboys ought to learn. The expressions and words he used made the schoolmaster's hair stand on end, but undoubtedly he spoke French, and with a fluency that was appalling. It was not in a school for the " sons of gentlemen " that he had learned it—nor in a school for the " daughters of ladies " either—but in a French *café chantant,* as it called itself, which had recently been installed in the Jews' quarter of the city.

The Jews of Morocco are a race apart. There are two distinct branches—the descendants of the original Berber Jews of the country, and the descendants of the Jews who migrated from Spain, mostly in the fifteenth century. While the latter have preserved Spanish as their native tongue, the former use the Shelha (Berber) or Arabic languages, according to the part of Morocco they inhabit. The type, as might be expected, is very different, and it is often difficult, and at times impossible, to distinguish between the Israelites of the Atlas and the neighbouring Moselm Berber tribesmen. They even dress alike, except for the small black cap which is common to the Jewish tribes. The origin of these indigenous Jews is unknown, but their presence in Morocco is of great antiquity. A tradition exists that they were driven out of Palestine by Joshua, the son of Nun, but it seems more probable that they were native Berbers converted at some very early period from paganism.

These original Jews inhabit the interior of the country, mostly in the towns, though many are scattered amongst the tribes. They live alone, and regard the more educated Jews of Spanish origin as leaning toward unorthodoxy, if not actually unorthodox. The circumstances in which they pass their existence amongst proud and fanatical Moslem tribesmen has naturally given to the native Jews none of the facilities nor the incentives for progress. In the case of the Jews of Spanish descent there has been a remarkable movement during the last fifty years. They have seized upon every form and kind of education in order to increase their social welfare. Schools have been built, professors from Europe engaged, and all this has been accomplished almost entirely from funds locally subscribed. The " Alliance Israelite " has largely found the personnel of the schools, but the wave of education has been the work of the intelligent Jews themselves. No sacrifice has been too great, no effort too vast, with the result to-day that there is scarcely a Jew in the coast towns of Morocco who does not speak and read and write at least two languages, while the majority speak three. These Jews of Spanish origin share with their co-religionists of the East the title of "Sephardim." When they were exiled, after a period of cruel persecution, from Spain, they sought refuge in Morocco. They were already an educated and civilised race, in learning and the arts far ahead of the majority of Spaniards, amongst whom they were no longer permitted to live. On their arrival in Morocco they found the Jews of Berber origin living in a position of inferiority, such as it would be quite impossible for them to accept. They therefore negotiated with the Sultan an "Ordonnance" as to the status they might hold in the country, which at the same time laid down certain rules for the guidance of their own conduct, lest life amongst their more ignorant native co-religionists might cause them to abandon some of their more civilised and civilising tenets. This "Ordonnance" is still adhered to, and is known to the "Sephardim" as the "Decanot." It contains, amongst many other clauses, rules as to marriage contracts, and on the question of succession of property.

The "Sephardim" of Morocco are a remarkable people, who have rendered and are rendering great services to the country. Hard-working, intelligent, keen business men, and capable organisers, the Spanish Jews of Morocco have progressed in civilisation, in education, and in fortune in a manner that is highly commendable.

But long before this modern "renaissance," the "Sephardim" Jews of Morocco, in spite of the great difficulties and drawbacks under which

they existed, had gained for themselves a position
in Morocco. They had become, as bankers and
money-lenders, indispensable to the country, while
they filled also many other professions. The
tailors, jewellers, tent-makers, and metal-workers
were practically all Jews. The " Mellah," as their
quarter is called, was the centre of trade. In
their shops there was nothing too small to be
bought: I have seen boxes of wax-matches split
up and sold by the half-dozen; while the same
shopman, or perhaps his brother, would lead you
to his house, and in an upper chamber, with the
door locked, offer you a string of pearls or a great
cabuchon emerald, or a diamond the size of a
shilling.

In many ways their position, persecuted though
they were as a race, was preferable to that of the
Moslem. They had their own laws, administered
by their rabbis. Their taxation was collected
apart by their own people, and paid in a sort of
offering to the Sultan. They were squeezed, of
course, and now and again their quarter was
pillaged, but there was never the individual
danger of persecution such as the Moslem was at
all times liable to. They were able almost at any
time to gain access to the authorities, and even
to the Sultans, who in their conversation with the
many Jews and Jewesses who worked—as tent-
makers and tailors—in the palace, were far more
intimate and affable than with their own people.
Both Mulai Abdul Aziz and Mulai Hafid had
personal friends amongst the Fez and Marrakesh

Jews, with whom they were on terms of considerable intimacy. The result was that the Jews of
Morocco as a race were far more often able, through
their friendships at Court and with the viziers,
to obtain justice for their wrongs than were their
Moslem neighbours, and even in the country
districts a Jewish trader was feared. He would
be mocked at perhaps, or sometimes a little
bullied, but seldom really ill-treated. An example
of the fear in which the Jews were held came to
my personal knowledge during my travels many
years ago. A Jew, travelling alone from country
market to country market, was murdered, and
his little stock-in-trade and his few dollars were
robbed. The murder took place in the thickly-
populated Gharb district, between two of the
most important markets, during the early hours
of the night. I knew the man well, and he was a
constant visitor of the " souks." For a day or
two nothing was known, except that he was no
longer seen at the markets. He might, it is true,
have gone back to Alcazar, his native town, to
replenish his stock, but it seemed certain knowledge that he had been done to death. His body,
however, was not found, though on those level
plains, thick with tent and hut villages, it would
be difficult to hide it. All that could be said for
certain was that he had disappeared.

Now, what had happened was this. The murderers, having robbed the body, laid it by night
just outside a neighbouring village. At dawn the
villagers found it, and terrified of being accused of

murdering a Jew, they concealed the corpse till night, when stealthily they carried it away and laid it on the outskirts of another village. Here again the same manœuvre was practised, and day by day and night by night the body was concealed and carried on. It mattered little that in time the state of the corpse would have clearly demonstrated that the murder had taken place already some time back. It would have been sufficient evidence of guilt merely for it to have been found near a village, no matter how decomposed. The inevitable punishment would have been severe—imprisonments and confiscations— for the innocent villagers. Had the murdered man been a Moslem, little heed would have been taken, but the murder of a Jew was far more serious. The matter reached my ears, for the inhabitants of a village confided in me that they had found the body that morning, and that, owing to death having occurred some weeks before, its transport to another village was a matter of extreme difficulty. I intervened, and notified the discovery to the authorities, and the villagers did not suffer.

The business instinct is naturally very strong amongst the Morocco Jews. Their existence has always been a struggle in the past, and life has been hard. One of the many friends I have amongst the race told, with a delightful sense of humour, an anecdote of his early childhood. He had just begun to study in Hebrew the details of his faith, and his soul was aflame with the idea that the promised Messiah might come at any

moment. Bidding good night to his parents and
his relatives, he whispered to his old grandmother,
a lady of great influence in the family, " Do you
think the Messiah will come to-night ? " She
patted his head gently, and said, " Don't worry,
my dear, about that. He will come in his own
day. Learn to add up ; learn to add up." She
was a practical old lady, and her grandson followed
her advice. He is to-day the leader of the Jewish
community in one of the most important towns in
Morocco, an honourable and wealthy man, of great
generosity, and of unswerving devotion to the
interests of his people.

The Jews keep very strictly to the letter of the
law, and though I have every respect for devotion,
I once was really very seriously annoyed by the
rigid adherence of an elderly Israelite to his
commandments.

I was camping in the Gharb province in winter.
The rain was falling in torrents, and the ground
deep in mud. During dinner a Jewish youth
arrived, and, bursting into my tent, began to
cry. As soon as he could make himself intelligible,
he stated that his father, who was camping in a
neighbouring village, was very ill. He had heard
of the arrival of a " Christian," and begged me to
go and see him. I went, my men accompanying
me with lanterns. It was a long walk, and it was
raining cats and dogs ; but at length we arrived
where the camp of the Jews was pitched—a
couple of big tents, such as the travelling Jewish
trader always uses. Everything was in darkness.

I was welcomed, by the light of my own lanterns, by the youth's father, who, surrounded by his bales of cloth and cotton goods, seemed the picture of health. After the usual compliments I asked what I could do.

It was Friday night, and therefore the Jews had already entered upon their Sabbath. With many apologies, the merchant informed me that the wind had put their lanterns out, and as it was the Sabbath they were not permitted to strike matches, so they could not relight them. The Moors—infidels, he called them—had refused to help them, and so he had been obliged to trouble me!—and I had walked a couple of miles through deep mud, late at night, in torrents of rain—to strike a match!

I struck it, and I pride myself it was the only thing I did strike. I left him with his lanterns alight, but I made him tip my men so generously for their long and tiring walk, that he would probably prefer in the future to spend weeks in darkness rather than risk disturbing another Christian.

A Moslem family that suffered many vicissitudes was that of a former Governor of Oulad Sifian in the Gharb. Haj Bouselham er-Remoush was at one time a great man. He owed his appointment to friends and to bribery at Court, and quickly became an influential and wealthy personage. As a matter of fact, he was not, as Moorish Kaids go, a bad Governor. Extortion he naturally practised, and his prisons were full, but the tribe he governed did not inordinately com-

plain, which meant that he must have had some
good points. Those good points certainly weren't
his sons. The elder, who was deputy-Governor,
was a thorough rascal. A fine horseman, always
beautifully dressed, he was to outward appearances
an attractive personality; but he drank copiously,
and no good-looking woman or girl in his jurisdiction was safe from his attentions. He was still
almost a youth when the crash came. There had
been complaints to the Sultan of his licentiousness,
and consequently the father was heavily "squeezed"
from Court, and his fortune could not stand the
pressure. When the viziers had extracted all he
had to give, a band of troops arrived, and arrested
all the male members of the family, while the
soldiers spent the following day or two in his
harem. His house was torn down stone by stone
in the search for treasure, and the Kaid and his
two elder sons were sent in chains to Marrakesh.
His home became a ruin, and his gardens were
destroyed. Still to-day, in the midst of a tangle
of " prickly pear," one sees the remains of what
was once the important residence.

Haj Bouselham, an elderly man, accustomed to
all the luxuries of wealth, succumbed quickly to
the horrors of the Marrakesh prison. His eldest
son died soon afterwards. The third, still a boy,
was released. Some few years afterwards, riding
across the hill-tops near Wazzan, a shepherd in
charge of a flock of goats spoke to me. " You do
not recognise me," he said ; " I am Mohamed, the
son of Haj Bouselham er-Remoush." I asked

him to tell me his history. Released from prison, penniless of course, he had taken refuge with his mother's people, who had suffered, too, in the general confiscation that had succeeded his father's fall. He was now a goatherd; and only a few years before how often I had seen him mounted on one or other of his fine horses, on a saddle embroidered in gold and surrounded by his slaves.

A few years later I met him again. His luck had turned. Part of his confiscated property had been acquired again, and he was a well-to-do young tribesman in a prosperous way. To-day, under a benigner rule, he is an important landowner and farmer, and once more rides fine horses.

As a rule, families held together for better or for worse. Their safety depended upon their cohesion and on their numbers. The moment a man was made Kaid he collected all his brothers and his uncles and his cousins, and installed them round him. He exempted them from taxation, and let them rob. It was the numerical strength of his retainers as much as his prestige that kept him immune from murder and revolt. Yet sometimes the families were split up, and then woe betide them.

Some thirty years ago, on the death of one of the great southern Kaids, his eldest son hurried to the Sultan's Court, with mules laden with money, to buy his succession to his father's post. There was a younger son who still was allowed in the women's quarters, and whose mother had been the old Kaid's favourite wife, and she had remained up to the time of his death his confidante. She knew well enough what would be her fate should the elder son succeed in buying the succession—that she and her boy would be driven out to starve, even if the youth was not murdered, for the feud between the members of the family was a deadly one. She held one trump card—almost always the winning card in Morocco. She and she alone knew where the dead Kaid's secret fortune was hidden. Under the charge of some of her relations she hurried her son to the Court. He arrived to find that his half-brother was already nominated to the Kaidship, and had left to return to his tribe that very morning. Not a moment was to be lost. The youth and his advisers sought the Grand Vizier, and asked how much the brother had paid for his succession. The sum was named, whereupon the younger brother offered a still greater amount in return for a letter from the Sultan appointing him to the post, with Imperial authority to take such steps as he might think necessary in order to dispossess his brother. The bargain was quickly struck, and, with a strong body of cavalry placed at his disposal by the Sultan, he set out in pursuit. They met outside the Kasba walls, and, overpowered by the troops, the elder son of the old Kaid was taken prisoner and thrown into a dungeon in the castle. Needless to say, he never emerged alive. The soldiers remained a few days, and returned to the Sultan, bearing the promised price of office, for the son had dug up, from under a great fountain basin

in the courtyard of the Kasba, the secret treasure
of his father.

There was no crime that the Maghzen would
not commit for money. The Sultans not unseldom
carried out their own bargains. Mulai Hafid had,
rightly, little confidence in his entourage—it was
a mutual sentiment,—and there was no financial
transaction, however doubtful its morality, that
he would not personally undertake, and nearly
always with success.

The whole atmosphere of the palace was permeated with extortion. The Sultans never hesitated playfully—but definitely—to take possession
of any article that took their fancy, if the owner
were on any but the most formal terms. Over
and over again I was the victim of these petty
thefts—pocket-books, sleeve-links, necktie pins.
One soon learned to take nothing of value with
one into the precincts of the Court. It must not
be thought that presents were given in return,
for it was rare indeed that any Sultan gave away
anything. Now and then they were generous with
some one else's property, and even that was rare.
Visits to the Court of Mulai Abdul Aziz and Mulai
Hafid were expensive. There were many who
thought that the few lucky persons to whom those
closely-shut gates were opened were making their
fortunes. Some were—those who had goods for
sale; but those who, like myself, were casual
visitors, paid dearly enough for their privilege
of the *entrée*. One of the commonest forms
of robbery was this. On arriving at the palace

gates one's horse was taken possession of by the black slaves. On emerging later on from the precincts of the palace the slaves were there, but the horse invisible. Protests and threats were of no avail ; a payment, and often a heavy one, had to be made in order to get it back. At one time my audiences with Mulai Hafid, who was then at Fez, were of almost daily occurrence, and this form of extortion became so expensive that eventually I " struck," for it often cost me from £2 to £3 to get my horse back. On one occasion I lost my temper, and cursed the slaves. Failing to obtain any redress, I returned in a justified burst of rage, and complained to the Grand Vizier. The Sultan overheard me, and I was summoned to his presence, where I spoke equally forcibly. I told him that in Europe people paid gate-money to go and see monstrosities in sideshows—fat women and tattooed men—but that I wasn't going to be robbed in this perfectly unjustifiable and wholesale way each time I came to see him. It was he, I added, who sent for me. As for myself, I was indifferent to these interviews, and was quite prepared not to come again if affairs were not put right. The Sultan soothed my injured spirits, spoke a little of kindness and charity, and finished up by saying, " You mustn't judge them too hardly. You see, none of them receive any wages, and they live on what they make. However, I will have them punished, so that they won't worry you again," and he ordered the Grand Vizier to have them flogged. Of course

I intervened, knowing what these floggings often were, but I needn't have troubled. They were flogged, but it was only a pretence—half a dozen blows each that would scarcely have hurt a small child. On reaching the door of the palace a few minutes later, my horse had disappeared again! It had been taken by the slaves who had administered the bastinado, and who now demanded payment for the punishment they had inflicted on their fellow-slaves for an exactly similar offence. There was nothing to be done. I paid.

It is all so different nowadays at the palace. The traditional and historical etiquette is strictly followed on all State occasions, but the organising hand is felt. The slaves and soldiers are beautifully dressed. The Court officials, in their long white robes, are politeness itself, and an official reception by the present Sultan at his palace is a sight worth seeing. In the outer courtyards are his black guards in scarlet and gold, cavalry and infantry, and his band of musicians in their " kaftans " of rainbow colours, and the long corridors are filled with the palace attendants. In the throne-room, seated on a divan, the Sultan receives his guests, an intelligent affable host. It is true the " surprises " are gone, but the rest remains, even to the lions that roar in their cages in a corner of the inner garden. The palaces are the same, but swept and cleaned and garnished, for in the old days only the portion of the great buildings actually inhabited by the Sultan was kept in repair. I visited the palaces at Fez and

x

Marrakesh soon after the abdication of Mulai Hafid. I had already seen certain parts of them, but the presence of hundreds of women under the old régime—many the widows and slaves and descendants of dead Sultans—prevented one visiting many of the courtyards and buildings. On the advent of the new régime other arrangements were made for these palace pensioners, much to their advantage, and the restoration of the palaces was undertaken. But there was much past restoring—courtyard after courtyard, where the ceilings of the rooms had fallen in, and where it was literally unsafe to walk. The impression that the ensemble gave one was that, with the exception of some of the oldest and some of the most modern parts, the Sultans had been terribly " done " by their builders and the men responsible for the upkeep. No doubt this always was so. The Court functionaries and the viziers demanded and received commissions—and what commissions ! —on all the work done at the palaces. As a rule, the decoration in the palaces is no better than that existing in the splendid private residences of Fez and Marrakesh, and the workmanship is often distinctly inferior. The greater parts of the existing palaces were constructed by Mulai Hassen, the grandfather of the present Sultan Mulai Yussef, who died in 1894. He must have destroyed, in order to raise these acres and acres of buildings, much of what existed previously. Of the palaces of former dynasties nothing but the merest ruins remains—a few walls at Fez of the palace of the

Merinides, and at Marrakesh the great walls and
enclosure of what must have been the finest of all
Moroccan buildings, the palace of the Saadien
Sultans, whose dynasty came to an end in the
seventeenth century. Their mausoleum, dating
from the sixteenth century, the most beautiful
building in Morocco, still remains intact as an
example of perfect Moorish art; and there is no
doubt, from contemporary descriptions, that the
neighbouring palace was of unparalleled beauty
and magnificence. The ground-plan of its great
courtyard, with its immense water-tanks and its
fountains, can still be clearly traced; while at one
end, facing a long straight tiled walk between two
of the great basins, are the ruins of the Sultan's
audience-chamber, a vast square room. The walls
are still standing, but the roof has fallen long ago.
The description of this palace in the days of its
glory reads like a page from the ' Thousand and
One Nights.' What had taken a century to build
was destroyed in a day. The Saadien dynasty fell,
and the cruel despot, Mulai Ismail, seized the
throne. His first act was to order the destruction
of this famous palace of his predecessors, and the
great building was looted by the soldiery and the
crowd. Many of the old houses in Marrakesh
to-day have doorsteps formed of small columns,
or parts of larger ones, of rare marbles—the
remnants of the colonnades that once decked this
magnificent palace of the most intellectual and
civilised dynasty that Morocco ever boasted.

Perhaps the most noticeable change that has

come about in Morocco is in the attitude of the
people to medical and surgical aid. The Moor
was often ready in the past to accept the assistance of European doctors, and had a certain faith
in their medicines, but the opportunities were few.
The Medical Missions at Fez and Marrakesh were
well attended and rendered great services, and
the doctors attached to the Sultan's Court had a
certain clientele. As a rule, the native's faith was
half-hearted, sufficient to accept medicines if no
charge was made, but rarely of the kind that
would pay a fee. Often, too, the medicine was
not taken, and secretly in his inmost heart the
patient had sometimes far more faith in the good
that might accrue from the presence of the doctor
than from the remedies he recommended. A short
time since I experienced a good example of this.
A Moor, a neighbour of mine, was very ill with
typhus fever, and at my recommendation his
women-folk summoned an excellent doctor to
attend him. I always accompanied the doctor
on his visits. The man was desperately ill. The
doctor and I carefully explained to the women
how his medicines should be taken, and they
apparently followed our advice to the letter.
But one day, arriving unexpectedly at the
house at the hour in which the patient should
have taken his medicine, I saw his wife carefully measure the dose into the glass and deliberately pour it away. I remained concealed for a
few moments, and then made my presence known.
I asked if the man had had his medicine. Hold-

ing up the bottle and pointing to the diminution in its contents, the woman replied, " Yes ; he
has just taken it." I told the woman that I had
seen her throw it away. She showed little or no
confusion, but said, " The doctor's presence is
sufficient without his drugs. His knowledge is
what is useful—who knows what his drugs contain ? " I have experienced many similar cases,
one that was so absurd that it is worth repeating.
Happening to meet an old native who had a
terrible sore on the calf of one of his legs, I
asked him if he would go as an out-patient to
the hospital to have it treated. He willingly
assented, and I wrote on a visiting-card a line
to the doctor in charge. The man took the
card and went his way. A day or two later I
met him—his leg was bound up with a filthy rag.
I asked him if he had been to the hospital.
" No," he replied, " there was no need. My leg
is already better." I insisted on seeing the
sore. Under the reeking bandage, bound across
the open wound, was my visiting-card ! I asked
the man why he had put it there. " Your kindness," he said, " and the knowledge of the doctor
to whom it was addressed is sufficient cure, so I
applied the card to the sore. It is better already."
It wasn't. If anything, it was distinctly worse,
so I took the old man by force and walked him up
to the hospital myself, where he was treated.
Finding almost instant relief from pain, he followed
the doctor's advice, and continued his visits until
his leg was healed. I attempted to show him the

follies of his own idea of cure, but he would only reply, " Your card was sufficient. It would have got well just the same if you had allowed me to leave it there."

The women were, and are still, the most difficult, but even in their case a great change has come about, and the Medical Mission to women at Fez, so admirably conducted by two estimable English—or rather Irish—ladies has rendered immense service. It is curious that it is at Fez, the most fanatical of all the Moroccan cities, that the most headway has been made in this women's medical work. Elsewhere there has been a considerable measure of success, but nowhere else, I think, have the houses and hearts of the native women been so opened to " Christians " as they have at the northern capital. No great function in any of the aristocratic houses is complete if the ladies of the Medical Mission are not present. Speaking the language with perfect fluency, they have succeeded by their good works—and perhaps still more by their good natures—in making themselves most justly and most sincerely beloved. Part at least of the secret of their success has been what is often so wanting, cheerfulness and love— which constitute, after all, perhaps the most important equipment of real Christianity.

Formerly the mass of the people were satisfied with the healing power of their Shereefs, and with the charms of the " tholba," or students of religion. They visited certain holy places, mostly tombs, where prayers were offered. Others, still more ignorant, summoned to the bedside of their sick, negro dancers and the devotees of the "Aissaoua" sect, the noise of whose music and chants should have been sufficient to drive away all the djinns of Morocco. At the same time there is a certain knowledge of herbs existing amongst the country people, and many of the remedies to which they have recourse are by no means to be despised. Bone-setting is regularly practised, and well practised, with splints of wood and cane.

The Moors have long been aware of the medicinal value of certain hot springs, which are largely resorted to for the cure of skin diseases and other maladies common to the country. Particularly famous are the hot baths of Mulai Yakoub, not far from Fez, and the benefit derived is unquestionable. I have known natives, scarcely able to ride to the spot and covered with sores, who, after a sojourn of from twenty to thirty days at this spot, have returned healed.

Apart from the venders of strange medicines who can be seen in any of the Moroccan markets, with their stock-in-trade set out before them— hideous dried animals and the skins of moth-eaten birds predominating—there are a certain number of native doctors. The most renowned are Shereefs from Dades, an oasis situated to the south of the Great Atlas. These men pretend to inspired and hereditary knowledge, and there is no doubt that there still exists amongst them some trace of medical learning. They operate for cataract, not by removing the cataract, but by dislocating it,

by which sight is often restored, but without any
certainty that the cure is more than temporary.
They are also skilful in removing portions of
broken skull. There is no actual trepanning of
the bone, but the broken part is removed and
replaced, the scalp having been opened and drawn
back by a portion of the dried shell of a gourd,
which, overlapping the uninjured part of the skull,
covers the aperture and protects the brain. The
scalp is replaced and sewn up.

Perhaps the most ingenious practice in use
amongst the Berbers of the Atlas is the use of the
large red ant for closing skin wounds. The art of
sewing up wounds is known and practised, but they
have no means of disinfecting the material used,
and they state that the stitches often either open
or form sores. They therefore employ the following method. Holding the two edges of the skin
together, so as to leave a little of both edges
protruding, they apply a living red ant to the
wound. The ant closes his strong mandibles on
the skin, and is promptly decapitated with the
aid of a pair of scissors. The mandibles remain
closed, holding the two edges of skin together.
As many as four or five of these " clips " are applied
to a wound of a few inches in length. By the time
the ant's head falls away the wound has closed.
This system is in common use in the Atlas, and the
Governor of Marrakesh, Haj Thami Glaoui, told
me that he insists on his men using it in preference
to sewing, unless the sewing can be performed by
a European doctor with disinfected material.

The Sultans Mulai Abdul Aziz and Mulai Hafid both took an interest in medicine and dentistry, and had confidence in their doctors. An English dentist, who attended the ladies of the palace in the reign of the former of these two Sultans, was only allowed to work on the mouths of the inmates of the Imperial harem through a small hole cut in the sheet, which entirely enveloped the patient as she sat in the dentist's chair. So successfully, however, did he mend up the teeth of the ladies of the palace that the viziers followed suit, and the dentist had a busy time. The Minister of Foreign Affairs sent for me one day, and after some general remarks, asked me if I knew the dentist. I replied that I did, and that he was an adept at his art. The Vizier continued that he knew personally very little about dentistry, and would I tell him whether every time his wife sneezed it was necessary to sneeze her new row of upper teeth half across the room. I replied that I doubted whether this was an absolute necessity, but I would ask the dentist. I did so, and the lady's set of teeth was quickly altered to fit her better. "It is wonderful," said the Vizier to me later on; "she sneezes and sneezes and her teeth never even rattle."

In the days of Mulai Hassen, before the advent of a resident physician to the palace, Kaid Maclean, then a young officer, used to dabble in medicine, and so great was the confidence that he inspired in the Sultan's eyes that even His Majesty allowed himself to be treated. Kaid Maclean's knowledge

was limited to the contents of his medicine-chest
and a book of explanations. On one occasion the
ladies of the palace had been suffering, from indi-
gestion probably, and at the same time some dis-
infectant was required for some one in the palace
who had been injured in an accident. Kaid Maclean
sent the two medicines, with instructions how they
were to be used, but by some mistake the ladies
swallowed the compressed tabloids of perman-
ganate of potass instead of the tonic. The tabloids
dissolved inside, but brought on violent attacks of
sickness, and to the horror of the Sultan and the
ladies themselves, they began to vomit what appeared to be vast quantities of blood. The more
sick they were the more terrified they became, and
in reply to an anxious message, Kaid Maclean
hurried to the palace. The Sultan was beside
himself with fear, but an explanation was forthcoming, and the ladies recovered.

Mulai Abdul Aziz's first experience of the use
of chloroform might easily have led to more serious
results. Dr Verdon, his English doctor, had
operated on a slave under chloroform, and the
Sultan had been present. The operation over,
His Majesty retired into the palace carrying with
him a large bottle of the anæsthetic. The doctor
tried to obtain possession of the bottle, but in vain,
and all he could do was to warn His Majesty to be
very careful with it. He no doubt was, for apparently nobody died; but rumour has it that his
ladies lay all over the palace as insensible as logs
of wood—for he had a grand chloroforming evening

all to himself. Mulai Hafid, too, quite appreciated the use of chloroform, and insisted on its being administered to a lion that was suffering from overgrown toe-nails. The lion, whose temper was not of the best, took none too kindly to the whole operation, which was, however, eventually successfully performed, to the satisfaction of His Shereefian Majesty.

To-day the people flock in thousands to the hospitals and dispensaries which the French have opened throughout the length and breadth of their Protectorate. There is yet room for more medical work, for disease is rife, but what has already been accomplished is admirable. The Moor, who would never have thought of accepting the assistance of a doctor in the old days, now hurries to the nearest dispensary as soon as he feels ill, and any man who meets with an accident is immediately taken by his fellow-workmen to the native hospital. Crowds patiently wait their turn in the gardens and corridors, and the women's days are almost as congested as are those for the men. Whatever may be the people's real sentiments toward Europeans, their confidence in " Christian " doctors is undisputable. Yet the very people who crowd to the flock for medical aid would probably not acknowledge that any change has taken place in their views. They don't realise that only ten years ago, even if the possibilities had existed, they would never have dared to show this outward respect for and belief in the skill of the " infidel." But the change has come gradually, and is unnoticed by those to whom it is owing. The same sequence of mentality is noticeable in many other ways. The " universities "—medarsas—of Fez and Marrakesh, closed for centuries to Europeans, are now open once more to the Christian visitor, who is allowed to enter and admire these gems of Moorish architecture. The religious authorities could no longer insist on their being kept closed when they acknowledged that a few centuries ago Christian scholars were actually being educated in their precincts, so after a little hesitation they decided to permit the " medarsas " being visited. The authorities of the Service des Beaux-Arts immediately set about the restoration of these architectural masterpieces. At first the students were shocked at the presence of the Christian, and on one of my visits to the beautiful " medarsa " of Ben Youssef at Marrakesh, they complained rather bitterly that the French architects were restoring the old work and taking liberties with the structure. They would rather, they said, have it left alone in its ruined condition than have it tampered with by " unbelievers."

A year later I returned to the " medarsa." The same, or many of them the same, scholars were there. The Service des Beaux - Arts had restored one side of the great courtyard, but were waiting for further funds before beginning the rest. Again the scholars complained, but their complaint was a different one—the French architects had abandoned their work. What right had they to leave it unfinished ? Would I use my influence to see that the restorations were continued and completed? I reminded them of their complaint of only a year ago, and of their objection to the work being undertaken at all. They laughed, and replied, "Well, you see, yesterday was yesterday, and to-day is to-day."

INDEX

Abda regiment, the, 70–71
Abrish, Shereef of, 24
Abyssinia, 232
Africa, North, 232
Agdal, park of, 4
Aissaouna sect, 285–6, 327; *see also* Sidi ben Aissa
Ahmed El-Aoufi, 218–25
Alcazar, 24, 213–14, 243, 312
Algeciras Conference (1906), 104, 106, 111–12, 212–13
Algeria, 287, 295
Amaati, Haj, 19–21
Amin Haj Abdesalam El-Mokri, 25
Amrani Shereef, 104
Anjera mountains: author imprisoned in, 75, 182–4, 194; and capture of British officers, 79; Sid El Arbi in, 255
Anjera tribe, 190, 248, 252
Arabia, 232
Arzeila, 24, 181, 234, 236, 239, 242, 246
Asia, 232
Atlas mountains, 5, 10, 32, 234, 289, 303, 327–8
Australia, 163
Azimour, 289

Baghdad, 284, 288
Bahya, the, 33
Beaumarchais, M. and Mme. (of the French Legation), 217, 219, 221, 224
Ben Ahmed, 252
ben Aissa Haj, Basha, 299, 301
Ben Youssef, 332
Beni Aros mountains, 289

Beni Aros tribe, 179, 242
Beni Hassan (mountain), 202
Beni Msaour Mountains, 202, 210
Beni Mtir tribe, 66, 298
Beni Zerual tribe, 284
Berber tribes, 32, 303–6, 308–9, 328
Berenguer, General (Spanish commander), 259
Berlin, 87
Bou Ahmed *see* Si Ahmed ben Moussa
Bou Jad family, 267
Bou Hamara *see* Omar ez-Zarhouni
Bouselham er-Ramoush, Haj, 315–17
Bu Jad, 290

Carleton, Edmond P., 198
Casablanca, 116–18, 293
Ceuta, 247, 253
Chaouia Campaign (1907–8), 165, 294
Cherisy, Comte de, 78
China, 232
Cranley, Lord, 198
Crowther, Captain, 79

Dades (oasis), 327
Deilan family, 248, 251–2
Deilan, Sheikh, 252
Delcassé, Théophile, 78
Derkaoua sect, 284–5; *see also* Mulai el-Arbi ben Ahmed el-Derkaoui
Doukkala regiment, the, 69–71
Drummond Hay, Sir Joh~ ~ 146
Dua family, 248, 251-

Duas, Sheik, 194–5, 197

Edward VII, King of England, 80–81
Egypt, 295
England *see* Great Britain
er-Remiki, Kaid, 243
Europe, 2, 212

Fahs tribe, 208
Fez: Mulai Hassen leaves, 10; as centre of Morocco, 19–20; author visits, 23–8, 89, 161, 234; court in, 53, 65, 67–8, 71, 74, 118, 240–41; foreign missions in, 78, 115; palace in, 98–9, 143, 321–22; famine in, 104–11; Pretender in, 113; Mulai Hafid in, 121, 123, 136, 149; Mulai Hafid leaves, 131; Raisuli and, 214; Kittanïin sect in, 288; Fichtala near, 289; Mulai Yakoub's tomb near, 290; water supplies of, 292; torture of Governor's wife, 299–302; Jewish community in, 311; medical mission in, 326; university in, 332
Fichtala, 289
France, 3, 75, 122–24, 160–78, 213, 220, 258, 294–5

"Gennaoua", sect of, 121–22
Germany, 173–74, 212–13, 257–58
Gharb region, 290, 312, 314–15
Ghurgaya region, 289
Gibraltar, 111, 160, 163
Gindafi, the (El Gindafi), 33
Glaoui (Glaoua), 304; *see also* Thami el Glaoui
Great Britain, 3, 7, 31, 75, 161, 174, 180, 213, 220, 258
Greece, 269

Hagenbeck, 136
Haj *see* individual names (*e.g.* Amaati, Haj)
Hamacha, of Meknès, the, 58
Hamacha sect, 286–7; *see also* Sidi Ali ben Hamdouch

Hamburg, 136
Hammou el-Hassen, Kaid of the Beni Mtir, 66
Hatton, Lieutenant, 79

India, 269
Islam, 268–73; *see also* Sheiya; Sufism; Sunni

Japan, 232
Jewish community in Morocco, 308–15; *see also* Sephardim, the
Jordana, General (Spanish High Commissioner), 259

Kaderia sect, 284, 288; *see also* Mulai Abdul Kader el-Ghrailani
Kaiser *see* Wilhelm II
Kasba-el-Maghzen, 10
Khalkhali, Kaid, 237
Khlot tribe, the, 243
Kimberley, John Wodehouse, Earl of, 26
Kirby-Green, Sir William, 1, 3, 6, 198
Kittanïin sect, 288; *see also* Sidi Mohamed el-Kitani

Laraiche, 190, 198, 244–45, 247–48, 261, 290
Lister, Sir Reginald, 31, 115, 255, 300–301
Loch, Lord, 45–6
London, 87
Louis XIV, King of France, 20
Lowther, Christopher, 217, 224
Lowther, Sir Gerard, 31, 78, 214–15, 217, 219, 224
Lyautey, General Hubert, 160, 295

M'al Ainin, Shereef, of Shingit, 287
Maclean, Colonel Sir Harry (Kaid), 23, 190, 213–15, 239, 241, 329–30
McLeod, J.M., 300–301
Madrid, 244–45, 247, 257

Maghzen, the (Moroccan Government), 28, 35, 72, 106–7, 199–201, 205–6, 220, 297, 303, 319
Maimounieh Palace, 4
Maizerieh, the, 25
Mannesmann brothers, the, 248
Marrakesh: British Mission to, 3–4, 44; author visits, 34, 234; court in, 41, 50, 53, 60; Mulai Abdul Aziz advances on, 120; Mohamed Hiba in, 287; tomb of Mulai Brahim near, 289; patron saints of, 289; water supplies of, 292; Thami Glaoui and, 304–6; Jewish community in, 311; Bouselham er-Remoush imprisoned in, 316–17; palace in, 322–23; university in, 332
Marrakesh region, 32
Marseilles, 162–67
Mazagan, 3
Meknès, 20, 25, 68, 88, 101, 112, 284–86
Melilla, 114
Menebhi see Sid Mehdi el-Menehbi
Mexico, 80
Mogador, 180
Mohammed El-Mokri, Haj, 25
Mohamed Hiba, 287–88
Mohammed Torres, Haj, 181
Mokri family, 26; see also Amin Haj Abdesalam El-Mokri; Mohammed El-Mokri, Haj
Mtougi, the (El Mtougi), 33
Mulai Abd es-Salam, 179
Mulai Abdesalam ben Mashish, 289
Mulai Abdesalam el-Amarani, 89
Mulai Abdul Aziz, Sultan: British Mission to, 6–9; accession of, 13, 17–18, 23; on his father, 15–16; and court intrigue, 18–21; author's mission to, 25–28; early reign of, 32–33, 36; and Bou Ahmed's death, 37–39; amusements of, 40–46, 50–53; author's audiences with, 44–49;

royal progress of, 53–64; and reform, 65–66, 303; campaigns, 67–72; and revolution, 74; and Raisuli, 76, 213–16; and foreign powers, 78–79; life-style of, 79–88, 91–111, 119, 135; and famine in Fez, 104–11; abdication of, 113, 121, 240; and Mulai Hafid, 116, 120, 153–54; plays bridge, 150–51; at dinner-party, 151–53; rumours concerning, 241; and M'al-Ainin, 287; and Rifs, 305; and Jewish community, 311–12; expense of visiting, 320; and medicine, 329–30
Mulai Abdul Kader el-Ghrailani, 284, 288
Mulai Abdullah, Shereef of Wazzan, 273
Mulai Abdullah II; Shereef of Wazzan, 287
Mulai Ahmed, Shereef of Wazzan, 189, 196–97
Mulai Ahmed ben Mohammed er-Raisuli: family of, 24; intrigues of, 75–6; as brigand, 79, 109, 112, 180–81; ancestry of, 178–9; imprisons author, 180, 182, 185–98, 251; personality of, 181–82; takes hostages, 198–99; as Governor of Tangier region, 199–210, 241–42; as outlaw, 211–38; British subject, 239; and Mulai Hafid, 240–42; and Spanish, 243–48, 259–63; and Germans, 248, 257–58
Mulai Ali Shereef, 289
Mulai Bou Shaib, 289
Mulai Bouselham, 290
Mulai Brahim, 289
Mulai Busseta el-Khammar, 289
Mulai el-Arbi ben Ahmed el-Derkaoui, 284
Mulai el-Kebir, 68, 71
Mulai Hafid, Sultan: abdication of, 18, 124, 322; accession of, 113, 121, 240, 305; and Pretender, 113–14; and treatment of

enemies, 115; revolt of, 116, 120; nature of his reign, 121–23; and debts, 123–39; life-style of, 140–59; and Mulai Abdul Aziz, 153–4; plays bridge, 154–5; in France, 160–78; and Raisuli, 240–42; and M'al Ainin, 287; and Sidi Mohamed el-Kitani, 288; cruelty of, 297–302; and Sid Madani Glaoui, 305–7; and Jewish community, 311–12; and Maghzen, 319; expense of visiting, 320–21; and medicine, 329–31

Mulai Hassen I, Sultan, 322

Mulai Hassen II, Sultan: character of, 1, 136; and Moroccan unity, 3; at reception of British Mission, 5–6; and Sid Fadhoul Gharnit, 9; and journey to Tafilet, 10–11; death of, 11–14, 23; and greedy tutor, 16–17; first-born son of, 67, 113, 212; and medicine, 329–30

Mulai Idris I, 179, 287, 289

Mulai Idris II, 289

Mulai Ismail, Sultan, 20

Mulai Mohamed, 67, 113, 212; see also Omar ez-Zarhouni

Mulai Mohamed (of the Wazzani), 274–6, 278

Mulai Taiyeb, 287

Mulai Thami, 278–82

Mulai Yakoub, 290, 327

Mulai Youssef, Sultan, 18, 123, 322

Nasaria sect, 288; see also Sidi ben Nasr

Nicolson, Sir Arthur, 6–7, 31, 44, 189, 191, 196–7

Omar ez-Zarhouni (Bou Hamara; the Pretender): origins of, 66–7, 112–13; defeats Mulai el Kebir, 71; and Raisuli, 75–6, 197, 199 215; dominance of in Eastern Morocco, 79, 109, 111, 211–12; overruns Sultan's camp, 87–9;

capture and death of, 113–15, 302

Omar Tazzi, Haj, 94–6

Ouezzan see Wazzan family

Oujda district, 75, 208

Oulad Sifian, 315

Ould el-Aoufi see Ahmed el-Aoufi

Ould Bakkasha, 76–7

Ould Boulaish, 79

Oum er-Rebia (river), 58–9

Paris, 30, 80–81, 224

Perdicaris, Ion, 76, 190, 198–9

Persia, 232

Plymouth, 161

Pretender, the, see Omar ez-Zarhouni

Rabat, 7, 13, 19, 60, 67, 123–4

Rahamna Kaid, the (El Rahamna Kaid), 33, 35

Rahamna tribe, 35–6

Raisuli see Mulai Ahmed ben Mohammed er-Raisuli

Rif region, 113–14, 211

Rif tribe, 305

Saint-René Taillandier, 78

Sanderson, Sir Thomas, 26

Satow, Sir Ernest, 23, 26–8, 30–31

Sebat er-Rejal ("the Seven Men"), 289

Sebou valley, the, 25

Sephardim, the, 310–11

Sheiya, followers of, 269

Shereefs: position and influence of, 265–8

Shingata sect, 287–8; see also M'al Ainin, Shereef, of Shingit

Si Abderrahman ben Sedira, 208

Si Ahmed ben Moussa, 9, 12–13, 18–21, 33–40, 44–5

Si Mohammed Soreir, 19, 21–3

Sid El Arbi bel Aysh, 252–5

Sid el Haj Abdesalam, 273–4, 282, 284

Sid el Haj el-Arbi, 273–7

Sid el Haj Mohamed el-Mokri see Mohamed el-Mokri, Haj

Sid Fadhoul Gharnit, 9–10
Sid Madani Glaoui, 304–7
Sid Mehdi el-Menebhi (Minister of War), 52, 87–8, 95–6, 99, 108, 113, 156
Sid Mohamed el-Amarani, 89
Sid Mohamed el-Kittani, Shereef, 288, 298–9
Sid Thami el Glaoui *see* Thami el Glaoui
Sidi Ahmed el-Tijani, 287
Sidi Ahmed ou Moussa, 287
Sidi Ali ben Hamdouch, 286
Sidi ben Aissa, 285–6
Sidi Ben Daoud, 290
Sidi ben Nasr, 288
Silvestre, General Fernandes (Spanish commander), 245, 247, 260
Spain, 3, 75, 158–9, 174, 243–8, 253–5, 257–63
Sudan, 58
Sufism, 269–70, 288
Sunni, followers of, 269
Sus region, 288
Syria, 232

Tadla region, the, 11
Tafilet, 10–11, 289
Taher ben Suleiman, 35–6
Taibiya sect, 287; *see also* Mulai Taiyeb
Tamgrout, 288
Tamshlat family, 267
Tangier: author travels to, 23–5, 75, 88, 223; French Mission to, 29; British Ministers in, 31; tennis-party in, 38–9; Kaiser visits, 77; Mulai Abdul Aziz's photo for sale in, 86; Mulai Hafid in, 125, 128, 131–2, 140–47; Governor of, 181; distance from Zinat, 182, 196–7; prisoners in, 190–92; Raisuli and, 212, 216, 244; author visited in, 215–16, 244–6; and security of Europeans, 255; and Armistice celebrations, 258; Spanish expedition against

Raisuli and, 260–62; Sid el-Haj Abdesalam and wife living in, 273, 282
Tattenbach, count von, 78
Taza district, 75, 88, 113, 208
Tazerout, 242
Tehret, 304, 307
Temps (journal), 224
Tetuan, 21–2, 179, 246–8, 255–6, 261
Thami el Glaoui (Sid Thami el Glaoui), Pasha of Marrakesh, 33, 304–6, 328
Tijania sect, 287; *see also* Sidi Ahmed el-Tijani
Times, The (newspaper), 30, 104, 300–301
Tunis, 295
Turkey, 232

Ulad Jamai family, 18; *see also* Amaati, Haj; Si Mohammed Soreir
Ulad Sidi Ahmed ou Mousa sect, 287; *see also* Sidi Ahmed ou Mousa

Varley, M., 76, 198–9
Verdon, Dr, 89, 330
Vichy, 166–74

Wad Draa, the, 288
Wad Ras, 259–62
Wad Ziz, the, 10
Wazzan family, 267, 273; *see also* Mulai Abdullah, Shereef; Sid el Haj Abdesalam; Sid el Haj el-Arbi
Wazzan region, 24, 234, 274–7, 278–83, 316
Wilhelm II, Kaiser, 77–8
Wyldbore-Smith, Edmund C., 198

Zarhoun mountains, 286
Zarhoun tribe, 112
Zimmour tribe, 68–70, 72
Zinat, 75, 180–5, 188, 193–4, 200–210, 215–25, 229, 242, 262

MEMOIRS OF A
BENGAL CIVILIAN

JOHN BEAMES
The lively narrative of a Victorian district-officer

With an introduction by Philip Mason

They are as entertaining as Hickey . . . accounts like
these illuminate the dark corners of history.
Times Literary Supplement

John Beames writes a spendidly virile English and
he is incapable of being dull; also he never hesitates
to speak his mind. It is extraordinary that these
memoirs should have remained so long unpublished
. . . the discovery is a real find.
John Morris, The Listener

A gem of the first water. Beames, in addition to being
a first-class descriptive writer in the plain Defoesque
manner, was that thing most necessary of all in an
autobiographer – an original. His book is of the
highest value.
The Times

This edition is not for sale in the USA

Previously published by

ELAND BOOKS

VIVA MEXICO!
CHARLES MACOMB FLANDRAU
A traveller's account of life in Mexico

With a new preface by Nicholas Shakespeare

His lightness of touch is deceiving, for one reads *Viva Mexico!* under the impression that one is only being amused, but comes to realise in the end that Mr Flandrau has presented a truer, more graphic and comprehensive picture of the Mexican character than could be obtained from a shelful of more serious and scientific tomes.
New York Times

The best book I have come upon which attempts the alluring but difficult task of introducing the tricks and manners of one country to the people of another.
Alexander Woollcott

The most enchanting, as well as extremely funny book on Mexico... I wish it were reprinted.
Sybille Bedford

His impressions are deep, sympathetic and judicious. In addition, he is a marvellous writer, with something of Mark Twain's high spirits and Henry James's suavity...as witty as he is observant.
Geoffrey Smith, Country Life

ELAND BOOKS
specialise in the literature of travel.
If you wish to receive details of forthcoming publications,
please send your address to
Eland Books, 53 Eland Road, London SW11 5JX

TRAVELS WITH MYSELF AND ANOTHER

MARTHA GELLHORN

Must surely be ranked as one of the funniest travel books of our time — second only to *A Short Walk in the Hindu Kush*... It doesn't matter whether this author is experiencing marrow-freezing misadventures in war-ravaged China, or driving a Landrover through East African game-parks, or conversing with hippies in Israel, or spending a week in a Moscow Intourist Hotel. Martha Gellhorn's reactions are what count and one enjoys equally her blistering scorn of humbug, her hilarious eccentricities, her unsentimental compassion.
Dervla Murphy, Irish Times

Spun with a fine blend of irony and epigram. She is incapable of writing a dull sentence.
The Times

Miss Gellhorn has a novelist's eye, a flair for black comedy and a short fuse...there is not a boring word in her humane and often funny book.
The New York Times

Among the funniest and best written books I have ever read.
Byron Rogers, Evening Standard

ELAND BOOKS
specialise in the literature of travel.
If you wish to receive details of forthcoming publications,
please send your address to
Eland Books, 53 Eland Road, London SW11 5JX

Previously published by

ELAND BOOKS

FAR AWAY AND LONG AGO

W. H. HUDSON

A Childhood in Argentina

With a new preface by Nicholas Shakespeare

One cannot tell how this fellow gets his effects; he writes as the grass grows.
It is as if some very fine and gentle spirit were whispering to him the sentences he puts down on the paper. A privileged being
Joseph Conrad

Hudson's work is a vision of natural beauty and of human life as it might be, quickened and sweetened by the sun and the wind and the rain, and by fellowship with all other forms of life...a very great writer... the most valuable our age has possessed.
John Galsworthy

And there was no one – no writer – who did not acknowledge without question that this composed giant was the greatest living writer of English.
Far Away and Long Ago is the most self-revelatory of all his books.
Ford Madox Ford

Completely riveting and should be read by everyone.
Auberon Waugh

ELAND BOOKS
specialise in the literature of travel.
If you wish to receive details of forthcoming publications,
please send your address to
Eland Books, 53 Eland Road, London SW11 5JX

Previously published by

ELAND BOOKS

THE CHANGING SKY

NORMAN LEWIS

Travels of a Novelist

He really goes in deep like a sharp polished knife. I have never travelled in my armchair so fast, variously and well.
V.S. Pritchett, New Statesman

He has compressed into these always entertaining and sophisticated sketches material that a duller man would have hoarded for half a dozen books.
The Times

A delightful, instructive, serious and funny book. Norman Lewis has the oblique poetry of a Firbank, the eye of a lynx.
Anthony Carson, The Observer

ELAND BOOKS
specialise in the literature of travel.
If you wish to receive details of forthcoming publications,
please send your address to
Eland Books, 53 Eland Road, London SW11 5JX

A DRAGON APPARENT
NORMAN LEWIS
Travels in Cambodia, Laos and Vietnam

A book which should take its place in the permanent literature of the Far East.
Economist

One of the most absorbing travel books I have read for a very long time...the great charm of the work is its literary vividness. Nothing he describes is dull.
Peter Quennell, Daily Mail

One of the best post-war travel books and, in retrospect, the most heartrending.
The Observer

Apart from the *Quiet American,* which is of course a novel, the best book on Vietnam remains *A Dragon Apparent.*
Richard West, Spectator (1978)

One of the most elegant, witty, immensely readable, touching and tragic books I've ever read.
Edward Blishen, Radio 4

ELAND BOOKS
specialise in the literature of travel.
If you wish to receive details of forthcoming publications,
please send your address to
Eland Books, 53 Eland Road, London SW11 5JX

Previously published by

ELAND BOOKS

GOLDEN EARTH

NORMAN LEWIS

Travels in Burma

Mr Lewis can make even a lorry interesting.
Cyril Connolly, Sunday Times

Very funny . . . a really delightful book.
Maurice Collis, Observer

Norman Lewis remains the best travel writer alive.
Auberon Waugh, Business Traveller

The reader may find enormous pleasure here
without knowing the country.
Honor Tracy, New Statesman

The brilliance of the Burmese scene is paralleled by
the brilliance of the prose.
Guy Ramsey, Daily Telegraph

ELAND BOOKS
specialise in the literature of travel.
If you wish to receive details of forthcoming publications,
please send your address to
Eland Books, 53 Eland Road, London SW11 5JX

Previously published by

ELAND BOOKS

NAPLES '44
NORMAN LEWIS

As unique an experience for the reader as it must have been a unique experience for the writer.
Graham Greene

Uncommonly well written, entertaining despite its depressing content, and quite remarkably evocative.
Philip Toynbee, Observer

His ten novels and five non-fiction works place him in the front rank of contemporary English writers ... here is a book of gripping fascination in its flow of bizarre anecdote and character sketch; and it is much more than that.
J. W. Lambert, Sunday Times

A wonderful book.
Richard West, Spectator

Sensitive, ironic and intelligent.
Paul Fussell, The New Republic

One goes on reading page after page as if eating cherries.
Luigi Barzini, New York Review of Books

ELAND BOOKS
specialise in the literature of travel.
If you wish to receive details of forthcoming publications,
please send your address to
Eland Books, 53 Eland Road, London SW11 5JX

Previously published by
ELAND BOOKS

A YEAR IN
MARRAKESH

PETER MAYNE

A notable book, for the author is exceptional both in
his literary talent and his outlook. His easy economi-
cal style seizes, with no sense of effort, the essence of
people, situations and places... Mr Mayne is that rare
thing, a natural writer ... no less exceptional is his
humour.
Few Westerners have written about Islam with so
little nonsense and such understanding.
Times Literary Supplement

He has contrived in a deceptively simple prose to
disseminate in the air of an English November the
spicy odours of North Africa; he has turned, for an
hour, smog to shimmering sunlight. He has woven a
texture of extraordinary charm.
Daily Telegraph

Mr Mayne's book gives us the 'strange elation' that
good writing always creates. It is a good book, an interesting book, and one that I warmly recommend.
Harold Nicolson, Observer

ELAND BOOKS
specialise in the literature of travel.
If you wish to receive details of forthcoming publications,
please send your address to
Eland Books, 53 Eland Road, London SW11 5JX

Previously published by

ELAND BOOKS

JOURNEYS OF A GERMAN IN ENGLAND

CARL PHILIP MORITZ

A walking-tour of England in 1782

With a new preface by Reginald Nettel

The extraordinary thing about the book is that the writing is so fresh that you are startled when a stage-coach appears. A young man is addressing himself to you across two centuries. And there is a lovely comedy underlying it.
Byron Rogers, Evening Standard

This account of his travels has a clarity and freshness quite unsurpassed by any contemporary descriptions.
Iain Hamilton, Illustrated London News

A most amusing book...a variety of small scenes which might come out of Hogarth...Moritz in London, dodging the rotten oranges flung about the pit of the Haymarket Theatre, Moritz in the pleasure gardens of Vauxhall and Ranelagh, Moritz in Parliament or roving the London streets is an excellent companion. We note, with sorrow, that nearly two centuries ago, British coffee was already appalling.
Alan Pryce-Jones, New York Herald Tribune

ELAND BOOKS
specialise in the literature of travel.
If you wish to receive details of forthcoming publications,
please send your address to
Eland Books, 53 Eland Road, London SW11 5JX

Previously published by

ELAND BOOKS

TRAVELS INTO THE INTERIOR OF AFRICA

MUNGO PARK

With a new preface by Jeremy Swift

Famous triumphs of exploration have rarely engendered outstanding books. *Travels into the Interior of Africa*, which has remained a classic since its first publication in 1799, is a remarkable exception.

It was a wonder that he survived so long, and a still greater one that his diaries could have been preserved . . . what amazing reading they make today!
Roy Kerridge, Tatler

The enthusiasm and understanding which informs Park's writing is irresistible.
Frances Dickenson, Time Out

One of the greatest and most respected explorers the world has known, a man of infinite courage and lofty principles, and one who dearly loved the black African.
E. W. Bovill, the Niger Explored

Told with a charm and naivety in themselves sufficient to captivate the most fastidious reader...modesty and truthfulness peep from every sentence...for actual hardships undergone, for dangers faced, and difficulties overcome, together with an exhibition of virtues which make a man great in the rude battle of life, Mungo Park stands without a rival.
Joseph Thomson, author of Through Masailand

ELAND BOOKS
specialise in the literature of travel.
If you wish to receive details of forthcoming publications,
please send your address to
Eland Books, 53 Eland Road, London SW11 5JX